SYSTEMS OF
VIOLENCE

SUNY series in Global Politics
James N. Rosenau, editor

SYSTEMS OF VIOLENCE

The Political Economy of
War and Peace in Colombia

NAZIH RICHANI

State University of New York Press

Published by
State University of New York Press, Albany

For information, address State University of New York Press,
90 State Street, Suite 700, Albany, NY 12207

Production by Susan Geraghty
Marketing by Jennifer Giovani

Library of Congress Cataloging-in-Publication Data

Richani, Nazih.
    Systems of violence : the political economy of war and peace in Colombia / Nazih Richani.
        p. cm. — (SUNY series in global politics)
    Includes bibliographical references and index.
    ISBN 0-7914-5345-6 (alk. paper) — ISBN 0-7914-5346-4 (pbk. : alk. paper)
        1. Violence—Colombia. 2. Violence—Economic aspects—Colombia. 3.
    Colombia—Economic conditions—1970- 4. Colombia—Politics and government—1974- 5.
    Colombia—Social conditions. I. Title. II. Series.

HN310.Z9 V5659 2002
303.6'09861—dc21
                                                                        2001041117

10 9 8 7 6 5 4 3 2 1

*This book is
dedicated to the
peasants of Colombia*

CONTENTS

ACKNOWLEDGMENTS

My nephews and nieces used to ask what I was writing about, and I would tell them that I am writing the story of the children of Colombia. Finally, I can say to Ryan and Yasmine, Yara and Nadine who are all a few years short of their teens, that I reached the conclusion of my story, and they will be happy to know that it ended with a hopeful note or at least that I hope it will.

My journey with this project started in the early 1990s with a letter I sent to Professor Gabriel Murrillo, then chairman of the Political Science Department at the Andes University, who generously extended to me a letter of invitation expressing his interest in my research proposal, which I submitted to the Fulbright Program for Scholars. I am deeply indebted to Gabriel and also Dora Rothersberger, Gary Hoskin, of the Political Science Department of Los Andes, who supported me in the subsequent years. I am also indebted to the Institute of Political Studies and International Relations of the National University of Colombia and Colciencias who offered me the financial and institutional support without which this project would have not been possible. At the IEPRI, I had the good fortune to meet a remarkable group of scholars who later became my colleagues and friends such as Gonzalo Sanchez, Alvaro Camacho, Fals Borda, Francisco Leal, Eduardo Pizarro, Luis Restrepo, Jaime Zuluega, Ricardo Peñaranda, Francisco Gutierres, Gloria Ines, and the other staff, all of whom were instrumental in supporting my research at all levels and made my four years staying in Colombia as fruitful and as pleasurable as the country's circumstances allowed. The IEPRI's "golgota," the weekly forum for intellectual exchange was an important schooling for a student of Colombia like myself. The staff of the Fulbright Commission in Bogotá were and still are like family to me. Their support extended beyond the grant period and helped me in making my staying in Colombia as comfortable and safe as possible. In particular I would like to thank Consuelo Valdivieso for her care and generosity.

My field research was made possible by a host of people who helped me travel to areas off-limits to most people for security reasons. I thank in particular Santiago Martinez, my student assistant, and his family (Gordis and Jorge) who opened their home to me in Barrancabermeja several times assuming with that the risks that my staying could have brought on them in a conflict prone city.

The workers, miners, and peasants that I interviewed also ran great risks, and to them I am deeply indebted for allowing me to share their lives. Their stories will remain carved in my memory and I only hope that the narrative presented in this book is faithful to the realities of their daily struggle and helps in bringing peace and justice to their beleaguered nation. I also express my gratitude to all the individuals who took the time an accepted to be interviewed for this research: the guerrillas, the interests groups, politicians, and military personnel.

I am also greatly indebted to professor James Rosenau, the chairperson of this series, for his confidence in me, generous support, and encouragement; he helped this project to bear its final fruit.

At the personal level, one of my greatest gratitude is for my life companion, my wife, Mona Kaidbey, who graciously and patiently dealt with her worries and concerns about my field research in Colombia and supported this undertaking; she has a profound love to Colombia and its people, and of course, to me.

I also thank Dr. Michael Rinella, Susan Geraghty, and Camille Hale of SUNY Press for their time and effort in bringing this manuscript into it current form. I thank also my dear friend Ida Audih who patiently edited the very first draft of this manuscript. Finally, words of appreciation to the comments and critics made by the two anonymous reviewers who helped in bringing my argument into a sharper focus.

A word to my dear grandmother, Bahia Haidar whose keen love of knowledge and affinity with the underprivileged have always been to me a source of inspiration and admiration. To her memory I say, Thanks, grandma.

CHAPTER 1

Introduction

Colombia is the fourth most populous country in Latin America after Brazil, Mexico, and Argentina and is fifth in the size in its gross domestic production after Venezuela. It was among the very few countries in the region with almost uninterrupted positive economic growth since the mid-1940s. Such development led to a common saying in Colombia that "it is a country of no busts and no economic miracles," allowing the country to avoid the demons of the "lost decade" and the debt crises of the 1970s and 1980s, which haunted most of the region. Such stable economic performance contrasts sharply with the country's political history marred with protracted wars and narcotrafficking. The country's violent history has led some social scientists and policy makers to believe that there is a kind of an inherent cultural character that has contributed to such violent outcome.

Such belief is based on the fact that Colombia is one of the most violent countries in the world because of its high rates of political violence, criminality, and homicides amounting to 63.7 per 100,000 in 2000.[1] The Colombian strand of violence has generated a fine literary genre, mostly in Spanish, attempting to address the root-causes of violence focusing on its socio-economic and political roots. The violontologos, as the students of violence are called in Colombia, have employed multidisciplinary approaches in their studies of this phenomenon that has caused in the last two decades more than 350,000 deaths and about 2 million internal refugees threatening the social fabric and the very existence of the country.[2] Moreover, in the last few years, Colombia's violence reached higher proportions, spilling over its borders into Venezuela, Ecuador, Peru, Brazil, and Panama and becoming a threat to regional and international security. Cross-borders military incursions, weapons contraband, and narcotrafficking are almost daily occurrences expanding the radius of the conflict increasingly involving new actors.

Furthermore, narcotrafficking and its political economy compounded the problem, drawing into the conflict the United States' "War on Drugs." By 2000 the Colombian conflict became more entangled than ever before with the competing interests of the different U.S. government organizations, agencies, multinational corporations, and politicians. Each

1

of these groups has found in Colombia something to capitalize on, particularly after Colombia became the third most important recipient of foreign aid after Israel and Egypt. Consequently, Colombia is a candidate to occupy a prime position in the U.S. foreign policy in the succeeding American administrations.

One will tend to assume that all of the above would have prompted more research and studies of the beleaguered country, but that was not the case. There is a serious paucity in the literature that almost every text written on Colombia starts by mentioning the lack of in-depth studies similar to the ones on Mexico, Peru, Argentina, Brazil, Venezuela, or Central America. This lack of interest in the United States has many causes, including the orientations and foci of the Latin American studies programs in the major universities, reinforced by the secondary position Colombia occupied in the U.S. foreign policy and strategic considerations. My study is an attempt to fill some of the scholarly void and also an attempt to advance our understanding of Colombia.

My focus in this book is the conflict that ensued since the 1960s which became the longest conflict in the country's history and in Latin America. The protraction of the civil war in Colombia is by no means unique today since there are 49 similar conflicts raging in Asia and Africa which makes this study urgent. According to a study group from the University of Hamburg, of the total 49 wars and armed conflicts, 26 had their origins during the 1990s, another 8 during the 1980s, 8 during the 1970s, 5 during the 1960s, and 1 started in the late 1940s.[3] This book addresses two key issues: why conflicts protract, and when they do, what type of socioeconomic and political structural configurations make their peaceful resolution difficult to obtain. Addressing these two issues also can be useful to guide studies of other prolonged interstate wars.

Most studies on revolutions and political violence are relatively silent on the causes of the protraction of civil wars and pay little attention to the functions of violence in the case of their long duration. The causes and outcomes of revolution received extensive scholarly attention during the last three decades, producing an impressive body of literature. Comparative studies of revolutions such as Barrington Moore, Jr.'s *Social Origins of Dictatorship and Democracy*, Eric Wolf's *Peasant Wars of the Twentieth Century*, Ted Gurr's *Why Men Rebel*, Charles Tilly's *From Mobilization to Revolution*, and Theda Skocpol's *States and Social Revolutions* explore agrarian structures, aggregate-psychological motivations for political violence, conditions of relative deprivation, and the interplay of domestic and international contexts that affect the breakdown of the *Ancien Regime states* and the buildup of revolutionary organizations.[4] These studies make important contributions to

general theories and hypotheses for comparative studies but are inadequate in explaining why some social conflicts are protracted and what
type of social transformations occur in such conflicts.[5]

Theories of protracted conflicts explore the relationship among four
clusters of variables—communal contexts, needs, governance, and the
role of the state and international linkages—all of which are precondi-
tions for protracted social conflicts.[6] According to Edward Azar, what
determine the initiation of conflict are communal actions and strategies,
state actions, and built-in properties of conflict. He argues that most
intrastate conflicts involve zero-sum outcomes in which winners and
losers can be differentiated. However, protracted social conflicts result
in negative-sum outcomes because of their innate behavioral properties:
protraction, fluctuation, and spillover. In his scheme, there are no winners; all parties to these conflicts tend to be victimized by the process.

This binary notion of winners and losers has been challenged by
new approaches employing theories on economic utility, cost-benefit
analysis, rational choice, and political economy to tackle different
dimensions of protracted social conflicts.[7] This book belongs to this
developing genre. It draws on the advancement achieved in this field of
inquiry to revise Azar's model to explain why and how certain class
structures and institutional arrangements contribute to the perpetuation
of violence for long periods of time. It proceeds to give an assessment of
the functional outcomes that organized violence tends to generate within
given social structures, political arrangements, and international political economy. Finally, it analyzes the protraction of conflicts in terms of
the best available arrangement given the dynamic interplay between balance of forces (structure) and actors' goals and strategies (agency).

In this book, a system is defined as a group of units or components
related by their common characteristics, where the latter are the quali-
ties of the components. The pattern of interaction between the units constitutes the thread that ties them in a systemic relationship.[8] Thus, a system is a set of interacting units.[9] In a war system, the common thread
between the actors is their exercise of violence, and this activity links
them together in a systemic relationship that in turn forms the dynamics
of the system.

This book argues that a war system is formed under three key conditions, all of which are present in Colombia. These conditions are (a)
the failure of the institutions, the channels, and the prevailing political
mechanisms to mediate, adjudicate, or arbitrate conflicts among antagonistic social and political groups; (b) the antagonists' success in adapting themselves to conflict by establishing a "positive political economy"
through accumulating political and economic assets that make the condition of war the best available option given the balance of power and

the higher costs of peace; and (c) a balance of forces among the conflicting groups or actors that results in a comfortable impasse.[10]

My main thesis is this: The convergence of these three variables leads to the establishment of a war system that tends to perpetuate itself; where any of these conditions is lacking, conflicts are most likely to terminate faster. Following Kenneth Waltz and Robert Jervis's lead and applying some of their key concepts at the domestic level, the attributes of the war system are determined by how its main units (guerrillas, state and organized crime) stand in relation to one another in the spectrum of power.[11] Thus, the relation of power becomes a core aspect of my theoretical model.

Analyzing power relations among actors is not possible without developing an appreciation of the assets that they acquire through war (political and economic) that they could not access under conditions of peace. This aspect is explored by assessing the political economy of scale of violence, That is to say an X increase in the input of violence applied by actor Z may increase Z political and economic assets by XY. Here, the war system's theoretical model guides us in exploring the dynamics and dialectics between the relations of power and the political economy, that is between the attributes of the system and its corresponding units.

Violence associated with protracted conflicts can evolve into a distinct system that theories of revolution and protracted civil wars cannot explain because such theories focus on causes and outcomes.[12] The interim period that lies after the initiation of a violent conflict and before its final conclusion becomes a "black box" overlooked by the majority of studies. This interim period deserves special attention particularly because of the number of ongoing protracted conflicts that have yet to be brought to a resolution: Angola, Afghanistan, Sudan, Rwanda, Somalia, Burundi, Algeria, and Congo, among many others. My main goal is to cast light on a dimension of violence that has received little scholarly attention and to recommend policies and devise new strategies for conflict resolution.

METHODOLOGY

This book is based on two types of information: structured interviews and literature review of primary sources supplemented with secondary sources. Two hundred interviews and dozens of informal ones were carried out in different regions of Colombia between 1994 and 1998. The interviewed were members of business groups, guerrilla commanders, military officers, state officials, Colombian analysts, peasant leaders, labor union leaders, and paramilitary informants. The objective of these interviews was to explore various political views on the causes of the conflict, perceptions of the warring actors, and opinions regarding the conflict's possible resolution. The interviews helped me in forming a fairly accurate assessment of the costs and benefits of war and peace as seen by the mentioned groups (see appendix).

In exploring the three key variables of the war system model, the book examines (a) failure of state institutions in mediating, arbitrating, and adjudicating the main sources of social conflict; (b) whether the antagonistic actors succeed in adapting themselves to a war condition— as the best available alternative given the power relations and the higher costs of peace—and managed to establish a *positive political economy (PPE)*; and (c) whether the balance of forces among the conflicting groups or actors does not allow any one group to establish its own hegemony.

In exploring the efficiency of states' institutions in mediating, arbitrating, and adjudicating social conflicts, it is relevant to invoke Barrington Moore's contention that determining the default axis around which social conflict is organized in a given society is imperative in social research. An example is agrarian structures, which promote labor-repressive and authoritarian tendencies within the landed oligarchy generating resistance within the peasants and wage laborers. I would add that passing the threshold from class antagonism to class violence is also largely determined by the role of states' institutions in mitigating or exacerbating conflicts. This study focuses on one salient source of conflict in Colombia: struggle over land.

In analyzing the efficiency of state institutions in solving social disputes, the research would investigate the reform strategies implemented before and during the civil wars. In this context, the research would analyze to what degree the dominant classes (or fractions of a class) blocked these reforms. Since the struggle over property rights is central, the analysis focuses on the role of the Ministry of Agriculture and particularly Instituto Colombiano de La Reforma Agraria (INCORA), the state agency in charge of the implementation of land reform. The effectiveness of state institutions is assessed by exploring (i) the number of land disputes that the state institutions were able to adjudicate during the last four decades; (ii) the number and size of land titles distributed to landless peasants in relation to the total fertile land available during the same period; and (iii) the extent to which these measures mitigated peasant-landlord conflicts.

The second component of the war system is exploring the political, economic, and military assets that the warring groups accumulate or lose during the civil wars. This will aid in evaluating the political economy. Three main scenarios drawn from civil war experiences can be sketched:

1. If the political economy is negative for one side (e.g., for the guerrillas), then the other side (e.g., the state) has less incentive to negotiate (other than the terms of surrender) since it has a better chance of prevailing. In fact, most civil wars (80 percent) fought between 1945 and 1990 ended in the capitulation of one side. If any of the main contending forces is registering a negative political economy, then the war systems are most likely aborted early on.[13]

2. If the contending forces, however, are recording a positive political economy—even if it is asymmetrical—the conflict is more likely to be protracted, particularly when the balance of power does not allow either side to decisively defeat its opponent. In this phase, the war system is more likely to consolidate.[14] I argue that Colombia's civil war has been in that phase since the 1980s. Under a PPE, the price of peace versus the political, economic, social, and military costs of war becomes higher because it could entail radical reforms (such as power-sharing formula and a unified reformed armed force) for the dominant classes. And given the balance of forces, the opposition is not likely to accept a settlement that does not consolidate the economic and political gains achieved during the war.

3. If the escalation of conflict inflicts higher costs on the main warring actors (in terms of fatalities, resources, loss of political assets, measured in terms of dissension and erosion of support base), this might lead to a negative political economy, which may create favorable conditions for mediation and a negotiated settlement.

These three scenarios or phases should be seen as a continuum and in a dynamic mode. Most civil wars pass through a combination of these phases. Thus, our assessment of the political economy is essential to evaluating the different phases of civil wars and the life cycle of the war system (inception, maturation, and decline). Hence, I modeled the war system as a function of the political economy of war and the power relations between the units.

In order to measure the political assets of the participants in a conflict, it would be necessary to take the political influence that a given group had prior to the outbreak of hostilities as a point of reference and compare that with the political status of the group during the different phases of the conflict. The indicators for the measurement of political influence are as follows: (a) contrast the areas, municipalities, and districts that were under the control of opposition forces prior to the initiation of hostilities with those after; (b) determine the increase or decrease in the opposition's capabilities to influence public policy, political reform, and electoral politics; and (c) evaluate if the opposition gained or lost political recognition nationally and internationally by exercising political violence.

The economic assets are the incomes that the warring factions generate through the extraction of protection rent from the population under their control. The state, the guerrillas, and organized crime each has an extraction strategy, and estimates of incomes are available in the form of increases in military spending and budgets during the civil war, salary hikes for soldiers and officers serving in areas of combats, the guerrillas' annual income, organized crime income through narcotrafficking, and arms sales.

This book assesses the interdependence among organized crime, the state, and the opposition. This evaluation is based on a number of indicators: available estimates of organized crime annual income, economic impact of such incomes at the macro and micro economic levels, available estimates of incomes of the opposition extracted from organized crime, and the degree to which organized crime has managed to penetrate state institutions (including the military), measured in terms of number of public officials serving sentences or investigated for receiving money from organized crime.

In order to evaluate the power relations between the guerrillas and the state, the research relies on the following indicators: (a) number of major military confrontations that involve more than 100 combatants on each side and changes in the fatality ratio between the two over the last fifteen years; (b) number of municipalities under the control of the guerrillas over the same period;[15] (c) ability of the state to regain lost territory; (d) changes in the political leverage the guerrillas enjoy in the elections of local officials, mayors, and governors; (e) changes in military strategies of both sides; and (f) changes in the types of armaments used.

Since power relations is a systemic attribute, the research explores the distribution of power among the warring parties in an attempt to investigate whether a change in this distribution affects the dynamics and dialectics of the war system and its stability and how this structural change affects actors' behavior, such as their rent-extraction strategies, and political assets (i.e., their political economy). Since, the relationship between the system and its units is not unilinear and is interactive, the research examines also how changes in the actor's strategies, goals, and assets could alter the system dynamics. Simply stated, the war system dynamics is studied in terms of symmetrical and complementary changes. The first leads to a conflict spiral, where actors become more aggressive and heavily armed (currently the situations in Colombia, Angola, and Afghanistan), or complementary, where one side becomes more appeasing in front of the other's growing power (the final stages of the civil wars in Cambodia and Lebanon fit this model). The latter leads to the breakdown of the war system, while the former destabilizes it, and its perpetuation becomes an open ended question depending on the case.

BOOK MAP

Chapter 2 provides a brief historical background of conflicts over land since the Spanish conquest and the institutional failure of the post-independence state in solving conflicts between landlords and peasants. This failure has been compounded by intraelite disputes, producing a perpetual hegemonic crisis of the state during most of twentieth century.

Chapter 3 introduces the military institution as a category with its own interest and points out the merits of discussing it on its own rather than under the "rubric of the state." The quasi-autonomy of the military in handling the civil war with little civilian authority oversight led to the development of a bloated military bureaucracy, military strategies, and vested interests contributing and reinforcing the comfortable impasse with the guerrillas. This chapter attributes the quasi-autonomy and the latitude of the military to the state's hegemonic crisis and the lack of consensus within the dominant class.

Chapter 4 discusses the second actor in the war system, the guerrillas. This chapter presents a brief social history and sociology of the guerrillas in Colombia and identifies their main base of support and leadership social composition. This chapter contends that the guerrillas—particularly, the Fuerzas Armadas Revolucionarias de Colombia (FARC)—as a peasant-led and peasant-based insurgency, embody the historical peasants' struggle for land. However, the political strategies of the FARC and those of the Ejercito de Liberacion Nacional (ELN) of building local power instead of seizing political power have contributed to the establishment of the war system. Of particular interest is analyzing the political economy the guerrillas built under the comfortable impasse that consolidated their local power, as well as the war system.

The role of organized crime in the war system is analyzed in chapter 5. This chapter focuses on narcotraffickers and their armed paramilitary groups. It demonstrates that since the consolidation of the paramilitary groups in the mid-1990s, the dynamics of the war system have changed, ushering in a new phase in the system's life cycle. The chapter argues that the post-1995 phase is characterized by a higher intensity war, and hence the positive political economy achieved under comfortable impasse is being eroded.

Chapter 6 investigates the economic and political implications of the war system on the interests of the dominant classes particularly on the conglomerate groups. This chapter postulates that the coincidence of the increased costs—especially after 1995—of maintaining the war system with a new configuration of the dominant class and the growing impetus of globalization provides the bases for the reconstitution of a new hegemony that could dismantle the war system. It argues that the elements of a "historic compromise" between peasants and the bourgeoisie are already in place. Finally, chapter 7 discusses three other areas of protracted violence: Italy, Lebanon, and Angola. The objectives of this last chapter are to cast the Colombian case within a broader context, examine the validity of the war system theory, and generate questions for future research on protracted conflicts.

CHAPTER 2

Institutional Failure: Genesis of the War System

A theory of the state or of revolution must assume a terrain of war to be normal."
— Antonio Negri, *The Politics of Subversion*

Theories of state and revolution as Negri[1] contends must assume that war is normal as long as class and other cleavages cannot be negotiated by peaceful means. Colombia's 19th and 20th century history is a case in point, where historical continuities and discontinuities can be seen in the several waves of civil wars that have engulfed the country. This research demonstrates that continuities and discontinuities are the two main dialectical poles of a historical process, which are constantly remaking the present and shaping the country's future. Purely uninterrupted or absolutely interrupted development is only a fantasy, as Ira Gollobin contends.[2] This chapter presents the historical antecedents, particularly the institutional factors, that contributed to the emergence of the war system in Colombia and how this latter has become to represent a discontinuity with previous patterns, or in dialectical terms represents a historical synthesis.

This chapter discusses how the failures of state institutions to resolve disputes in property rights and land distribution engendered a new set of rules that were mostly sanctioned by state and nonstate actors. Institutions, be they the formal rules of political arenas, channels of communication, language codes, or the logic of strategic situations act as filters that selectively favor particular interpretations either of the goals toward which political actors strive or of the best means to achieve these ends.[3] This chapter attempts to explain why social actors such as peasant squatters (colonos) and large landowners found that prevailing state institutions invariably disfavored their class interests. Consequently, they created parallel violent institutions in their struggle to achieve their opposing goals.

In the economic sphere, when the institutions that organized the production process and property rights and regulate the relationships among the participants prove ineffective in protecting the interests of the participants in the production process, actors are left to build their own resources to protect their own interests. Since the turn of the 20th century, violence in Colombia can be explained partly in terms of failure of the state (defined as an ensemble of institutions) to adjudicate and resolve social conflicts, particularly in the distribution of income and resources and especially in the agrarian sector.

PEASANT REVOLTS AND LANDLORD RESISTANCE

In Colombia, as indeed in most Latin American countries, the formation of the haciendas (large farms) and the emergence of the peasantry were long processes that can be traced back to the evolution of the colonial regime.[4] During the New Kingdom of Granada (1564–1718), the original systems of Indian exploitation introduced by the Spanish were the *encomienda, concierto,* and *mita* (mining). The *encomenderos* extracted tribute in kind from the Indian communities in exchange for protection and religious instruction. Under the *encomienda* system, the indigenous peasants owned the land. *Concierto* was a kind of forced labor by which crown officials allocated workers to neighboring settlers who had received land leases, or *merced de tierra*. Later, the Indian population was granted communal lands as resguardos while land leases became private property. The *mining mita* system was forced procurement of Indian and later African slaves in the mines. Due to the decline of the Indian population and other economic factors, the periodic reduction of these *resguardos* was carried out, and land was transferred to landowners. By the 18th century, the *resguardos* could no longer provide significant surplus output or labor. Consequently, during the viceroyalty of Nueva Granada (1718–1810), the remaining *encomiendas* and the *concierto* system were abolished and the hacienda system was introduced.

The hacienda system was a self-sufficient unit of production satisfying the needs of provincial towns of food and meat and responding to commercial impulses. The hacienda production system depended on servile labor and on the limited access to land. Hacienda included the mestizos who did not qualify for land in the Indian *resguardo* due to their ethnic mix, and were incorporated as *agregados,* a category that included different types of tenants, sharecroppers, and peons tied in by bondage debts. The *resguardos* were liquidated in 1780 by the Bourbon reforms which decreed their privatization and by 1820 a republican decree ordered the repartition of communal lands among its members which contributed to an intense landowner's drive to acquire the *res-*

guardos lands. Some Indian communities, such as those in Cauca, Caldas, and Tolima, rejected parcelization and kept their communal land properties largely intact.

In the eastern Andean mountains, some mestizos accepted privatization but managed to resist landlord pressures and maintained their control over the land.[5] During the hacienda system, the class configuration in the rural areas was a class of landlords, servile peasants, and a free peasantry resisting their incorporation into the hacienda system. The hacienda system was coupled with a process of land colonization and defection where free peasants, Afro-Colombians escaping slavery, those escaping the haciendas, and poor settlers were trying to gain lands on the slopes and plains of the Andes. For all those groups, land was their ticket to freedom.

Many of these public lands were granted to landlords by the crown, were given to them as reward for their participation in the war of independence, or were obtained through speculation. Such conditions laid down the framework of the agrarian conflict in the 19th century and early parts of the 20th century between free peasants seeking to colonize lands and the landlords who resisted this process. The colonization of land and the emergence of colonos were symptoms of the decomposition of the hacienda system. The hacienda system created its own "grave-diggers": the *colonos*, the landless squatters.

The result of this phase of the struggle was a class structure based on sizes of land ownership that in the early 20th century appeared as follows: minifundia in the highlands, mixed patterns of production in the slopes, and latifundia in the plains.[6] These patterns of production still characterize the rural production system of the country. The contradictions within and without these distinct modes of production, their class structures, and their responses to the general capitalist development (including their relation with world markets) and their respective interaction underpinned the class conflicts in the rural areas. The coexistence of these three main modes was uneasy and was characterized by overt violence. Although Leon Zamosc claims there is no evidence of peasant revolts, Catherine LeGrand in her study of the process of peasant colonization counted more than 450 separate major confrontations between colonos and landlords from 1875 to 1930. This new evidence leads us to question Zamosc's conclusion that the landlords were able to control the peasants and safeguard the property structures.[7]

LeGrand provides evidence not only about the failure of the legal system but also for the period she studied about how the conflict was more often than not resolved by violent means. Violence was used not only to repress peasants in interclass conflicts but also by landlords in their intraclass disputes. Violence was thus used to solve disputes among the landowning class and among peasants, as was the case during "La Violencia" (1948–1958) when the landowning class split along political, ideological, and regional lines.

An example of how the failure of the justice system to resolve land disputes led to violence is the case of Salmina in the portion of Antioquia that later became the department of Caldas. In 1801, the crown granted Don Jose Aranzazu vast areas of land between Rio Buey on the north and la Vieja on the south, an area that contained only two settlements, the ancient town of Arma and the more recently established Sonson. Notice was given to the owners of adjacent properties to vacate these lands. In 1824, when the district judge at Rio Negro decreed that the land belonged to the Aranzazu family, but this was opposed by the citizens of Arma. The matter remained suspended until 1828, when the Supreme Court ruled in favor of the opponents. In 1829 the citizens of Arma concluded a transaction making them owners of the land between the San Lorenzo and Honda.

In 1833 Aranzazu ceded to the citizens of Salamina some of the lands belonging to him but kept the more valuable lots. But in 1843 the peasants challenged the property rights of the donor taking the case to court. The litigation lasted for fourteen years and led to government intervention and the imposition of a "compromise" that was not accepted by the peasants; one of the plaintiffs was assassinated in 1853. The period of litigation was marked by assassinations, burnings, imprisonments, and dispossessions.[8]

Similar cases were recorded in Tolima (1906), Sucre (1906) and Majagual (Bolivar). In the latter, in 1907, cultivators settled on territory the government designated as *baldios* (public lands) found their grant application by an alleged proprietor and the municipal judge, a cultivator warned President Rafael Reyes, " The inhabitants, who are angry, intend to take justice into their own hands." The state response was to use police forces to stop the settlers who threatened to disrupt what they referred to as the illegal proceedings perpetrated by the alleged proprietors Sres. Leiva."[9] Colonos of Margarita Bolivar expressed clearly the choices they faced given the power relations and institutional arrangement: "If the law will not protect our property rights, if because we are poor and weak we can not defend ourselves, if honorable labor is not to be respected, we know which road we must follow: either the path of crime or that of migration."[10] For most of the 20th century, colonos and peasants chose a combination of both paths.

Colonos did try legal avenues to protest or contest landlords' illegal claims, but this approach was predicated on the assumption that the central government would support them only if it were informed of the situation. This "peasant logic" was consistent not only with Latin

American history as LeGrand believes but also with worldwide peasant history, where peasants would raise their case to governments expecting that adjudication will come in their favor.[11] In Colombia, incrementally, this approach was replaced by violence as a method of resistance and counter-resistance employed by the contending social forces. The following sections discuss why.

LAND LAWS, HEGEMONY, AND CONFLICT

Laws are not neutral but rather embody the class, political, and ideological interests dominant in a given social structure and historical context. Laws that are designed to organize a polity in a manner consistent with the prevailing power and social structure can hardly be applied efficiently without what Antonio Gramsci termed "the exercise of hegemony."[12] Hegemony becomes a central piece in the puzzle of maintaining social peace in differentiated societies with discriminatory power structures. Simply stated, laws and their institutions become dysfunctional without an effective hegemony exercised by a dominant class—or fraction of a class—which projects moral authority and leadership that is accepted by the dominant as well as the subordinate groups.[13]

The Land Laws promulgated during the 20th century were not only contested by peasants but also were disputed by sectors of the dominant classes.[14] It will be argued that the dysfunction of institutions (in this case the legal framework) in Colombia stemmed in part from an endemic lack of hegemony. In general property rights laws and particularly land laws reflect to a large degree the socioeconomic level of development and the pace at which institutions are evolving to accommodate and facilitate this development.

The advent of coffee as an export crop and its rapid expansion from 150,000 sacks in 1894 to 2 million sacks in 1920 led to radical transformation of the subsistence peasant economy, particularly in the rural areas of Antioquia, Caldas, Valle, Tolima, Cundinamarca, and Santander, where coffee production was concentrated. The exports of coffee in the first three decades of this century laid the foundations for the national industry and accelerated capitalist accumulation.[15] The sociopolitical consequences of coffee expansion and the subsequent emergence of an agro-commercial sector manifested themselves in a new class configuration represented by two parties: the Conservative and the Liberal. Bourgeois-reformist factions were inspired by the social democratic ideas of the welfare state that gained momentum after the Great Depression in Europe and the United States; Alfonso Lopez Lopez Pumarejo, a wealthy banker, elected in 1934, represented at the time such a trend within the Liberal Party and started flirting with a "welfare" concept of the state. Some noted that he had been influenced by Franklin Roosevelt's "New Deal."[16]

In Lopez Pumarejo's opinion, the neglect of the poor class was not only wrong but also dangerous, because the masses would sooner or later demand a larger share of the national wealth. He believed that the Liberal Party should take the initiative and espouse the demands of the underprivileged classes and hence avoid social revolution if for no other reason. The banana strike against the United Fruit Company of 1928, which ended in a workers' massacre and increasing unrest in the rural areas added a sense of urgency to Lopez Pumarejo's concerns.

The reformist wing within the bourgeoisie was propelled not only by the developing coffee-export commercial bourgeoisie but also, and more important, by the industrial sector, which increased its contribution to the GDP from 8.9 percent in 1930 to 16.5 percent in 1945, the period of highest increases occurring between 1931 and 1939.[17] This industrial expansion was largely stimulated by the Great Depression, which had made the prices of foreign products out of reach for most consumers and thus stimulated the demand of local products, which were available at much lower prices. It should be noted that trade protectionism was exercised by the Conservative Party, which ruled from 1886 through 1930, a period known as the "Conservative Hegemony."

Lopez Pumarejo's election was the product of tactical political alliances within the Liberal Party and in no way indicated the defeat of its strong large landowner faction. We have to consider that the Liberal Party was in opposition during the long period of the Conservative Republic and became more in tune with the aspirations and demands of the growing urban middle class and working class. The Liberal Party incorporated within its ranks a radical student faction, the urban middle class, and members of the industrial and merchant's bourgeoisie, in addition to its traditional land-owning class. Thus, the Liberal Party became the stage for class alliances depending on the political conditions and the perceptions of the leader's factions of how to tie their personal ambitions to a broader political program without antagonizing the traditional class blocs. But incorporating these social groups did not mean by any stretch of the imagination that their political and class interests were reconciled or aggregated in the party program.

The Liberal Party efforts to reconcile contradictory interests became more difficult when it assumed political power. Lopez Pumarejo launched his proclaimed program, La Revolución en Marcha (a marching revolution), which in essence tried to accommodate the interests of the peasants and the urban middle class without undermining the interests of the bourgeoisie and large landlords.

The industrialization process coupled with rapid urbanization enhanced the power of the working class and urban middle class. The emergence of the Confederation of the Colombian Workers (CTC), as a unified union under the leadership of Communists and radicals from the Liberal Party, however, exerted pressure that strained the precarious alliance that brought Lopez Pumarejo to power. During 1934 and 1935, there was an increase in the number of strikes in the cities and in the pace of union organization of rural workers and the peasant leagues. By 1936, the government presented two packages of laws: constitutional reform and land reform.

The first package contained an article in which the state consecrated the social function of private property and gave the state the right to expropriate land for public use or for social purposes but required a legal due process and compensation. This package contemplated expropriation without compensation provided that both chambers of Congress approved such an act by a two third majority vote. This last requirement made it almost impossible for land to be expropriated without indemnification. This was a product of a balancing act given the strong representation of large landowners in Congress.

Lopez Pumarejo's objectives were clearly stated in his 1935 presidential message to Congress:

> Technically, then we are faced with the juridical alternatives of turning the nation to a socialist orientation or of revalidating the deeds to private property by purifying them from imperfections. The government has chosen the second. The project of the land law has no purposes other than to strengthen property rights, organizing them on the basis of principles of justice, and of resolving the conflicts which have grown out of the vagueness of existing titles.
>
> Some landowners when confronted with agitation, often justified, sometimes unjust, but understandable, have solicited from the state armed forces of public order to clear the title to the property or even the land itself from dangerous ideas. The law provides for this to be given in accordance with the decisions of the judges and makes the alcalde the agent of reaction. The eviction notice should be followed by the machine gun to prevent resistance. My government serves notice that is not its criteria, neither with respect to the evicted campesino nor with respect to the squatter who has invaded uncultivated lands supposing them to be in the public domain . . . land ownership should be acquired by two titles, whose provisions should be established by law: by labor and by public deeds, but without the latter giving endless right of possession of undeveloped lands. The government wants the law to define how, when and for what reasons one is a landowner, so as to prevent property being held by usurpers and so as to establish the validity of the titles of the large landowner who is putting his holdings

to use and also to clarify those of the colono who with tremendous energy, wrests from the jungle a plot of land on which to build his home and raise a family."[18]

The "Land Law 200" was designed to modernize the agrarian structures particularly by eliminating the non productive *latifundios* and called for a more efficient use of the land. The main objective of this program was to organize the land titles and put an end to the chaotic conditions of land ownership that had characterized the countryside since colonial times. The political objectives of the president were to eliminate the most backward sector of the agrarian oligarchy and to respond to the growing pressures from below.[19] The program did not call for the abolition of *latifundios* but rather for synchronization of the use of land with the country's capitalist development.

Simply stated, Lopez Pumarejo's attempt was a capitalist modernizing project, but the state also had to respond to other impulses and social antagonisms unleashed by the same process. On several occasions, the state sided with strikers against owners of enterprises and with colonos against landlords. Lapses of state "autonomy" exhibited some impartiality in land conflicts, particularly by the executive, and were strongly opposed by large landowners and the political opponents of Lopez Pumarejo. This opposition became more vocal when it joined forces with the church, which also was aggravated by Lopez Pumarejo's attempts to curtail its role in the education system. Consequently, a faction in Congress boycotted the reforms attempting to bring Lopez Pumarejo's program to a halt.

At another level, the working class also became an active political force. In 1938, the working class amounted to 753,000 workers. Workers mobilized their forces in support of Lopez Pumarejo's reforms.[20] Under such social and political polarization, Law 200 passed the Congress but not without an important amendment giving the large landowners until 1946 to cultivate the land or their lands would be expropriated. Law 200 did not affect property relations in any fundamental way, but the law was designed to rectify the "defects" of the preceding law that required land owners to provide land titles in the event of a dispute over ownership. Law 200 eliminated this requirement on the condition that land had to be used for a period of ten years or it would be transferred to public ownership. None of these properties ever became public property without compensation. Law 200 stipulated in Article 12 that whoever occupies the land for five years could claim it as his/her own. Law 200 also gave evicted colonos the right to be compensated for the improvements that they may have made on the land. Article 12 opened a Pandora's box where landlords and peasants struggled for land titles. The landlords, to avoid the loss of their lands, started to expel their sharecroppers and tenants. This process of expulsion was in most of cases effected through violent methods.

Law 200 was particularly important because it stipulated the creation of *jueces de tierras (land judges)* with the responsibility of arbitrating land disputes. From 1937 through 1943, the judges acted expeditiously, and according to the Ministry of Industries, more that 80 percent of existing disputes had been decided by the end of 1938.[21] LeGrand, however, found no concrete evidence in the records of the land courts to substantiate this claim, but the evidence she collected shows that land judges in their interpretation of the law tended to side with large land owners. After 1936, land judges called for the eviction of colonos from occupied haciendas in various regions. Other colonos managed to stay on the land they tilled but on terms that are not entirely clear.[22] In some places the landowners simply did not remove colonos from lands whose legal status remained undefined. Landlords also succeeded in reclaiming land from colonos supported by provisions of Law 200, particularly when colonos failed to purchase their shares.

Law 200, a very limited attempt to settle land disputes, revealed the incapacity of the state institutions to enforce the law. Local landlords who exercised their political power through municipal governments, the police, and district judges were able to circumvent the law and even to offer a different interpretation of its provisions. When local landlords were the local political bosses, land judges found it difficult to adjudicate disputes in favor of colonos and tenants. The peasants mistakenly interpreted Law 200 to be consistent with the bill of 1933, which granted land to those who cultivated it. Paradoxically, the interpretation of the peasants coincided with that of landlords who opposed Law 200 and stressed the provisions relating to the social function of property and the protection of colonos.[23] As a result, two opposing social classes in effect cooperated in subverting Law 200. At the general level, the different interpretations meant that district judges and land judges were subject to pressures of local social classes and that their modes of adjudication largely depended on the local balance of power between peasants and colonos and landowners.

At the general level, the state ineffectiveness in enforcing its interpretation and overseeing its execution reveals one manifestation of the crisis of hegemony. In consequence of the state's failures, the way was opened for different interpretations of Law 200 and to various modalities of execution negotiated by local actors. In most of the cases, large landowners got away with their own execution of the law. Where the large landowners were not present or were weak, colonos and poor peasants prevailed, particularly in the Andean slopes and highlands, generally the less productive areas.

In the end, Law 200 left the latifundios intact but accelerated in some areas the transformation of sharecroppers and tenants into wage laborers. The large landowners strategy was to rid themselves of tenants and sharecroppers to avoid land claims. Some tenants and sharecroppers tried to assert property rights inside some latifundios, which generated conflict with landowners. Thus, buying out sharecroppers' shares or forcing them to sell became an institutionalized mechanism of violence that laid some of the ground rules of the war system of the 1970s and beyond.

Land conflicts led to the transformation of large estates into pasture and cattle ranches, which were less labor intensive, causing disruption of production, reduction of food stuff, and an increase in land prices, outcomes that the reform was designed to avert. In the coffee regions, land tenure was not considerably affected, and the country became more dependent on this cash crop to import food stuff.

LAW 100 OF 1944: "LA REVANCHA"

President Lopez Pumarejo's shy attempts at reforms were exhausted by the end of his first term (1934–38). His successor, Eduardo Santos (1938–42), although he belonged to the same bourgeois faction of the Liberal Party, was more conservative in his approach. He did not change the course of the reforms introduced by Lopez Pumarejo, but he toned it down to satisfy the landlords' opposition. When Lopez Pumarejo was reelected in 1942, his flirtation with "welfare" became a costly enterprise and caused him to back away from the stances he assumed in his first term. Although Law 200 did not affect the latifundios, and large landowners managed to circumvent the negative impact it would have brought on their class interests, they were not satisfied and sought *revancha*, "revenge."

This revenge was made possible by the convergence of several factors. The first was the inability of the Liberal Party to reconcile the contradictory interests of the dominant groups and the demands of the subordinate classes. Lopez Pumarejo was outflanked by a leftist-populist group led by Jorge Eliecer Gaitan, by a rightist group led by Santos within his party, and by Laureano Gomez, the leader of the Conservative Party. All along, large landowners viewed the reformist inclinations of Lopez Pumarejo either with suspicion or outright animosity. Also, the increasing mobilization of the working class alarmed sectors of the industrial bourgeoisie who feared the political advancement of the left in labor unions. From 1940 through 1945 about twenty strikes per year were recorded. That was a significant increase from the

1920 through 1930. Within the working class—particularly the oil workers—unions— the struggle took an anti-imperialist tone against the American multinationals such as Tropical Oil and against the United States' investments in the country. This coincided with the onset of the Cold War which created a favorable condition for the right wing to launch a political counteroffensive.

The country's economic condition from 1940 through 1945 was characterized by high rates of inflation. In Bogota, for example, the living costs climbed 82 percent and in Medellin by 88 percent; prices of primary consumer goods increased by 108 percent and workers salaries fell by 50 percent between 1939 and 1942.[24] Agricultural production also went down, for example, wheat fell from 146,000 tons in 1942 to 68,000 in 1943. This decline can be explained in part by the crisis in the hacienda system and the landlords shifting from labor-intensive food stuff production to cattle ranching in a bid to avoid land claims by tenants and sharecroppers.

Under such conditions the Liberal Party was unable to contain its internal contradictions any longer. In 1943, for example, the party could not come up with a unified list for the municipal election in Bogota. Instead, twelve lists were presented. Of course, Laureano Gomez, the leader of the Conservative Party jumped at the chance to exploit such discord in his vehement campaign against Lopez Pumarejo. Thus in effect, the program of Lopez Pumarejo was not only significantly weakened but was also under enormous pressures to introduce a series of proposed laws that favored large landowners and the industrial bourgeoisie. The result was Law 100 and labor reforms that limited workers' rights to strike.[25] It is important to note that Lopez Pumarejo was also subject to an unsuccessful military coup in 1944, and in 1945 he finally gave up the fight and resigned his position one year before the end of his term. With his resignation, the attempt of a bourgeoise led democratic revolution with peasant support was finally put to rest and with it the prospect of a hegemony based more on persuasion than coercion ended, for a long while.

Thus, Law 100 was passed with the reformist-bourgeoisie position weakened and with heightened internal divisions within the Liberal Party. A political realignment between the rightist groups of both parties started taking shape. These groups were interested in the removal of Lopez Pumarejo and in redressing the balance in the rural conflict. Such rightist realignment was also aided by the Cold War ideology and regional politics, which called for the control of workers and peasants, the social bases of communist parties.

Law 100 was designed to correct the shortcomings of Law 200. Whereas Law 200 was to create a class of agrarian farmers following

Western models of agrarian capitalist development and shifting agrarian relations from tenancy to wage labor, the objectives of Law 100 were to reorganize the relationship between landlords and tenants, particularly those that tried to assume colono status in order to claim land and maintain sharecropping as a viable mode of agrarian production and exploitation. Law 100 also defined the rights and obligations of tenants in a way that secured landlords' control of the land.

What conditions and actors were instrumental in the production of Law 100 and its outcome (i.e providing a proper legal institutional framework to adjudicate, arbitrate and mediate rural conflict that was acceptable to the contending social groups), and what was the type of relation between the state and the contending actors? Two groups, Asociacion Patronal Economica Nacional (APEN) (Employers' National Economic Association) and the Sociedad de Agricultores de Colombia (SAC) (Farmers Association of Colombia), which includes the large landowners, with the help of the Federacion Nacional de Cafeteros (Federation of Coffee Growers), in 1944 succeeded in pushing for Law 100, which denied tenants and sharecroppers the possibility of becoming landowners. Law 100 guaranteed the protection of landlord's contracts and properties, prohibited the cultivation of permanent crops, restricted land exploitation of tenant-farmers and sharecroppers in their assigned parcels, and put in place a rapid legal instrument to expel the tenants and colonos after determining the improvements they might have made during their occupation of a given disputed land.

Law 100 reflected two main developments. It showed the ability of the landlords to regroup and strike an alliance with the agro-industrial elite represented by the large coffee growers tipping the balance in their favor, particularly for maintaining a labor repressive sociopolitical order whereby extra-economic modalities of exploitation are maintained, particularly sharecropping. The second interrelated factor was the weakness of the peasant movement, which was debilitated by internal fractures and lacked a unifyng political force. Under such a balance of forces, the state relented to the wishes of the alliance of landlords and agro-industrial alliance.

The new law was a major reversal for the peasants' struggle against the hacienda mode of production and, more important, it demonstrated the significant weight of the agrarian and agro-industrial elite in shaping and determining state policy. Law 100 also indicated the weight of the agrarian elites within the dominant class. The other segments of the dominant class—namely, the industrial, financial, and commercial elite—were acquiring power due to their respective growth in the post 1929 depression but were not yet strong enough to establish their hegemonic project of capitalist development. In retrospect, Law 100 did not significantly helped to reverse the trends of capitalist development and to avoid the transition from sharecropping to wage labor, nor did it produce a legal-institutional arrangement capable of reducing the intensity of agrarian conflicts. In fact, large landlords in areas of contention in Tolima, Cauca, and Cundinamarca launched a fierce war against sharecroppers and tenants, ostensibly to avert any claims after the lapse of ten years, which Law 1936 stipulated for non exploited *latifundios*.

Finally, even though the state, during Lopez Pumarejo's first government (1934–38) and due to a particular set of international and domestic conditions, had managed to adopt a relatively autonomous position toward large landowners, this relative autonomy was short-lived. Large landowners managed to change the battle lines and to generate a balance of forces in their favor and then to capitalize on the factionalism of the Liberal Party by playing on the fears of the bourgeoisie of radical labor; this took place against the backdrop of the evolving cold war between the U.S. and the U.S.S.R., which redrew local political alliances. Thus, given the inability of the state to produce acceptable institutions backed up by a "hegemonic consensus" to solve the agrarian question by the end of the 1940s, the stage was set for more conflict and violence.

LA VIOLENCIA (1945–58)

Three years after the resignation of Lopez Pumarejo, in 1948 Eliecer Jorge Eliecer Gaitan, the leader of the radical faction of the Liberal Party and a presidential candidate who was favored to win the election of 1950, was assassinated. The levels of political violence increased significantly since the mid-1940s but reached new high in the wake of Eliecer Gaitan's death ushering in what is referred to in Colombian historiography as "La Violencia," a civil war between partisans of the Liberal Party and Conservative Party. Most of the fighting was in the countryside where peasants fought against peasants in a sectarian fight that was exacerbated by personal vendettas and parochial interests. More than 200,000 people perished from 1945 through 1958. La Violencia was the logical outcome of the sociopolitical crisis and the inability of the prevailing institutional arrangement to contain it. It was also a manifestation of a political realignment between the different factions of dominant class bent on repressing the peasant, labor, and middle-class movements.

When the objectives of the civil war are measured against the outcomes, one concludes that the dominant classes were partially successful. The changes brought by the civil war were contradictory and did not correspond to any uniform logic or interpretation. The civil war did not accelerate capitalist transformation, reinstitute the feudal system of the hacienda, or enhance the state's hegemony. The sociopolitical outcome varied from one department or region to another, depending on a host of variables such as the correlation of forces between the landlords and the peasants, the level of political organization, the degree of influence of traditional political parties, the economic performance of the hacienda prior to the outbreak of violence, and the impact of state policies in tipping the balance to one side or the other. In this fashion, the net outcome from the different regions and departments for the 1948–1965 period were contradictory.[26]

Gonzalo Sanchez discusses five different outcomes of La Violencia as seen in terms of changes in property structures and relations of productions. The first outcome manifested *structural continuity* in the western parts of Quindio where haciendas escaped the ravages of La Violencia. Here landlords established informal arrangements with local and regional forces, or they had diverse sources of income from other investments that helped them avoiding economic ruin. These were mostly coffee haciendas based on sharecropping that capitalized on the high prices of coffee, low costs of labor, and opportunities that war could offer.[27] The second outcome was *regressive transformation* manifested in the north of Tolima where the hacienda system was reinstituted after it was practically dissolved by the socioeconomic changes that took place during the first administration of Lopez Pumarejo. But Tolima also witnessed capitalist transformation though direct investment from the urban bourgeoisie.

In the third outcome, the *progressive transformation*, the development of agro-industrial capital was coupled with violence. A Case in point was the department of Valle and particularly the high Cauca. The fourth outcome, according to Sanchez, was what happened in Sumapaz. In this particular case, the peasant path as opposed to the capitalist one prevailed at least for a while.[28] The fifth and final outcome was the *expansive transformation,* which took hold in the south of Tolima and in the Cauca departments, whereby large cattle ranchers expanded their properties at the expense of peasants and the Indian population. The relations of production in the expansive transformative mode did not change during La Violencia, but the *hacendados* derived significant political power from their territorial expansion.[29]

This scheme captures the various modalities of capitalist development induced by La Violencia, but three questions remained unanswered. How did these various outcomes affect the configuration of class forces and alliances in the rural area and the overall capitalist development? What was the class configuration of the dominant class within the state after the Violencia? And finally, did La Violencia lay the institutional foundation for dealing with social conflict, that is, a war system?

Answering the first two questions lies outside the scope of this book, but some observations can be made. At the end of the civil war, the same dominant classes emerged in control, and their biparty system was revived. The large landowners and other factions of the dominant class formed a political alliance (National Front) ostensibly to put the state under their political control and avoid "lapses of state autonomy" such as the one experimented with under Lopez Pumarejo's first government. The state under the National Front inhibited any expression of social conflict and excluded the subordinate classes from politics. Another consequence of the civil war was that it blocked the way for populism in Colombia by eliminating Jorge Eliecer Gaitán's populist option.

The civil war was an expression of various contradictions among the dominant classes and political elite and between those and the subordinate classes. The civil war revealed that the then prevailing institutional arrangement (electoral democracy) was strained by increasing polarization between members of the political elite resulting from pressures from peasants and workers' mobilization and populist tendencies (represented by Jorge Eliecer Gaitan).[30] Thus, the contestation of political power by constitutional electoral means could have entailed a populist revolution that might have undermined the interests of the dominant classes. In hindsight, the National Front eliminated that possibility by limiting government succession and alternation only to its handpicked members, thus becoming the institution through which the dominant class negotiated and resolved its differences.

This mechanism proved to be effective in solving intraelite conflicts and controlling the state, but it failed to project its hegemony over the subordinate classes. The National Front did not envisage similar effective institutions to resolve one important source of conflict, namely the agrarian question. On the one hand, this shortcoming led to the incremental institutionalization of violence to complement the exclusiveness of the political system, and, on the other hand, violence started to assume different functions incorporating new dimensions and actors, as a function of the socio-economic and political changes and shifts that occurred thereafter.[31]

The issue becomes how to define the relationship between institutions of violence and other types of political, social, and economic institutions and how they interact in a complementary fashion under given social structures and historical conditions. Institutions generally are thought of as arrangements, patterns of interactions that regulate different spheres of social, political, market, and cultural life. But we rarely consider violence as an institution with its functions within the overall social structure and institutional arrangements.[32] The National Front was an example of an institution that regulated aspects of political life (intra-elite relations) complemented by "accepted levels" of sociopolitical violence where those who were excluded from the political process and those who were included interacted to produce a complementary institution.

Within this framework of analysis, the remaining parts of this chapter discuss how the success of the elite in resolving their political differences within a legal constitutional frame ushered in since the National Front sharply contrasted with the elite failure in establishing the proper institutional channels to settle antagonisms with the subordinate classes by peaceful means. The National Front unwittingly inaugurated a new phase in the institutional history of the country by allowing two institutions (violence and restricted democracy) and two political modalities (election and excessive repression) to interact and coexist within the framework of the same socioeconomic political system. Now our task is to define the different historical conditions under which the evolution of such institutional duality became integrated in the socioeconomic structure and how this duality has allowed the sustainability of an "electoral democracy" since 1958. Then political exclusion and the inability of the state to address the agrarian question propelled the institution of violence, particularly when an armed opposition emerged. This is the subject of the following chapters.

LAW 135 OF 1961 AND COLOMBIAN INSTITUTE OF AGRARIAN REFORM (INCORA)

During and after the formation of the National Front, none of the factions of the dominant class enjoyed a hegemonic position in a sense that would have allowed the construction of a consensus around a set of "ideas" to solve key problems pertaining to the country's model of capitalist development. Nowhere is this clearer than on the agrarian question. The bourgeois-reformist ideas of President Carlos Lleras Restrepo did not have better reception than those of Lopez Pumarejo almost three decades earlier. The internal balance of forces upon which the National Front was based made it imperative for the industrial bourgeoisie and agro-industrial and large landlords to reinforce their class representation through their respective associations to take the initiative in representing and defending their interests.

For example, the political influence of Federación Nacional de Cafeteros de Colombia (FEDECAFE) (National Federation of Colombian Coffee Growers) the group that represents the wealthiest coffee growers, was unquestionable during the coffee bonanza and when coffee constituted the backbone of the economy. But growth of the industrial sector in the 1940s and 1950s, which grew from 14.8 percent of the GDP during 1945–49 to 21.1 percent of the GDP by 1965–69, diminished the status of the coffee sector and the agrarian sector at large. The agrarian sector contribution to the GDP including coffee, decreased from a 40.5 percent 1945–49 to 26.6 percent for 1965–69. This structural change was accompanied by an increasing political assertiveness of the Asociación Nacional de Industriales (ANDI) (National Association of Industrialists), which became the articulator of the industrial bourgeois interests.

During La Violencia, ANDI and FEDECAFE sided with an authoritarian solution and supported the extreme-rightists from the Conservative Party, such as Ospina Perez (1946–50) and Laureano Gomez (1950–54). Both were tough antagonists of labor unions and the leftist opposition but differed on protectionism economic policy.[33] ANDI and FEDECAFE did not share the same position regarding trade protectionism because coffee as an export-oriented crop depended on the openness of international markets, particularly to U.S. market. Thus, it became a prime consideration that the Colombian government protectionism would not undermine FEDECAFE access to the U.S. market. This conflict of interest between FEDECAFE and ANDI was long and contentious, but ANDI gained the upper hand after the mid 1940s.[34]

Sociedad de Agricultores de Colombia (SAC) (Society of Farmers of Colombia), which represented the landed oligarchy and agro-industrialists, felt that protectionism adversely affected its prime import such as fertilizers and machinery which in turn increased local prices of food products. The state conducted a policy that satisfied the needs of the industrial bourgeoisie by providing some protectionism and by giving FEDECAFE a wide margin to determine the marketing strategies of coffee and by leaving to SAC decisions in the area of land reform. An example of how land policy was managed by the state under the National Front was the approval the Agrarian Social Reform Law (Law 135) in 1961, which only passed after a consensus was reached between the dominant classes represented by the above mentioned groups.[35] When the law was submitted to a Congress divided between Liberals and Conservatives, only a few Conservatives opposed it. The law passed only after large landowners toned down the criteria for land expropriation and instituted proper indemnification procedures and payments.

Law 135 was designed also to assist the minifundios and colonization movements, to improve productivity through technical assistance, to increase incomes through the promotion of peasant cooperatives, and to provide better services. These lofty goals, which remained largely unfulfilled, were intended to reestablish the authority of the dominant classes in rural areas which was shaken during the civil war. Some projects under the newly found INCORA, however, were initiated in areas of conflict, such as in the departments of Tolima, Huila, Cundimarca, Santander, North Santander, and Antioquia and in new areas of colonization in Caqueta, Ariari Meta, and Sarare Meta.[36] In areas of latifundios, very little was done even where reform should have been introduced. The latifundios particularly on the Atlantic Coast and with the exception of Eastern Llanos, were largely spared by La Violencia.[37] This was because most large landlords on the Atlantic Coast were Liberals and the region is separated from Santander and the interior by the mountain ranges and plains, and the low population density made it even more difficult for the civil war to spread.[38]

The terms of land distribution were so ambiguous that the Ministry of Agriculture was given leeway to determine which land was subject to expropriation. That compromise was worked out after the state gave in to the demands of FEDECAFE and other business enterprises that areas under their tutelage be excluded from any land expropriation.[39] By 1971, less than 1 percent of the lands subject to expropriation were distributed, and most of that was public land. Moreover, the distribution of these lands was marred by a complex list of requirements that colonos had to complete in order to qualify for credit and to settle legally land boundaries. Such requirements impeded any meaningful advancement in land reform, and the prime land of latifundios was out of reach of the law. Thus, Law 135 was not any better than the previous laws, and again institutional failure exacerbated land conflicts.

During the 1960s, the peasant subsistence economy was in a steep decline. Such decline was marked by an increasing mobilization of the peasantry championed by the National Association of Peasant Users (ANUC) established in 1967 and other leftist political groups such as Fuerzas Armadas Revolucionarias de Colombia (FARC) founded in 1964 and the Ejercito de Liberacion Nacional (ELN), founded in 1965. By the mid-1960 the Colombian economy entered into a recession, and the industrial sector reached the limits of what import-substitution policy could offer in the national market. The market for consumer goods had been saturated in the 1950s, and industry was then completing a program of import substitution of intermediate and capital goods.[40] A drop in the international prices of coffee, at the time, contributed to a decline in foreign reserves badly needed to buy equipment from abroad.[41] These conditions led to the stagnation of the industrial sector and to the rise in urban unemployment, which reached 13 percent in 1967 up from a 4.9 percent in 1964.[42] Under these dire economic conditions, class struggle became eminent in both a regional and an international environment characterized by revolutionary movements and cold war politics, which increasingly internationalized local conflicts.

In this environment, the populist and exmilitary dictator Rojas Pinilla gained political ground and threatened to undermine the regime of the National Front. In the late 1940s, Jorge Eliecer Gaitan had posed a similar threat and the dominant classes had plunged the country into a civil war to avoid that path. Later, the dominant classes chose to close ranks behind Carlos Lleras Restrepo (1967–1971), a reformist bourgeois very similar to Lopez Pumarejo, who led a very different Colombia. Some segments of the dominant class thought that solving the economic crisis, was the key to checking the political appeal of Rojas Pinilla and his ANAPO movement. Many measures were taken to deal with the economic crisis which I will not discuss here, except for one of its main components: agrarian reform. Carlos Lleras Restrepo proposed that, in order to solve the unemployment problem, it was necessary to tackle the crisis in the subsistence peasant economy, which was propelling the rural migration to the cities (It is important to mention here that Carlos Lleras Restrepo was also one of the main architects of Law 135 of 1961 and a force behind its passing through Congress).

The Carlos Lleras Restrepo administration proposed a set of laws that called for the compulsory distribution of land in all haciendas where rent and sharecropping were the pattern of tenancy, as discussed earlier in the chapter. This was resisted by landowners who had managed to abort all previous reform attempts either by direct political opposition in Congress or through the use of their local power to subvert the implementation of reforms. Landowners worked through the Conservative and Liberal Parties in Congress to modify the bill known as Law 1 of 1968, which recognized the rights of sharecroppers and tenants to the land, by introducing many restrictions that made it virtually impossible to apply. In response, Carlos Lleras sought peasant support by establishing the ANUC as a quasi governmental organization in order to overcome landowners' resistance by creating new social realities on the ground. This was another rehash of Lopez Pumarejo's bourgeois reform faction alliance with the peasantry, but this time with an organizational base: the ANUC.

The main function of ANUC was to coordinate a "massive land reform."[43] This was in direct violation of the National Front agreements and was viewed with apprehension by large landowners and other factions of the dominant class. According to Zamosc the role of the reformist's faction was "to create external pressures to undermine the position of the landowning class, thus changing the balance of forces within the National Front and creating a more favorable climate for the implementation of agrarian reform"[44] In this analysis the peasantry was the only social force and the logical ally of the reformist-bourgeois faction. But Zamosc understates the importance of pressure from below stemming from the armed insurgency and the persistent peasant struggle for land in various departments during the 1950s and 1960s. A more plausible interpretation could be that Carlos Lleras Restrepo's bourgeois faction, in a bid to undercut the left and the right, capitalized on the agrarian conflict, to pull the peasantry toward its bourgeois project. Carlos Lleras Restrepo's failure in gaining the peasantry, therefore, did not stem only from landowners or peasants but also from the dynamics of class struggle and its gravitation toward an armed solution given the inability of state institutions to contain the conflict. The "peasant republics" of the 1950s and 1960s had a significant impact on the political discourse of the dominant classes and consequently on state policies a few months before the election of Carlos Lleras Restrepo.[45]

The military campaigns of Guillermo Vallencia's government to eradicate the peasant defense leagues, or the so called independent republics established in Marquetalia, El Pato, Guayabero, and Riochiquito during 1964–65 undercut the reformist-bourgeois faction efforts to pull the peasants to the bourgeois project away from an emerging peasant revolt.[46] These military campaigns radicalized the peasants and provided the backdrop against which the divisions between a radical and a conservative faction came to sweep ANUC in the 1970s. The dynamics of class conflict reached a point that neither the institutional framework (land laws) nor the organizational vehicle (ANUC) was capable of ameliorating. This led to the defeat of Carlos Lleras Restrepo's program and subsequently to violent state repression institutionalized in 1978 through the Statute of Security, which complemented, the legalization of paramilitary groups (1962) as tools to combat the radicalization of the peasantry and the peasant-based armed groups. Moreover, in the regions where ANUC witnessed its greatest mobilizations, its subsequent decline validated the guerrilla movement as a political alternative. This was the case along the Atlantic Coast, Sucre, Bolivar, and in Magdalena Medio and the eastern plains.[47]

In the 1990s, most regions where the peasant movement disputed land ownership became battlegrounds between the armed insurgency and paramilitary groups with occasional participation of the state's army.[48] Such development provides strong evidence supporting my central argument that historically the institutional and organizational arrangements could not contain the social antagonisms, and in turn, their failure exacerbated the conflict. To provide context for the social conflict that ensued in the past three decades, how it played out within the departmental structures, and why the institutional framework became overwhelmed by the recalcitrant position of the landowners and the radicalization of the peasants, one should look at where the conflict did occur.

About 76.9 percent of the land conflicts in 1971 took place in the latifundios of the Atlantic Coast, in the inner valleys, and in the eastern Llanos where large cattle latifundios and agrarian capitalism were developing.[49] The rest of the land conflicts occurred in the Andean departments on minifundios. In the 1980s and 1990s capitalist development was accelerated by the advent of African palm plantations and illicit plantations. It is important to emphasize that the contours of Law 135 and the Laws of 1968 did not provide an efficient mechanism to distribute land, nor was INCORA able to cope with the increasing demand for land. This was all occurring in an environment characterized by rapid capitalist transformation in the rural economy where greater concentration of land and less labor-intensive methods were being used, and the stagnated industrial sector was unable to absorb the resulting excess labor. To make matters worse, there was the National Front, a rigid exclusive consociational system that did not give breathing space for dissent. When it did allow dissent, and reform was attempted—such as under Carlos Lleras Restrepo—it was unsuccessful because the reform ideas of Carlos Lleras Restrepo did not garner a support base within the industrial bourgeoisie nor within the agri-businesss for the land reform measures.

THE AGREEMENT OF CHICORAL: ANTIREFORMISM

President Misael Pastrana started a counter-reform path supported by the industrial bourgeoisie, agri-business, large landowners, and cattlemen. The land invasions of 1971 sponsored by the radical Sincelejo faction of ANUC alerted the mentioned groups to the difficulty, if not the impossibility, of containing a mobilized peasantry within the sociopolitical contours of traditional party politics, which was Carlos Lleras Restrepo's original intention. The class struggle and antagonisms became difficult to contain within the framework of the agrarian reforms espoused by Carlos Lleras Restrepo. Both state organizations INCORA and ANUC were overwhelmed by the events.

A telegram from the American Embassy in Bogota at the time described the events: wave of land invasions begun October 8 (1971), continues unabated October 12 brought new invasions by thousands of campesinos in Boyaca, Huila and Tolima, no violence reported but some arrests. ANUC, communist infiltrated campesino group originally created by government, issued a manifesto October 13, calling for freedom of association and end of the state of siege and military tribunals, in addition to usual calls for land, credit, better markets and reduced inter-city transport costs."[50] A month later, another dispatch from the American consul in Cali described the escalating land conflict in the following manner:

> Early in the morning of November 14 approximately 50 families invaded six acres of land owned by the Papayal sugar mill in Palmira, Valle, about 20 miles from Cali. The families are landless rural poor who exist as economic scavengers, working when work is available, eating when food can be obtained. Police and troops were dispatched to remove the squatters. A pitched battle ensued, boiling water badly scalded several soldiers. One squatter was shot dead. The invaders were finally evicted and the ringleaders arrested.[51]

Under these conditions, and on January 1972, Pastrana's government called representatives from both political parties as well as business groups for a meeting in the town of Chicoral. The outcome of the meeting was a pact to reverse the land reforms of Carlos Lleras Restrepo's government. In exchange for paying taxes on their properties, landowners were guaranteed a limited land distribution to the peasants and unequivocal support for the expansion of agro-businesses through favorable credit and loan policies. Accordingly, Law 135 was modified to assure compensation for expropriated land based on market value and not on census value; a greater proportion would be paid in cash, and the rest in higher interests rates. Laws 4a and 5a of 1973 and Law 6a of 1975 further diluted the standards of underexploitation of land, which made it even more difficult to expropriate.

Law 6a, or the Sharecropping Law, put an end to the possibility that sharecroppers could claim compensation for the improvement introduced during their tenancy. Laws 4a and 5a were complemented by the creation of the Agricultural Financial Fund to provide services to agri-business. These laws demonstrated, on the one hand, the government commitment to agrarian capitalist development and on the other hand, a total disregard for the peasantry's most basic interest. This implied the adoption of a clear path of brutal suppression based on state violence. It also showed that when dominant classes and the political elite feel any serious threat to their interests, they close ranks. This was the case during Lopez Pumarejo's second term and again under Carlos Lleras Restrepo's administration. The class/political realignment in the 1940s, as in the late 1960s, demonstrated that within the dominant classes, the "reformist factions" were anomalies and never gathered enough support within the bourgeoisie to tip the balance in favor of their policies.

The latifundios of the Atlantic Coast, the nemesis of any land reform measures, were satisfied with the new pact but the peasant threat was not yet overcome. During the land colonization and conflict of 1971, which was mainly in their dominion, the latifundios' response was to take matters in their own hands by employing organized violence targeting peasant leaders and organizers and leftist figures. This repressive behavior was sanctioned by the state and often coordinated with its coercive apparatuses, namely, the military. This marked yet another phase in the process of institutionalized violence, which reached higher degrees of institutionalization in the 1980s and 1990s with the emergence of an agrarian narco-bourgeoisie. The large landowners developed their own paramilitary force, especially after 1961. By 1965, paramilitary groups were granted legal status by the state to combat the then emerging radical peasant-based guerrilla movement. Thus, the institutional failure set the stage for a war system that became the the main modality to negotiate and settle social conflicts.

The failure of the dominant classes to produce a hegemonic faction, for better or for worse, produced a consociational power arrangement that circumscribed the state's political autonomy. One would expect that the state would become more autonomous if a balance of forces within the dominant class did not allow the emergence of a hegemon. Notwithstanding the short-lived autonomy under the first term of Lopez Pumarejo, this was not the case in Colombia particularly because peasant, working-class, and middle-class alliances were weak, and their resistance was not strong enough to represent a countervailing power against the dominant classes and to give the state more autonomy in enforcing a more egalitarian distribution of land, income, and political power.[52] The result was that the National Front guaranteed the dominant classes a firm control over state institutions and policies through a complex process of political and economic compromises that favored landowners.

LAND REFORM IN THE 1980S AND 1990S AND THE EMERGING RENTIER ECONOMY

INCORA grants titles and administers the agrarian reform, including acquisition, distribution, and the delivery of supportive services. By 1990, it had acquired 1.3 million hectares through purchase or expropriation, and another 4.8 millions hectares through the annulment of ownership of underutilized or abandoned land. INCORA has two programs for land distribution: one operates in agrarian reform zones and targets poor peasants with inadequate lands, and the other targets well-to-do peasants and farmers. Between 1961 and 1990, INCORA distributed 1.07 million hectares to about 60,000 families in the agrarian zones and issued more than 300,000 titles covering 9.2 million hectares of public land. In addition, it established, more than 256 reserves, covering 25 million hectares and benefiting some 37,000 indigenous families.[53] However, INCORA's land distribution was minimal in contrast with the agrarian "counter reform" resulting from budgetary constraints and market forces.

Perhaps the most notable force behind counter reform was the new landed stratum who built their fortunes through narcotrafficking and emerald smuggling and who acquired immense amounts of fertile lands, mostly in contested areas such as Middle Magdalena, Cesar, Uraba, Putumayo, Meta, Cordoba, Bolivar, and Boyaca. It is estimated that the narcobourgeoisie acquired in a few years more land than INCORA distributed in thirty years.[54] In the 1980s and 1990s about 4.4 million hectares were acquired by narcotraffickers with an estimated value of $2.4 billion.[55] Hence, the narcobourgeoisie accelerated a rentier-capitalist development of the agrarian sector, particularly in the forms of cattle ranching and land speculation (see chapter 5). In this rentier type of economic development the accent is on the speculative value of land rather than on its productivity, which partially explains the increasing decline in land used for agricultural production. Cases in point are the large ownerships which constitute about 43 percent of the country's agricultural land of which 9 percent only is planted, and the remaining (more than 5 million hectares are good for agriculture) are left unattended or underutilized; and about 800 thousand hectares owned by middle to small peasants more were left without plantations in the 1990s (see table 2.1).[56]

This rentier trend is transforming Colombia into a net importer of its main foodstuffs and ruining its traditional cash crops. Since the early 1990s, this trend received an important impetus from the economic liberalization policies carried out by the successive governments, which reduced tariffs and customs on imported products against which local producers could not compete. An example is cotton which was until the late 1980s a main cash-crop and vital for the national textile industry lost grounds for cheaper imports, consequently, from 350,000 hectares that were planted with cotton in 1980, in 2001 only 35,000 were left. Consequently, the economic liberalization helped the economic shift in the use of land for speculation and extraction of raw resources at the expense of production, since this latter became increasingly non competitive by the end of the 1990s.

It is also important to keep in mind here that during the 1980s, major oil, coal, and gold discoveries were made, leading to an increase in multinational corporations' investments in rural areas. This factor along with the economic liberalization, led to significant changes in

TABLE 2.1

	Percentage of fincas		Percentage of arable land		Percentage in agricultural use	
	1988	*1996*	*1988*	*1996*	*1988*	*1996*
Very small 0–5 ha	48.5	50.2	3.7	3.7	49.4	32.8
Small properties 5–20 ha	28.5	27.8	11.4	9.9	32.9	19.8
Medium sized properties 20–50 ha	11.6	11.8	14.4	14.0	18.3	11.2
Large properties 50–200 ha	9.4	8.0	34.8	28.2	10.6	7.3

Source: Based on data of the Ministerio de Hacienda for 1988 through 1996. Bogotá, Colombia.

the social and economic functions of land. With the increasing integration of the national economy with global markets, the social configurations of land conflict also began witnessing important changes. The new fault line of conflict that started taking shape in the 1980s is between a rentier economy and a subsistence peasant economy represented by poor peasants, colonos, and indigenous and Afro-Colombian communities whose lands became the target of speculators (such as narcotraffickers, real state companies, and wealthy individuals), and multinational companies.[57] The traditional landed oligarchy that had led the conflict since the 1920s started giving way to new social forces: land speculators, agribusiness, multinational corporations (such as oil, gold and coal mining companies), and the narcobourgeoisie. The implication of this change on the dynamics of the conflict is elaborated in chapters 5 and 6.

For now, however, it is important to stress that both the changing socioeconomic functions of land and the social configuration of the social forces in conflict did not halt the process of land concentration (referred to as "counter reform") which started in the wake of the Chicoral agreement but rather accelerated it. The concentration of land reached new highs by the end of the 1990s: large landowners increased their ownerships from 32.5 per cent of the country's agricultural land in 1984 to 35.7 percent in 1988, reaching 43.1 in 1996 and 45 percent in 1997 (see table 2.1).[58]

CHAPTER 3

The Military and the Comfortable Impasse

This chapter introduces the military as one of the organizations that helped in creating and perpetuating the war system. It addresses three main questions: 1) Why did the military choose a containment military strategy instead of one designed to eliminate the guerrillas? 2) How did this containment strategy contribute to the formation and consolidation of a comfortable impasse? And finally, 3) What type of institutional interests did the military form under the impasse contributing to the emergence and consolidation of the war system?

My choice of discussing the Colombian military institutions, particularly its armed forces is grounded on Theda Skocpol's assumption that people situated in state's agencies and institutions could articulate their own goals and at times carry them through.[1] The core issue is determining the conditions under which this is made possible and how the goals and interests of a particular state organization intersect with those of other interest groups and social classes. Before tackling the core objectives of this chapter, it is important to provide some historical background about the military and its relationship with the other sectors of the state, complementing my discussion of the hegemonic crisis of the state discussed in the previous chapter.

THE MILITARY'S AUTONOMY

Since the two military governments of Rojas Pinilla (1953–57) and of the Military Junta (1957–58), the military was gaining latitude in managing two core areas: state defense and public order. These two areas joined with the Doctrine of National Security adopted by the military. The military consolidated their integration into the regional security system through their linkages with the United States, which provided training, technical assistance, and political indoctrination. Paradoxically, however, while the military became more integrated with the regional security system, it became more autonomous versus the executive and legislative branches of government.[2] This was due to the deep rifts among the main sectors of the political elite, who had agreed on leaving the area of national security outside their political bickering since the 1958 National Front.

The interelite agreement on leaving the military outside their political disputes as a condition to maintain political stability after La Violencia (1948–58) became one of the most enduring legacies of the National Front (1958–74), surviving well into the 21st century. The National Pact and the return to civilian rule resulted from an agreement with then ruling Military Junta. The military accepted the persecution of Rojas Pinilla in return for granting them latitude in managing its resources and public order. Consequently, the military became the only guarantor of political stability, since the police forces took sides with the Conservative Party during the civil war. This arrangement was seen as political necessity and was executed during the consociational regime of the National Front. This interelite arrangement began to bear fruit in the 1970s and 1980s, when the state hegemony was further challenged by the rising power of the insurgency and the menace of organized crime. The military was the one to respond to these threats, since the areas of security and defense lie within its almost exclusive mandate.

The relative autonomy of the military is not peculiar to Colombia, and for that matter to Latin America, but rather most militaries enjoy some independence within democratic constitutional orders. In Colombia, however, this condition acquired a peculiar character due to an inherently weak state with a pronounced hegemonic crisis. This condition provided even more autonomy for the military in Colombia than in the rest of Latin America. The irony is that the military's extended margin of freedom in managing its own affairs, defense, and public order policy may explain why the Colombian military shied away from seizing political power. It was reaping the benefits of this political order without the costs of being at the political front. It learned its lesson from the military dictatorships of Brazil and Argentina which suffered significant losses in their military prestige, power, and economic resources during their rule forcing them to retreat to their barracks. Perhaps the best explanation to why the military shied away from seizing power in Colombia was presented by the former attorney general, Alfonso Valdivieso, who said: "The military always had its way by less drastic measures than taking power through the application of the strategy of the sabre-rattling (Ruidos de Sables)."[3] Under this strategy, "the military were able to extract concessions from the presidents and avoided losing their privileges," Valdivieso concluded.[4] In this manner the threats of a coup was as effective and less costly than a coup, Valdivieso explained. Hence, the several "rumors of coup attempts" that circulated during the Samper period as well as in previous periods could be understood better using Valdivieso's "sabre-rattling" analogy.

The causes of the military gaining more autonomy were due to two 1.) NO
intertwined processes. One was the lack of a coherent policy decided by DIRECT
the civilian authorities that defined clearly the ground rules of civil-mil- POLICY
itary relationship. Why the civilian authorities did so could be explained ON
by the lack of political consensus within the ruling elite still tormented CIVIL-
by sectarian politics compounded by the interelite war. The second inter- MILITARY
related process is the inertia that the pattern of delegating security issues RELATION-
created in front of any future change if it was not in the interest of the SHIP
military. If the military interests were threatened its reaction was sabre 2.) MILITARY
rattling which in most cases worked to expand its power.[5] INTEREST WERE 1ST

The outcome was two institutionalized domains of public policy
where the military almost exclusively determines and formulates strategies regarding national security, public order, and designing and executing military budgets. This allowed the military to articulate and pur-
sue its interests with relative ease and without public scrutiny. The
bifurcation of public policy led to a divergence in interests among the
state agencies, which at times caused conflicts. In no area was this
clearer than in the attempts at peace negotiations with the different
guerrilla groups carried out by the respective governments during the
1980s and 1990s.

When the executives were committed to a peace negotiation, the
military had a competing agenda that it sought to implement. Three
examples support the above argument. One is the infamous 1985 attack
on the Supreme Court of Justice in the center of Bogota and few meters
away from the presidential residence, Casa de Nariño. The then active
M-19 seized the building and took the magistrates and some visitors as
hostages.[6] The military who was not keen on President Belisario Betancur's negotiation with the M-19 nor on his policy in the area of security,
decided to attack.[7] According to different sources, the attack was not
ordered by the president and the outcome of the such event, which led
to the killing of almost all the people inside the building including the
judges, and the guerrillas, led to a virtual coup. The military regained the
upper ground in defining policy in the areas of defense and security and
its antithesis, peace negotiation. Betancur finished his term, and his
peace initiative died in the ruins of the Justice Palace.[8]

Another major case illustrating divergence between the military and
the civilian authorities was the 1991 attack on Casa Verde in La Uribe,
the headquarters of FARC since 1984, amidst peace negotiations and on
the same day of the Constitutional Assembly election, which was authorized to draft a new constitution. This attack of course derailed the
negotiation in spite of two attempts to save it in Caracas, Venezuela, and
Tlaxcala, Mexico.[9] The most plausible version of the event was presented by then Minister of Defense, Rafael Pardo, who contended that

the attack was not authorized by the president and himself, but rather carried out by the military in light of its granted latitude in fulfilling its constitutional duty in the area of defense and security.[10] In this context, according to Rafael Pardo, the military is not obligated to clear all operations with the executive since the decision to attack was within its "constitutional duty." What is more important is that the attack led to the protraction of the conflict, and the military retook the political initiative due to the escalation in the civil war that followed.[11] Pardo, who was also the chief peace negotiator (consejero de paz) in 1989, described the type of relationship that the government of Virigilio Barco developed with the military to avoid the mishaps of Betancur as "always strong and we sought to keep it close, not only in important policy making issues, but also we sought agreement on the operative details even the most trivial ones"[12] Pardo, added that "the peace process required articulation and decisions that involved the military at the command level as well as those at the medium and lower levels that are needed to safeguard the process." Peace negotiations are complex matters which involve a great number of agencies, institutions, and interest groups. In Colombia the military, because of the power amassed by their autonomy, became the maker and breaker of peace, as Pardo implied.[13]

During Ernesto Samper's (1994–98) government, the conflict became more evident, and the military gained the upper political ground. Armed with the scandal of narcotraffickers financing Samper's presidential campaign and the inability of the Congress to remove him, the military emerged as the most important remaining symbol of the "state's legitimacy." This notion was reinforced by the U.S. policy during that period that maintained its relationship with the military, while the president himself was ostracized and even denied a visa to visit the United States. Consequently, the military became more daring in its confrontation with its "deligitimized" president, which was epitomized with a showdown over the FARC precondition for the negotiation the army withdrawal from La Uribe. The military expressed its vehement opposition to this condition, which in turn led President Samper to question who was really governing the country by exclaiming in one of his speeches, "Aqui mando yo," "I govern here!" Samper's government was entertaining the idea of the demilitarization, which the following administration did carry out but not without confrontations.

Alfonso Valdivieso, who was then Attorney General during the Samper administration, explained that the schism between the government and the military reached very serious proportions, which threatened the country's constitutional order. The president and Harold Bedoya, then head of the military charted two parallel policies that more often than not were irreconcilable. Valdivieso added, that the general refused to resign in spite of his opposition to the president, and the president did not have enough political support to remove him.[14] Valdivieso concluded that this period strained the institutional division of labor propelling a crisis, which was not resolved until the end of Samper's term.[15]

Last but not least is the evident strain between President Andres Pastrana (1998–2002) and the military, which reached high levels when most of the army leaders (16 generals, 30 colonels, and many officers) threatened to resign their posts in support of the Defense Minister Lloreda, who was protesting the government's peace negotiating strategy.[16] The outcome of the "sabre-rattling" was the resignation of Lloreda in 1999, and the president in his turn promised to revise the government plan to reduce military retirement benefits, pension funds, and the military justice system (under which military personnel are only subject to military justice) and to consult more closely the military in the area of peace negotiation with the guerrillas.[17] Perhaps the most revealing aspect of this crisis was that the military did not limit its concerns to the government peace policy, but extended them to others, including the areas that also define the institutional interests of the military, that is government allocation of resources.[18]

In 2001, the military emboldened by the United States "anti-drug" 1.3 billion aid-mostly in military hardware—managed to pass through Congress a National-Security bill that aims to increase the armed forces legal freedom, reduction of outside scrutiny of their actions, limiting investigation of human rights abuses to the military branch of the prosecutor's office, and greater judicial power to retain civilians when prosecutors are unable to accompany military operations; it also exempts the military from government spending cuts. This bill demonstrates again that the military does not cease from attempting to expand its influence and interests whenever the chance arises. If approved by President Pastrana, the bill would be a severe blow to Colombia's shaky democracy and to what is left of civil liberties and freedoms.

CONTAINMENT, LOW INTENSITY WAR AND THE COMFORTABLE IMPASSE

From 1958 through 1990, the appointment of the Ministry of Defense was the prerogative of the military. Normally an active duty military was appointed to the position of minister of defense. This practice only stopped in 1991 and was reinforced by constitutional reform of the same year when a civilian was appointed to this position following consultations with the military. Before 1991, the military commanders articulated the institutional interests of the military and the defense minister carried out these goals with no oversight from the other branches of government.

In a condition of civil war, such arrangement provided the military with a wide margin to articulate a counterinsurgency strategy that classified most of the opposition under the rubric of "enemy of the state," thus subject to suppression and even physical liquidation. But this counterinsurgency strategy was primarily one of containment rather than all out war. The containment strategy was based on keeping the guerrillas out of the strategic economic areas and political centers. This strategy drew its principle from the doctrine of low-intensity war. It concentrated on maintaining tight control over key urban areas by suppressing union leaders, activists, guerrillas' allies, and the political opposition in general. In part, this strategy was affected by three main factors: (a) limited resources and poor equipment at the military's disposal; (b) U.S. support of a containment strategy rather than a costly high-intensity warfare; (c) the perception that the guerrillas did not pose any serious threat to the security of the state and the economic base of the country since most of the insurgency activity was fought in rural areas.

The containment strategy and the low-intensity war prompted the pragmatic interests of the military such as pressuring the civilian to maintain the flow of resources without straining the state budget but enough to satisfy the military's increase in salaries and pensions. More than 60 percent of the military force is dedicated to protect key economic sectors, and about 70 percent of the defense budget is spent on salaries and other benefits and the rest in upgrading its armament. This skewed structure of military expenditures inhibited the development of a proactive strategy to combat the insurgency. Instead, the institutional interests of the military became articulated around a strategy of low-intensity war, allowing an uneasy coexistence with the guerrillas.

The 1991 constitution did not make any serious changes in defining or restructuring civil military relations. Only one article of the 1886 constitution was reorganized, without changing its spirit. The causes behind this reluctance were the pressure that the military brought to bear on the drafters of the new constitution. The military accepted the constitutional change on the condition that its privileges and power were left intact, a promise that was fulfilled by the Constitutional Assembly members some of whom were ex-guerrilla members of the M-19. In essence then, Cesar Gaviria's government left the military role intact assuming an attitude of business as usual. This was the main constitutional change since the 1886 constitution; thus, a historical chance was missed.

Nonetheless, Gaviria's government introduced some measures such as the creation of the Presidential Council for Security and Defense and the appointment of a civilian to the Ministry of Defense, the first in forty years. It also created the Unit for Justice and Security within the Department of National Planning in charge of strategic planning, conducting feasibility studies, evaluation, and policy recommendations in areas of security and defense. Finally, there was the appointment of a civilian to the directorate of the National Security Department (DAS). These attempts to restructure civil-military relations were indeed overshadowed by the escalation of the armed conflict in the years that followed.

In hindsight, these measures had potential if they were to be put into practice, particularly in determining that the areas of "security and public order" are in the final instance the prerogative of the president in a democratic system. These new institutions were created but without altering in any fundamental way the military political dominance in the areas of security and public order. But when Gaviria finished his last year in government with the declaration of the "Integrated War"—all out war against the insurgency and narcotraffickers—the military was able to circumvent the institutional changes and thus managed to maintain its privileges.[20] In sum, Barco's and Gaviria's security emergency measures complemented the Legislative Decree 1923 (Estatuto de Seguridad), introduced during the government of Turbay Ayala. This latter was one of the most repressive government in the country's 20th century. All these security measures enhanced the power of the military.

One of the most relevant aspects to my investigation is that the military not only maintained its autonomy in conducting the military aspect of the civil war, but was very influential in determining its budgets. This important aspect was protected by Decree 1314 of 1988, which allowed the General Directorate of Budget and the National Department of Planning to specify to the military the maximum limits allocated for the operational costs, investment, and external credit. The military was entitled to allocate these funds the way it wished with no civilian oversight or any accountability to civilian authorities. At least once the military came close to overthrowing a civilian government, mainly because of civilian interference in deciding the military budget. That was in 1973 when General Guillermo Pinzon Caicedo criticized in an article the president for meddling in the defense budget, which led to his dismissal by President Carlos Lleras. But, because of his dismissal, according to a 1973 airgram from the United States Embassy in Bogotá, ". . . brigade commanders of all 20 general officers in the Bogotá area were prepared to overthrow (Carlos) Lleras, but Pinzon told them bluntly that he did not want a government brought down on his account. Nevertheless, the generals did go to Carlos Lleras and they demanded (and obtained) a letter of apology from Carlos Lleras to Pinzon."[21] This document reveals how vehemently the military defended its privileged role in deciding its budget. Twenty-six years later, in 1999, a similar crisis occurred in part caused by the Pastrana's government plan to cut the military budget and pensions as discussed above.

The military defensive posture mentioned earlier, was partially the result of structural factors and options chosen by the military leadership. On the structural side, we can highlight the limited resources diverted by the state to defense, which is attributed to the inability of the political elite to project leadership, that is hegemony, particularly in articulating a proactive counterinsurgency strategy and rally accordingly the resources needed to carry it out successfully. Now, however, it is important to analyze the choices made by the military leadership and their impact on the protraction of the conflict and the formation of the war system.

The first and most important choice was to assume a defensive posture, which meant that key strategic areas were kept under the protection of the army and the police force, devoting little attention and resources to enhance the military offensive capabilities.[22] In this fashion the guerrillas' state-building capabilities remained virtually unchecked with the exception of some military operations carried out intermittently. The structure of the military forces in the 1970s and throughout the first half of the 1990s was based on brigades and battalions distributed into some departments considered strategic with little mobile capability suitable for counterinsurgency. By 1997, the total number of soldiers (army, airforce, and navy) amounted to 131,000 with less than 20 percent (about 22,000) of those are professional soldiers deployed for defensive purposes and/or in occasional incursions against the guerrillas. The remaining are in administrative and logistical support positions. The proportion of personnel dedicated to administrative functions is very high as compared with the national armies of other countries. The ratio of administrative logistical support to combat soldiers is 6:1 in Colombia, while the international ratio is 3:1.[23]

This is not the most essential aspect of the issue in focus, but rather the function of the administrative posts in the ascendancy of the military personnel. The administrative posts tend to be the most appreciated and favored within the institution. Military commanders that are distinguished in combats are awarded administrative positions. In this manner, in order to move in the military hierarchy, administrative posts become key, since in that position one establishes a political network.[24] In this mode, we can infer that the low-intensity conflict has allowed the military to develop an institutional setup that was relatively comfortable within the context of a civil war. The key components of the setup are a defensive posture reinforced by a bloated administrative body. If we complement this finding with the increases in salaries, benefits, and pensions received by the military in the last two decades, then a better understanding can be achieved.

Military expenditures increased from 1.2 percent of the GNP in 1985 to 2.16 percent in 1996 and to 3.5 of the GNP in 1999. The increase was three times higher than its 1985 level in pesos. This was in addition to more than $600 million in debts, which constituted one-third of the total public debts, incurred in 1997.[2] But these increases did not improve the combat capabilities of the military forces as the coordinator of the Commission of Rationalization of Public Expenditures, Gabriel Rosas argues. A view concurred by the ex-director of National Planning, Armando Montenegro, who added that the attempts to rationalize military expenditures by establishing civilian oversights (such as the Unit of Security of the National Planning) were lost because of the lack of cooperation of the military.[26] The military instead, managed to increase its expenditures with minimal accountability, which also opened the doors for corruption.[27]

Since Gaviria's government, which inaugurated a civilian as minister of defense, salaries and other benefits to the military multiplied by 2.2 to 3.4, depending on the rank.[28] These increases applied also to the 90,000 retired personnel. Gaviria's government introduction of Law 4 led to a two-fold annual increase in the expenditure per person between 1991 and 1996, (from about five thousand dollars per year per person to ten thousand in 1996.[29] The bulk of the defense expenditures, more than 70 percent is spent in salaries, pensions, maintenance, logistics, medical services, and housing and less than 20 percent is invested to upgrade armament.[30] In 1991, for example, the salaries of the military and the police forces constituted about 1 percent of GNP, by 1996 they increased to 1.5 percent of the GNP, representing more than 53 percent of the total government payroll.[31] Such increases of the military salaries affected negatively the salaries of other government employees, including those working in health and education.[32]

The fact that the greatest proportions of resource increases to the military went into its administrative budget explains why the performance of the military in its combat of the insurgency has not changed since the 1980s. The army/guerrilla ratio of fatalities is an indicator to whether these increases in budgetary allocation led to an improvement in combat performance. If anything, this ratio changed in favor of the guerrillas in the late 1990s, from 1:1.52 in favor of the military recorded in 1984 to 1:1.21 in favor of the military in 1999 (see table 3.1). Note the success of the guerrillas in closing the fatality gap increasingly to its favor. The reason behind this decline in army performance lies in the structure of military forces, which did not change with the increasing power of the guerrillas in the 1990s. The army has only

TABLE 3.1

Fatalities: Armed Forces (FFAA) versus Guerrillas

Year	1986	1987	1988	1989	1990	1991	1992	1993	1994	1995	1996	1998	1999
Armed Forces	219	285	65	205	541	656	521	363	383	409	478	581	505
Guerrillas	335	457	49	464	727	1460	1404	1210	909	696	740	704	806
Fatalities Ratio Armed Forces/ Guerrillas	1:1.52	1:1.60	1:1.33	1:2.2	1:1.34	1:2.22	1:2.69	1:3.3	1:2.37	1:1.70	1:1.54	1:1.21	1:1.59

Source: The fatality figures were obtained from the Ministerio de Defensa, Estado Mayor de las Fuerzas Militares. The calculations of the fatality ratio are those of the author. The data for 1997 were unavailable.

— LOW # OF PROFESSIONAL SOLDIERS

about 23,000 professional soldiers (out of an institution with about 179,000 personnel) combating and insurgency that doubled its fighting force from 10,000 rebels in the 1980s to more than 20,000 rebels in the late 1990s.[33]

If the number of combats between the guerrillas and the military are factored in, then a better understanding of the military balance emerges. In 1986 there were 85 reported combats (see table 3.2), whereas the number of combats jumped to 552 in 1992 and remained approximately at that level for the rest of the decade. The probability of suffering higher fatalities increases with the number of combats sustained; hence, in 1996 the guerrillas confronted the military in 584 occasions, yet the ratio of insurgents killed remained at 1:1.54, which is close to the ratio of 1986 (1:1.52) when only 147 combats occurred between the military and the guerrilla groups.

This trend in fatality ratios reveals the existing correlation of military forces between the two contending forces indicating the guerrillas' improved combat performance between 1986 and 1999. This was against the backdrop of the military's reluctance to alter its structure, strategy, doctrine, and armament to respond to the guerrillas' growth until the late 1990s when the dynamics of the civil war changed due to the emergence of the paramilitary groups (see chapter 5).

The strategic choices made by the military to invest in its administration more than in raising its combat capabilities have contributed to a military impasse with the insurgency. This impasse was comfortable enough to allow the military to develop its institution by inflating the size of its bureaucracy— third in size only after the largest business conglomerates, Antioquian Syndicate and the Santo Domingo Group— and increasing salaries, pensions, and other benefits. Simply stated, the comfortable impasse allowed the military to accumulate significant resources that could not have obtained under a condition of peace or under a high intensity conflict. This explains the vested institutional interests in maintaining a low-intensity conflict characterized by containment rather than an all-out war, which is more costly. Therefore, the military forces' defensive posture, structure, and interests contributed to the emergence and consolidation of the war system. A question is in order here: did the military adopt the low-intensity war and the containment strategy as pragmatic responses to the lack of state resources? Or was it also responding to some other factors?

MILITARY CONTAINMENT
AND THE COMFORTABLE IMPASSE

Documents newly declassified by the Department of State may help to provide an answer to this question. According to a 1972 country assess-

TABLE 3.2
Guerrilla Military Activity 1985–1996

	1985	1986	1987	1988	1989	1990	1991	1992	1993	1994	1995	1996
Military-guerrilla combats	94	47	88	254	222	216	298	552	632	592	546	584
Ambushes	100	143	155	91	57	89	154	136	73	91	75	97
Sabotage	98	80	95	271	155	190	566	490	175	325	189	340
Attacks against population centers	96	78	52	35	12	19	51	34	15	22	13	25
Attacks against installations	50	46	62	56	20	24	44	65	8	34	28	35
Assaults on entities	49	44	52	74	54	48	50	49	31	18	13	15
Road blockages	59	54	48	41	32	29	54	63	34	50	26	16
Skirmishes	na	19	17	44	60	75	124	161	107	242	137	140
Total	546	611	669	866	612	690	1341	1550	1075	1374	1027	1252

Source: Consejeria de Paz, Presidency of the Republic.

ment study report "The Reasons for Discarding the Objective of Elimination of the Insurgency" which stated "when measuring the level of insurgency in Colombia [one must consider] (a) the current effectiveness of the insurgency including its impact against the established government and, (b) the potential of the insurgency," it was concluded that the guerrillas did not constitute a serious menace in the 1970s. Accordingly the Department of State report of 1972 recommended maintaining the same course of U.S. policy by stating " These considerations are still valid today, and limit the obtainable goal for both the Colombian and the U.S. governments to one of *containment in lieu of elimination.* The combination of Colombian-US resources are designed to reach this goal, whereas elimination would take vast amounts of resources which are better utilized elsewhere (emphasis added)."[34]

Hence, U.S. hesitation to commit more resources for warfare was underpinned by the assumption that the guerrilla threat was minimal (less than 700 insurgents in the early 1970s). Thus it would be cost effective to invest aid in social projects that could enhance the political power of the state.[35] The U.S. tailored containment policy has had a strong influence on the Colombian military security doctrine and its corresponding structure, considering that most members of the Colombian military were trained in the United States or in a U.S. base in Panama where the doctrines of "containment and low-intensity warfare" were central in the programs they studied.[36]

This finding calls for revisiting most of the literature on Colombia's military, which focuses on the impact of the doctrines of National Security of the U.S. and those elaborated by the bureaucratic-military models of the Southern Cone on civil-military relations.[37] But few made the analytical link between the Doctrine of National Security and the containment military strategy, which is our main concern in this chapter. While the Doctrine of National Security defined the ideology of the military as the guardian of the sociopolitical and constitutional order, it had little bearing on the military strategy formulated.[38] In my view, the military was responding to the actual capabilities and resources available at its disposal (adequate only for a containment strategy) more than to the ideological impulses of national security.[39]

The irregular guerrilla war that the military was fighting was difficult to win without reduction in its bloated administrative body, making costly changes in the military command, control, and communication system, and creating mobile ground forces with its logistics suitable for guerrilla warfare supported by an effective air force and navy. Neither Colombia nor the United States was willing to assume these costs. Furthermore, the institutional resistance of the military to change was an important variable that impeded the restructuring of its forces. Old habits die hard, as the saying goes; hence, the containment strategy that dominated the military discourse for three decades was not about to be abandoned without resistance from individuals, standard practices, and the bureaucracies developed under it.

Thus, the state's inability to commit more resources, the prevailing guerrillas warfare, and the U.S. policy largely shaped the alternatives available to the military. In this context, the containment military strategy became the optimal option given the mentioned structural constraints. In its turn, the National Security Doctrine became the ideological tool deployed to maintain and stretch the military's autonomy in managing public order, security, and its budgets. Within this context, we can understand the constraints as well as the set of practices and interests developed by the military under a low-intensity war. All of these factors contributed to the protraction of the civil war and to the conformation and consolidation of the war system.

THE MILITARY AND SECURITY ENTERPRISES

One of the most important outcomes of the civil war's comfortable impasse illustrating the type of economic and political interests formed is the mushrooming of security companies contracted to protect business enterprises, banks, and individuals. These companies extend their services to most residential buildings in middle-class and upper-class neighborhoods in Colombian cities. This characteristic is not peculiar to Colombia since the privatization of security—a function previously reserved to the state—is becoming common in most of the industrial world.[40] But in Colombia the privatization process has a different dimension since it has taken place within the context of a civil war underlying a chronic crisis in the state's hegemony, manifested by its inability to extend its authority over the totality of the national territory. It is estimated that about 40 percent of the territory is under the control of the guerrilla and other private armies.

The proliferation of these companies started in late 1993 and early 1994 when then President Cesar Gaviria introduced two decrees: Decree 2535 regarding guns, ammunitions, and explosives; and Decree 356 regarding "Private Security and Surveillance." Gaviria's government designed these two decrees to compliment the government's "Integral War" against the insurgency. In effect, as Francisco Leal and Eduardo Pizarro argue on this issue, the Gaviria government succumbed to the war drums played by the military circumventing the reforms it proposed in its first years.[41] The most intriguing aspect of the burgeoning private security companies is that many retired members of the military find in them a source to supplement their salaries and increase their retirement pensions. Needless to say, that the condition of civil war and the criminal violence it foments makes this sector one of the country's fastest growing businesses. About 300 companies were founded in the 1990s, with about 104 branches spread throughout 627 departments; there are 7 agencies that specialize in the protection of securities (such as banks), with 49 branches. By 1997, the total number employed by these agencies numbered 89,159 employees, plus 5,210 administrative personnel.[42]

A high percentage of these companies' owners, employees, and trainers are retired military officers and are regulated by the Directorate of Security and Surveillance of the Ministry of Defense, which provides the licenses. Increasingly these companies became revolving doors for military personnel seeking to supplement their retirement pension or salaries if they were contracted while in active duty. It has been estimated that by 1998 private groups (both business and individuals) spent about $150 million (0.3 of the GNP) to protect their properties and ensure their personal safety. The tendency of business enterprises and individuals to contract private security companies reveals that the state is unable to fulfill one of its main fundamental functions: protecting the economic interests of the dominant groups and their personal safety in class-divided societies.[43] This ineffectiveness of the state in protecting its main clients and their interests legitimizes the reticence of individuals to pay protection taxes to the state while paying to private companies in urban areas, or to guerrillas/and or paramilitary groups in rural areas.

The irony of this situation is that the state (represented by the executive and legislative branches which legalized these companies) and the military, who not only applauded the measures but also has direct interest in their adjudication, contributed to the weakening of an already weakened state. In economic terms, the approximately $150 million spent by the dominant class and the middle class on protection is a transfer of income to about 100,000 employees in the security companies, making this sector a viable source of employment, investment, and capital formation on which the military personnel cash. This sector is also tied to other multinational security and insurance companies that found in Colombia a lucrative market due to the high premiums they charge because of the risks.[44] In political terms, these companies allow members of the military (by proxy through ex-military) to penetrate deeper into the civil society structures giving them more latitude and authority in handling the privatize side of "public order" and thus benefit from a condition they helped create.

In addition to the privatization of security, in 1996 the government of Ernesto Samper (1994–98) promoted the creation of private vigilante groups, "CONVIVIR," a decision revoked two years later succumbing to political pressures. The CONVIVIR were under the Directorate of Security and Surveillance of the Ministry of Defense. The legal foundation of these organizations were the Decrees of 2535 and 356 mentioned above. Their objective was to provide logistical support and information gathering to the military forces. In a span of less than a year, more than 500 CONVIVIR were founded with about 9,633 armed men. The total cost of the Convivir was estimated to be $32 million.[45]

Even after their ban in 1999, some CONVIVIR still function in rural areas controlled by large landowners and narcotraffickers, their two staunchest supporters. CONVIVIR provided the legal cover for their paramilitary groups. The state has yet to recover the arms and ammunitions distributed to these groups before they were banned. If there is any lesson to be drawn from the CONVIVIR experiment, it is that it exacerbated both the state's hegemonic crisis and violence levels by further curtailing the prerogatives and functions of the government and the military.[46]

The CONVIVIR experiment was not yet concluded when in 1999 the Ministry of Defense introduced a pilot plan for Antioquia of creating "Peasant Soldiers" units. Their legality stems from the Law 48 of 1993, which allows peasants to serve their mandatory military service in their areas of residence, rather than in other cities. The "peasant-soldiers" are to perform civilian activities, gather military intelligence, and participate in combats. The plan entered into effect in October 2000. This plan is nothing but another rehash of old themes, but this time the goal is to create peasant organizations linked organically with the military similar to the peasant defense groups that were erected in Peru (Rondas) and Guatemala during their civil wars.

THE MILITARY AND
MULTINATIONAL SECURITY COMPANIES

Another important area that is critical for our understanding of the scope of interests developed by the military under the low-intensity war was that of the multinational security corporations operating in Colombia. The low-intensity war did not disrupt the country's economy in any fundamental way since the initiation of the insurgency in the 1960s allowing the country's economic growth to continue until the mid-1990s. The economic trade liberalization policy of the 1980s and early 1990s and the impetus of new discoveries of oil, gold, coal, emeralds, and other raw minerals led to an increase in capital investments by foreign companies.

With the advent of an increasing number of multinational companies came an increasing number of multinational security and insurance companies. Chapter 5 focuses on aspects of the multinational corporations operations in Colombia and the risks they take when meddling with warring actors in areas of conflict. Here, however, the focus is on the military personnel, particularly the retired officers, whose previous experience and personal relationships with high-level military officers allow them to carve for themselves a niche within the multinational security companies in Colombia.

An example of this is Enrique Urrea, a former Colombian officer and currently the chairman of a security committee that includes sixty-five of the most important multinational companies operating in Colombia, most of which are from the United States. Urrea also heads the security operation of Esso, a Colombian subsidiary of Exxon. According to Urrea, most of the security chiefs working in the private sector are retired military officers like him who have access to the most senior officers in the Colombian military command.[48] On the one hand, this access allows information sharing and collaboration with the state's security agencies. And on the other hand, these companies are interested in recruiting influential ex-military officers to facilitate their operations and consolidate their market share. The more connection an ex-officer has, the more access he has to sensitive security information, which improves the company services, increasing the amount it charges, and also helps the company in securing contracts and expediting licenses.

The study of multinational security companies also uncovers an important aspect of the modus operandi of foreign companies in a country where protection rent-seekers range from multinational security companies to military, paramilitary and guerrilla groups,[49] hence, exacerbating competition in the protection market and accentuating violent conflicts among local and international actors.[50] This example offers us another glimpse of the types of interests that the military (retired) or potential retiree developed under the low-intensity war and the systemic complexities of the war system.[51]

A different modality of protection rent was the one extracted directly from multinational corporations operating in Colombia. It is very difficult to assess the magnitude of the protection rent extracted, but some evidence suggests that this practice began as early as 1973 with Battalion 18 (twelve hundred officers and soldiers) of the Fourth Brigade, camped on the outskirts of Bagre camp, protecting the Consolidated Gold Dredging Limited on the Nechi River in Northeast Antioquia.[52] The multinational company paid about $80,000 per month to the battalion which was equivalent to the battalion's monthly food bill. Three decades later, British Petroleum and Oxy (a subsidiary of Occidental Oil) also financed the creation and maintenance of a battalion and two platoons (about one thousand soldiers and officers) by paying about $70 million a year to secure the protection of their operations in Colombia. It is plausible that there are other cases that have not come to the public eye yet.

At another level but noteworthy is the military's inability—given its political power, financial resources, and autonomy—to build an industrial-military complex similar to that of Brazil, Argentina, and Chile. The Colombian military owns only about thirteen institutions and business enterprises, which are humble in regional terms. This can be attributed to the level of the country's industrial development, which tallies behind the mentioned cases, and to the limited resources allocated for defense given the country's high levels of violence.[53] These two factors can partly explain why the military tended to extract protection rents from private sources (security companies) and through subcontracting security (such as its relationship with BP and Oxy).

MILITARY, PARAMILITARY, AND LANDOWNERS

Before concluding this chapter it is imperative to cast some light on the social class origins of the subalterns and the commanders of the military and how this variable comes into play with the ones already discussed. The military is predominantly drawn from the rural intermediary and small villages. The recruitment from these areas was not accidental but rather was a policy designed by the United States and accepted by the army. The political/ideological bases of this policy stemmed from the belief that recruiting army subofficials and officials from the middle class in cities could entail a security risk, since the urban centers are highly politicized and affected by leftist ideologies. In this mode, the armed forces became predominantly drawn from the middle peasants and small peasants. This recruitment was also underscored by financial and educational requirements to qualify to one of the following three categories: soldier, subaltern, and officer. From the latter the armed commanders are drawn. In general the class differential between the high command and the soldiers is not very wide, since all are drawn from middle to poor peasants. The children of the landed oligarchy as well as the urban bourgeoisie stayed away from an institution they did not need either for social or political ascension. These classes rather viewed the officers with condescension, which made it difficult for the high officers to be fully integrated with the traditional dominant classes.

The military served as means of social ascension to those originating from petty landed peasantry who possess the financial resources to pay the fees and who fulfill certain educational requirements. These financial and educational requirements attracted a certain social stratum that is politically conservative and keen in maintaining its privileges won

[handwritten margin note: — PREFER SOLDIERS FROM RURAL SECTOR = NOT VERY EDUCATED & WILL NOT REVOLT]

the hard way. The social class backgrounds of the military leadership and the new interests and ideologies acquired along the way in their ascending process within the army facilitated building closer social links and political alliances with the landed oligarchy. Such links acquired more importance in a country locked in struggle over land property for most of the 20th century.

In consequence, when the landowning class built its own self-defense militias or when the narcobourgeoisie built its paramilitary organization in rural areas, the army found no trouble in building alliances with these groups to fight the main enemy of the social order: the guerrillas. In fact, the military has been instrumental in fomenting these groups since the 1960s as an integral part of its counterinsurgency doctrine. Active and reserve officers played leading roles in building paramilitary groups. As late as 1999, a paramilitary group known as the Calima Front (Frente Calima) in Valle del Cauca was founded with the participation of active duty, retired, and reserve military officers attached to the Third Brigade along with paramilitaries from the Self-Defense Group of Cordoba and Uraba.[54] This is not an isolated incident, since many other groups were formed with the active participation of local commanders, including that in Puerto Boyaca and Cordoba as discussed in chapter 5. It is not surprising that half of the commanders of the Colombian army are investigated for alleged links with the paramilitary groups given the peculiar class and social and ideological makeup of this force.[55] Moreover, this finding reveals also the type of interwoven relationship between some actors (military, paramilitary, narcobourgeoisie, and landlords) under the peculiar conditions of the war system in Colombia.

The increasing importance of these paramilitary organizations in the 1980s and 1990s was a function of the "real or perceived" threat of the opposition forces. In the 1980s for example, the paramilitary groups were instrumental in liquidating the Patriotic Unity, a leftist political organization that included communists, union leaders, independents, and guerrilla who were seen as serious political threat.[56] And after these organizations were outlawed in 1989, the military did not sever its ties. On the contrary, these ties are as strong as ever.[57]

The military relationship with narcotraffickers is based on the belief that they do not constitute a threat to the social order as is the case with the guerrilla groups. The guerrillas threaten the very foundation of the social order that allowed the army leadership to ascend socially and politically. Moreover, the guerrillas' political project calls for a radical change of the military institution in terms of its role (national defense and not acting as a police force as is now case under the National Security Doctrine), orientation, and trimming its size, as mentioned before.

It is no surprise that the guerrillas (FARC and ELN) have the reform of the military institutions as one of their primary goals in any negotiation process, which adds an important element in defining the nature of the institutional antagonism between these forces.[58]

The military reluctance in fighting narcotrafficking organizations has social, political, ideological, and pragmatic foundations. The social base of this affinity is the class root of the narcotraffickers mostly in lower urban classes (with the only exception the Cali Cartel).[59] The view of the military, which has resonance within the "popular sectors" has been a sort of sympathy with these "Robin Hoods." This notion was not baseless, but it rather drew on the "populist" discourse of narcotraffickers such as Rodriguez Gacha and Pablo Escobar who espoused public projects in poor neighborhoods such as building sports facilities, hospitals, and schools and providing employmemt opportunities in their front business organizations.[60] Rodriguez Gacha and Pablo Escobar among other Colombian narcotraffickers, were perceived by some social sectors as "generous, good men, simple, and were persecuted because they ascended from humble class origins and because they help the poor."[61] Then the military reluctance to fight narcotraffickers can be at least partially attributed to a complacent political culture that accepts contraband and money laundering as a normal state of affairs.[62]

But more important, the military found also in the ascending narcobourgeoisie social allies that could strengthen their counterinsurgency because of their vast financial capabilities. It is a marriage of convenience as seen in the cases of Puerto Boyaca, Cordoba, Mapiripan, and finally Calima, among many others attest to the validity of this argument.[63] The military-narcotraffickers-paramilitary linkages correspond also to the National Security Doctrine of containing the guerrillas' threat by going after their peasant-base of support and their urban supporters. It is part and parcel of the low-intensity war underscored by the constraints discussed above namely, resources available and the inefficient military structure. It is a type of war that is convenient since it does not involve costs on part of the military or the state. At any rate, the narcotraffickers and large landowners primarily sustain these costs.

Finally, a vast network of relations exists among drug traffickers and the military which required as late as 1998 drastic changes in the air force command because many officers were implicated in narcotrafficking in what was called as the "Blue Cartel" a reference to their blue uniforms.[64] Air force officers were involved in two widely publicized foiled drug-trafficking attempts, in one of which they used the presidential plane and in the other an air force plane on a training mission to the U.S. The corrupting influence of the hugely wealthy drug traffickers and organized crime in general can not be underestimated in our analysis of their relationship. In March 2000, for example, Colonel Luis Alberto Alvaran, director of intelligence of the Department of Administrative Security (DAS) which coordinates the security functions of the military and police; and Major Luiz Eduardo Pedraza, head of its counterintelligence unit, and Romer Salazar Sánchez the coordinator of security operations, were implicated in the trafficking of arms and embezzling of public funds, among other charges. This was not an isolated incident. In cities such as Cali and Medellin, some military commanders were/ and probably still are on the payroll of narcotraffickers. Corruption, then, adds another important dimension to the interdependent interests between organized crime and sectors of the military.

CONCLUSION

In the above discussion is established a causal relationship between the resources available and the military choice of a containment strategy underscored by a low-intensity war. Nonetheless, this strategy did not hamper the growth of the military institution, nor did it affect its prerogatives in mastering public order and security, increasing their budget, and salaries, and expanding their sphere of interests onto private security companies. All these suggest that the impasse between the armed forces and the guerrillas was comfortable enough to allow the accumulation of political and economic assets that would have been inaccessible under a condition of peace or under a high-intensity war. Succinctly stated, then, the comfortable impasse permitted the formation of a positiv￼ political economy, which defines the institutional interests of the military in the formation of a war system.

But since protracted wars are dynamic open systems, the condition of comfortable impasse and the assets accumulated in one phase could erode under an escalation of warfare. During the second half of the 1990s, a grave escalation of war took place, which impacted the political economy of the war and the dynamics of the war system (discussed in chapters 5 and 6). For now suffice it to mention that after 1995, the civil war increasingly shifted away from a low-intensity war to a higher level of warfare underlying higher levels of violence in the country. The military's response was to adopt a new military strategy more apt for the new conditions.

This new strategy was based on reducing the size of the non-professional soldiers, increasing the number of mobile units, modernizing the military command and control and communication, and upgrading the role of the air force and the navy. Again this change of strategy was precipitated by the internal new dynamics of war but also in response to a policy shift in the United States, which is increasingly committing more resources and personnel to fight the menace of drugs. The irony is that United States, which was instrumental in promoting the containment military strategy in the 1970s fearing the costs of an all-out war, three decades later is promoting a more aggressive military posture, which is substantially costlier.[65] The estimated costs of modernizing the military forces is more than $400 million between 1999 and 2002, increasing the number of professional soldiers to 60,835 from 34,831 in 1999. These professional soldiers are backed up by a force of another 60,000 volunteers, making the total 120,000. Thus,the military did not witness any reductions in size in the new plan, only a restructuring in its composition. The salary of soldiers in this new plan increases from the minimum monthly salary of about $300 to about $600 between 1999 and 2002.[66] This is a very significant increase in a country suffering one of its worst economic crises since the Great Depression of the 1930s with skyrocketing unemployment levels reaching more than 20 percent in late 1999 and a negative economic growth of 6 percent.

Based on the above, it does not appear so far that the privileges of the military have been negatively affected by the escalation of the conflict caused by a destabilized war system. This could be attributed in large part to the increasing military aid and assistance of the United States mitigating some of the negative economic costs of the war. The core question is for how long would the U.S. sustain its involvement? Given the current level of the U.S. involvement, the question is whether the new conflict dynamics could undermine the military privileges acquired under the comfortable impasse and a stable war system or not? In the short term, the answer is obviously negative as demonstrated above but at the middle and longer terms is not clear. The following chapters, however, will help provide a more conclusive answer.

CHAPTER 4

Guerrillas and the Impasse

This chapter is grounded on my interviews with guerrilla leaders and informants as well as on a host of other primary and secondary sources. The interviews, which were conducted in 1997 and 1998, sought to gather information about the social composition of the guerrillas as well as their current political goals. Another set of interviews was carried out between 1994 and 1996; these were chiefly explorative and designed to familiarize myself with the subject matter, and actors involved, establish the necessary contacts, and assess the feasibility of this research. This chapter has two main objectives. It presents a brief history of the two major active guerrilla groups in Colombia, the Revolutionary Armed Forces of Colombia (Fuerzas Armadas Revolucionarias de Colombia; FARC) and the National Liberation Army (Ejercito de Liberacion Nacional; ELN), and a small group, Ejercito Popular de Liberacion (EPL), within the context of the crises of the peasant economy and the failures of the state institutions in resolving the conflict that these crises generated. The chapter's main argument is that the signing of the Pact of Chicoral in 1972 and the formal establishments of FARC (1964–66) and ELN in 1965 were no coincidence. The Pact of Chicoral and the guerrilla movements represent two diametrically opposed responses to the same institutional crisis whose genesis lies in the land struggles of the 1920s as discussed in chapter 2.

The second objective of this chapter is to analyze how the comfortable impasse with the state allowed the guerrillas to achieve a positive political economy (PPE), endowing them with political, military, and economic assets significant enough to increase their incentive to maintain the status quo rather than seeking an outright victory or a negotiated settlement. Seeking either an outright military victory, or a negotiated settlement carried risks that outweighed the benefits of the status quo. Keep in mind that this position of the guerrilla is grounded on the past experiences of the Patriotic Front and other guerrillas who agreed to surrender their arms and participate in the political process later to become subject to a systematic liquidation campaign by the state's (particularly its armed forces) sanctioned paramilitary groups.[1] In systems analysis, outcomes are in most cases different from the actors' original goals and interests. In this mode the chapter argues that the guerrilla organizations lend themselves inadvertently to a war system dynamics. I analyze the guerrilla groups in terms of their social composition, strategies, and military strength because I maintain that the war system is driven by the actors' incentives, goals, interests, and calculations. However, one can only evaluate an actor's behavior in connection with its impact on other actors' behavior and incentives.

FARC FROM MARQUELALIA (1964) TO CAQUETA (1998)

FARC evolved from the defense organizations that peasant squatters (colonos) and poor peasants set up in order to defend their parcels from the encroachments of large landowners and the state. The regions of Sumapaz and Taquendama (areas of strong communist presence) in the eastern part of the department of Tolima and southwestern part of Cundinimarca, which included large coffee estates, formed the bedrock of the FARC. These areas witnessed a struggle for land since the 1930s. After the assassination of the Liberal Party leader, Gaitan, in 1948, the Communist Party instructed the formation of self-defense leagues in these areas.

A few months before the 1950 election, president Ospina Perez (1946–50) declared a "state of emergency" in the country in an effort to control the riots protesting Gaitan's assassination. The Liberal Party in its turn declared a boycott of the presidential elections and called for a general strike. Consequently the army occupied Villavicencio (capital of Meta) and Puerto Lopez and armed supporters of the government occupied San Vicente de Chucuri in Santander on election day. Armed resistance spread to various departments and especially to the eastern plains. Liberal Party partisans, many of whom were related such as Los Parras, Los Bautista, Los Fonseca, Los Villamarin, Los Calderon, and others, joined forces with peasant leaders such as Eliseo Velasquez, Franco Isaza, and Guadalupe Salcedo, in their fight against the Conservative government. In the southeast of Antioquia, the resistance symbol was Juan de Jesus Franco; and in southern Cordoba the resistance was led by Jose Guerra; and in the northeast of Cundinamarca, it was led by Saul Fajardo.

In southern Tolima the guerrillas were drawn from members of the Communist Party and Liberal Party. The Commnunists were led by Isauro Yosa (alias Major Lister) and Jacobo Pias Alape (alias Charro Negro), all of whom were peasants. Among this latter group, the current legandary leader of FARC, Manuel Marulanda Velez (Tiro Fijo) started his revolutionary career. For four years, the Liberal guerrillas fought against the army and the Conservative partisans. In 1953, General Rojas

Pinilla led a successful military coup. He ordered the cessation of the military offensive and promised a general amnesty to those who gave up their arms. As a result a good number of Liberal guerrillas in the Llanos, Antioquia, and Santander surrendered their weapons to the government, some of whom were subsequently assassinated, including guerrilla leader Guadalupe Salcedo. The guerrillas of Cundinamarca and Tolima, particularly the Communists, refused to surrender their weapons, and consequently the state continued its military campaign against them.

In 1955, Pinilla declared Sumapaz and eastern Tolima to be military objectives. At that time, Manuel Marulanda Velez and Ciro Trujillo Castano were organizing peasants in southern Tolima and Tierra Adentro (Cauca). They decided to mobilize their forces, which included their families, and moved from Bejucales, El Doa, and Galilea to El Pato in Caqueta and Guayabero in el Meta, and some went to Alto Sumapaz. Consequently, these areas became guerrilla strongholds for the rest of the century.

In 1958, after the collapse of Rojas Pinilla's regime, the new National Front government issued the Plan of Rehabilitation, which offered a general amnesty to armed peasants who surrendered their weapons. The guerrillas of Sumapaz declared a cessation of hostilities and suspended their military operations but decided to keep their weapons and to maintain the self-defense league's organizational structures. (Many of the peasants of Sumapaz were veterans or children of veterans of the 1920s land struggles.)

Despite the cease fire, many of the peasant leaders were targets of an assassination campaign, and peasant leaders Silvestre Bermudez, Hermogenes Vargas, and Jacobo Parias Alape were killed. From 1958 through 1963, armed militias working for local landowners or the state carried out a terrorist campaign against the peasant leaders and their supporters in an attempt to break the resistance. Hence, this provided the ground work for a conflict in which paramilitary groups and armed peasants fought in different localities such as in Gaitania and Planado. In 1964, this led to the renewal of the state military campaign under the pretext of fighting the peasants' "Independent Republics" of Marquetalia, Riochiquito, El Pato, and Guayabero, regions of traditional peasant colonization.

This time, however, the fight against the "Communist" peasants had more international and regional resonance because it occurred in the wake of the Bay of Pigs crisis and the growing "specter" of Marx over the region.[2] The U.S. Doctrine of National Security taught to Latin American armies dominated the Colombia army's discourse and strategy. The guiding precept of this doctrine in Colombia became to fight peasant guerrillas and communism. In 1964, the army launched an offensive against the "independent peasant republics" with U.S. military assistance and political support. Anticipating an attack, the peasants evacuated children, elderly people, and women who could not fight. Forty-four women and men combatants remained. In a show of support and to coordinate the peasant defenses, the Communist Party dispatched a member of its central committee, Jacobo Arenas and a student from Universidad Libre and member of the Communist Youth Organization, Hernando González, who was killed a year later in Riochiquito.[3] The government forces dislodged the armed peasants, who in turn decided to shift their military strategy. Since the 1950s, they had operated through "self-defense leagues" in fixed localities; in the mid-1960s, the leagues were transformed into an armed movement that combined the agrarian reform experiments of the radical liberal Juan de la Cruz Varela and the organizational and military experiences of the Communist Party.[4] After the military offensive, armed peasants regrouped in southern Tolima and held an assembly in 1965 in which they adopted a guerrilla war mobile strategy instead of their defensive posture and an agrarian reform plan (Programa Agrario de las Guerrillas), which was later incorporated into FARC's political program. The official date of FARC foundation was in 1966, when the second conference of the guerrilla group was held to discuss military strategy and its political and agrarian plan. The first conference was held in 1965 when the peasant defense leagues retreated from its villages and regrouped in southern Tolima.

GENDER AND CLASS COMPOSITION OF THE FARC

The commanders of FARC were then Manuel Marulanda Vélez y Jacobo Arenas, Rigoberto Lozada ("Joselo"), Carmelo López, Rogelio Díaz, José de Jesús Rivas ("Cartagena") and Ciro Trujillo. All were of peasant origins, with the exception of Jacobo Arenas who was of working-class urban origins. The FARC's social base has not changed significantly since then, its social class composition remains predominantly peasant, and its strongholds are in areas of peasant colonization.[5] Only 30 percent of recruited combatants in the 1990s were from large cities and the lower middle class (see table 4.1). Since the 1970s, the number of women combatants has increased from less than 20 percent, to about 30 percent of FARC's forces.[6]

FARC's rank-and-file composition is also consistent with its leaders except for the fact that there is no female representation in its leadership (see table 4.2).[7] The social class composition of FARC leadership distinguishes it from the other guerrilla groups in Latin America, where the middle-class intellectual component was more pronounced. Such was

TABLE 4.1
FARC's Rank and File Social Composition (1998)

Class		Areas of orgins		Gender	
Peasants (mainly agricultural workers)	70%	Rural 90%	Urban 10%	Women 30%	Men 70%
Working class, students, and school teachers	20%				
Middle-class intellectuals	10%				

Sources: Yazid Arteta, FARC member of the Estado mayor Bloque Oriental interview with author, Bogotá, 1998; also based on FARC's urban leaders' accounts, interview with author, Bogotá December 1997.

TABLE 4.2
Social Composition of FARC's Leadership "Secretariado"[8]

Name	Area of Origin	Social class (father)
Manuel Marulanda	Village	Small propertied peasant
Raúl Reyes	Village	Small propertied peasant
Alfonso Cano	City	Middle class (professional)
Iván Márquez	Small city (Florencia)	Lower class
Jaime Guaracas	Village	Small propertied peasant
Mono Jojoy	Village (Nariño)	Small propertied peasant
Timoleón Jiménez	Village	Small propertied peasant

Source: Interview with FARC informant, Bogota, December 1997. The social category "small propertied peasant" refers to those with land properties of less than twenty hectares. This research adopts the classification of the Ministry of Agriculture of Colombia.

the case in the Cuban 26 of July Movement, FMLN (and its parties) in El Salvador and Sandanistas in Nicaragua, Shining Path in Peru, and URNG (and its parties) in Guatemala.[9] And in contrast to its counterpart in Colombia, ELN, the second most important active guerrilla group, has a less pronounced peasant composition, particularly in its

Central Command (the highest authority in the ELN) where the urban middle-class intellectuals outnumber the peasant and other lower-class members. But like the FARC, the commanders of fronts and columns are from peasant origins.[10]

Most revolutionary movements have drawn substantial support from intellectual urbanites, whereas FARC has done less so. There are a number of reasons why FARC remained predominantly a peasant movement. The first is the historical conditions under which FARC was formed and the social class composition of its founders. The peasant leaders of the defense leagues who later constituted the core group of FARC helped in cementing its peasant roots. It is no coincidence, therefore, that where once existed the "independent republics," FARC has succeeded in maintaining a solid support base for over three decades (see table 4.3). Subsequently, the areas of colonization have become the main areas where FARC exercises its major influence.

The second factor is the organizational divisions between the Communist Party(CP) and its former military arm, FARC. The party incorporated most of the urban intellectuals, students and working class, whereas FARC, because it operated in rural areas, attracted those living in the rural areas. This functional division of organizational/political labor was exacerbated when the CP and FARC relationship was severed in the late 1980s. The CP remained with a predominantly urban social base and FARC with a peasant one.

The third factor is that the political program and political tactics employed by the FARC did not address the class and political concerns of

TABLE 4.3
Guerrillas Rent Extraction (1998–1999)
($ million) (exchange rate $1=1,800 pesos)

	FARC	ELN
Tax on narcotraffickers	180	30
Ransom-kidnapping and extortion	198	40
Diversion of government resources and investments	40	60
Assaults on financial institutions and banks	30	20
Total	448	150

Source: Consejaria de Seguridad de la Presidencia, estimates of the National Police and the Military. See Camilo Granada and Leonardo Rojas, "Los Costos del Conflicto Armado," *Planeacion and Desarrollo* 26(4) (October-December, 1995): 119–51.

the urban middle class, particularly, after the collapse of the Soviet Union in 1989, which "discredited" the guerrillas' ideology and armed struggle with segments of leftist intellectuals.[11] The dialogue between the guerrillas and the majority of leftist intellectuals was practically severed in the 1990s. Consequently, the guerrillas lost an important political conduit in urban centers, which weakened their abilities to mobilize within the cities.

The fourth factor that locked FARC in the rural areas is related to the systematic liquidation campaigns exercised by right wing paramilitary groups allied with the military against important leftist leaders and activists, particularly in urban centers. Such campaigns have claimed more than 4,000 lives since the mid-1980s, and have left FARC as well as most insurgents without an urban political cover. The counterinsurgency tactics of the state and the paramilitary groups proved to be effective in denying the guerrillas a foothold in the urban centers where political and economic power is concentrated. This "political cleansing" of the key urban economic centers permitted the adaptation of the dominant classes and the political elite to a civil war mainly fought in rural areas, and allowed them to avoid the costs of any serious economic and political reform if peace is sought. This explains why the military impasse was comfortable to key sectors in the Colombian society, primarily the dominant classes as well as the military.

Most of FARC middle-class intellectual members are from urban areas, and most probably started their political life with the CP and then moved to guerrilla groups because of repression or for other reasons. FARC started a concerted effort in the mid-1980s to organize in urban centers through the Patriotic Union (UP), but as mentioned before, the UP was a target of state repression and paramilitary groups. Nonetheless, UP allowed FARC to expand its political activism in urban centers and gain some foothold within sectors of the working class and urban middle class. In the mid-1990s, FARC again revisited its organizational strategy within urban centers. One of its key tasks was to break its isolation from urban classes. Toward that end, it created the Bolivarian Movement for the New Colombia, a broad democratic movement with a broad agenda based on principles of democracy and social justice. According to Ivan Rios the political coordinator of FARC in San Vicente del Caquan, the new movement seeks to attract a cross-section of academics, artists, and intellectuals and it is not associated with the Communist Party as was the UP. Thus far, this front has received a lukewarm support among the middle-class intellectual circles.

FARC, COLONOS, AND CAPITALIST DEVELOPMENT

To understand the processes of colonization, it is imperative to identify the major trends in agrarian economic relations and how they corresponded to the impulses of national and international markets. I argue that colonization and the guerrilla movement are two forms of peasants' resistance against the capitalist transformation of production relations in the countryside. The levels and magnitude of this resistance depended also on the type of relations of productions that characterized each region: class relations and structure, political contingency, the pace of the region's integration into the global capitalist system, and the role of state institutions.

Colombia experienced three main waves of colonization in the 19th and 20th centuries. In the first wave(from the mid-19th century until the early 20th century) landless peasants escaped the haciendas in search of lands.The second wave occurred during La Violencia when peasants escaping from Pato, Riochiquito, and Marquetalia in el Meta fled persecution from the state and the Conservative forces and sought refuge in peripheral regions, such as Guaviare, Caqueta, and North Santander. This marked the beginning of the peasant struggle; its early proponents were Liberal partisans, but the CP gradually gained influence by propagating revolutionary ideas among the peasants and building the foundation of what later became known as FARC.

The third wave started during the 1970s, expanding the colonization process in Guaviare, Putumayo, Caqueta, South Bolivar, North Santander, and Meta with the rise of the illegal drug economy (marijuana, coca, and opium poppies) and the discoveries of oil (Putumayo) and gold (South Bolivar). The processes of capitalist development and the pace of integration of Colombian markets into the world economy invariably propelled these three waves. Although the waves of colonization were precipitated by different sociopolitical and economic conditions, they can be viewed as a defense mechanism employed by peasants to safeguard a subsistence economy against the expansion of the capitalist mode of production and capital accumulation at their expense.

Capital accumulation necessitated introducing changes in the modes of production (such as wage labor, concentration of land, and mechanization) and consequently new class structures. For example, sharecropping, the hacienda remuneration system,[13] and land colonization were obstacles to the advancement of more efficient systems of production. Karl Marx wrote:

> One of the prerequisites of wage labour and one of the historic conditions for capital is free labour and the exchange value of free labour against money, in order to reproduce money and to convert it into values, in order to be consumed by money, not as use value for enjoyment, but as use value for money. Another prerequisite is the separation of free labour from the objective conditions of its realization-from the means and material of labour. . . . This above

all means worker must be separated from the land. . . . This means the dissolution both of free petty landownership and of communal landed property.[14]

Peasants in some regions of Colombia developed resistance strategies to the capitalist transformation processes described by Marx. For example, armed colonization, of new lands has been an important tool of resistance, which has had a profound effect on the country's socioeconomic and political development over the last forty years. The Afro-Colombian and indigenous communities both with communal landed property also resisted the encroachments of capital and the privatization of their properties. In this respect, the guerrilla groups became crucial agents in this resistance process. They helped in galvanizing the petty and landless peasants enabling them to acquire lands in defiance to the logic of capitalist development which necessitates transforming them into wage-labor. The guerrillas also protected the communal landed properties of indigenous and black communities in their areas of operations.[15]

During the 1930s two patterns of class conflicts emerged. In regions such as Taquendama where property relations became capitalist in the sense that property rights were defined and consolidated, the conflicts were the typical ones over wages, work, and renting conditions. In Tolima and Cundinamarca, conflicts developed between landlords and sharecroppers—who worked in the coffee haciendas. Sharecroppers struggled for the right to cultivate coffee in their own parcels, to sell it in the market, and to move freely within the Hacienda. Sharecroppers also demanded to be paid with money instead of shares.The sharecroppers were in effect trying to deconstruct pre capitalist economic relations and sought to supplant them with a capitalist mode. The agrarian leagues of the 1930s played a major role in organizing peasants and in articulating their interests. These leagues were constituted by poor peasants and drew on the reform experiments of the radical Liberal Juan de La Cruz Varela and that of the Communist Party gradually became an armed movement. Subsequently, FARC emerged from these leagues and was capable of consolidating a social base and maintaining a tradition of resistance in the eastern parts of Tolima and southwestern Cundinamarca for most of the 20th century.[16]

The class conflict assumed another dimension in Sumapaz. Property rights were not yet defined, and public lands were subject to dispute among colonos, sharecroppers, poor peasants, and landlords, who were integrating these lands into their properties. That led to conflict and a reconfiguration in class relations and contributed to the emergence of small propertied peasants as an obstacle to capitalist expansion. In these areas armed resistance emerged as a tactic employed by peasants to negotiate land tenure and property rights. Peasants from parts of Sumapaz and Tequendama converged with peasants driven out from Chaparral, El Libano, and Rovira, in central Tolima, who lost their lands to landowners who in turn contributed to the nucleus of the FARC.

The waves of colonization in Guaviare, Caqueta, and Putumayo started during the period of La Violencia in the 1950s. Liberal and Communist guerrillas sought refuge in these areas escaping from the Eastern Plains (Llanos Orientales). Guerrillas generally were accompanied by their families; at times entire villages trying to escape persecution migrated to new areas. Soon after the pacification of the Llanos, some peasants decided to stay and start a new life away from the economic and political pressures of latifundios and "outside the logic" of capitalist development.[17] These areas were sparsely inhabited and had plenty of public lands to colonize.

There are two forms of land colonization: one targets public or privately owned land (internal colonization), and the other targets the border rainforest areas (frontier colonization). Land conflict in areas of internal colonization originated in 1920 and acquired new dimensions in the following decades. By1985, FARC was militarily active in 62 percent of the municipalities classified as undergoing processes of internal colonization and in 44 percent of the municipalities of frontier colonization. In 1995, the guerrillas extended their military presence to 93 percent in internal colonization and to 81 percent in the frontier colonization (see table 4.4).[18]

The colonization in the departments bordering Peru, Ecuador, Brazil, Panama, and Venezuela did proceed without conflict because the land claims were not disputed. However, after the 1980s colonization became violent with the rise of commercial drug plantations, narco-dollars investments in land, and the discovery of oil reserves, coal and gold. For example, Casanare was calm until the prospects of oil production were accompanied by an armed conflict. From 1987 through 1989, 33 armed confrontations were recorded, and from 1993 through 1995, 103 armed confrontations took place among guerrillas, state military forces, and paramilitaries. FARC established in Arauca a military presence after 1982, when it became a major region of oil production. By 1998, FARC trippled its fronts from one to three supported with a mobile force.[19] Subsequently, Arauca became a contested area with state forces and paramilitaries competing to deny the guerrillas their protection rents accrued from oil multinationals and political influence among peasants. Between 1989 and 1994, 1,115 persons were killed for political reasons, the highest in the region. Most of the victims were colonos, small peasants, and indigenous people who became subjects of forceful evictions

TABLE 4.4

Increase in Guerrilla Presence by Municipality, Economic Structure, and Activity 1985–1995

Type of economic structure and activity	1985		1991		1995	
	Number of municipalities	Percentage of total	Number of municipalities	Percentage of total	Number of municipalities	Percentage of total
Deprived Minifundio Andino	26	13%	83	42%	111	56%
Stable Minifundio Andino	18	13%	45	31%	76	53%
Minifundio Caribbean Coast	2	6%	4	13%	8	26%
Latifundio cattle raising and agriculture, Caribbean Coast	9	8%	40	37%	63	59%
Marginal rural	6	15%	12	31%	19	49%
Colonization						
Frontier colonization	32	44%	47	65%	58	81%
Internal colonization	36	62%	51	88%	54	93%
Small Peasants, noncoffee producers	26	15%	75	43%	100	58%
Middle-class peasant, coffee producers	1	2%	18	30%	32	53%
Agribusiness in predominantly rural areas	6	13%	19	42%	32	71%
Agribusiness in predominantly urban areas	8	25%	14	44%	18	56%
Urban structures						
Secondary cities	1	3%	12	39%	26	84%
City centers of Relieves	2	10%	12	57%	20	95%
Regional city centers	—	—	5	100%	5	100%
Total municipalities	173	17%	437	43%	622	61%

Source: Adapted from Jesus Bejarano Avila et al., *Colombia: Inseguridad, Violencia y Desempeno Economico en las Areas Rurales* (Bogotá: Fonade and Universidad Externado de Colombia, 1997), p. 133.

and assassinations in light of the rising economic importance of the region and the consequent valorization of its lands. The increasing speculative value of land after the 1980s ushered in rentier-capitalism (some describe it as savage capitalism) as an important force reshaping agrarian structures, causing class conflicts and changing the dynamics of the war system.

FARC AND ILLICIT PLANTATIONS

The colonization of Guaviare and Putumayo was accelerated in the early 1980s because of the advent of coca plantations. This new wave took place under different political circumstances than the one of the 1950s and 1960s but within the orbit of the same historic process: the steady economic decline of the agrarian sector. This sector contributed 40.5 percent to the national economy from the 1945 through 1949; it declined to 33.6 percent from 1950 trough 1954, and it reached 22.5 percent by 1984.[20] The guerrilla movement in general and FARC in particular (because of its predominantly peasant base) served multiple functions in rural areas. First and foremost it defended the colonos and their areas of colonization and attempted to protect the subsistence peasant economy.[21]

In Putumayo, Caqueta, and Guaviare, FARC managed to secure a stable economic base for the colonos and small peasants by regulating the market relations and prices and by providing financial and technical assistance to the peasants and protection to the colonos. In these regions, small peasants mostly rely on coca plantations to supplement their meager incomes. FARC forces the narcotraffickers to pay the peasants and wage laborers *raspachines* the market prices of coca leaves and labor.

FARC urges peasants to dedicate parts of their parcels for foodstuff production and to retain only a part for coca growing. Finally, FARC polices its area of influence by checking criminal and delinquent activity and the possession of weapons and adjudicating social conflicts and disputes between individuals, such as marital problems and domestic violence. For these services FARC imposes a progressive income taxation system. Poor peasants are mostly exempted from this tax. FARC levies, for example, a beer tax and the revenues are used to support local schools and other projects. Usually an elected committee from the locality decides on disbursement and allocation of the taxes collected. In Remolinos del Caguan, a locality where this beer tax is levied, an elected committee of students and teachers was set up to recollect the tax and disburse it for construction of a local school. FARC members enforce the system if payments are irregular.[22]

According to Yazid Arteta, a FARC commander in the Caguan area, his movement performs the role of a government in areas under its influence and extracts protection rent for this service from local merchants, narcotraffickers, medium-size and large land owners, and cattle raisers. Since 1996 written codes of taxation have facilitated accountability.[23] In various municipalities of Guaviare, Caqueta, Putumayo where the FARC influence is strongest, it manages to protect the peasant subsistence economy by fighting the large landowners, cattle ranchers, and narcoborgeoisie against expanding their landholdings at the expense of colonos and small peasants.[24] By providing market stability and protecting peasant coca plantations, FARC made it possible for the subsistence economy to incorporate into the international markets with minimum "structural adjustment" and economic dislocations as opposed to the experience of peasants subjected to the market forces of the legal economy. One peasant from Monterrey (south Bolivar), an area controlled by guerrillas, explained why coca plantations (which started in his region about ten years ago) are lucrative: "To market one sack of potato or yuca costs the peasant between 3 and 5 mil pesos (about $3.50) and is sold in the market between 10 to 12 thousand pesos depending on demand. Whereas the coca paste is much easier to plant and process and there is no need for transportation since the narcotraffickers buy in the town at 1,500.000/kilo of paste and export it to other destinations."[25]

By protecting its peasant base, FARC was also compelled to accept the peasants' shift to illicit crop plantations as a supplementary income. Coca and other illicit plantations extended the life of the peasant subsistence economy, particularly since economic liberalization policies reduced tax protection; as a result, foodstock products were unable to compete in the national market with cheaper imports. Coca and other illicit plantations became the only economically viable alternative under the new market conditions. Other contributing factors coincided with the economic liberalization policies and made Colombia a viable alternative for illicit production: (a) the traditional coca plantations in Bolivia and Peru were under increasing pressure from U.S. antinarcotic military policy through erradication, fumigation, and interdiction of narcotraffickers' air routes; and (b) Colombia's protracted civil war with a balance of forces favorable to narcotraffickers. Keep in mind that neither the guerrillas nor the state commands full control of the national territory. These two factors will be elaborated in the chapter on organized crime, but for now it is important to emphasize that the government liberalization process given the balance of forces produced an unexpected outcome: the shift of a segment of the peasantry to illicit plantations.

Constrained by the balance of forces and resources available at its disposal, FARC could not provide the peasants a viable economic alternative other than illicit plantations and in turn had to contend with the ripple effects of the economic liberalization measures on the poor peasants and colonos in areas under its control. Consequently, FARC's policy to protect and regulate the market relations between peasant coca growers and narcotraffickers and their merchant intermediaries generated in its turn wide-ranging systemic effects; such as changing the dynamics of the armed conflicts among guerrilla, state, and organized crime. The armed conflict became more violent and spread onto larger areas and became increasingly affected by the shifts in the global economies of drug and legal cash crops alike. These are just examples (discussed in chapter 5) of how a complex war system operates and how the action of one actor can generate ripple effects that are difficult to predict and that we can only comprehend with systemic analysis.

Coca and other illicit plantations generated a reverse migration process; the unemployed migrated from cities to areas of colonization. The sociopolitical implications of such processes have been multifaceted, affecting the social fabric of these areas whereby the relatively stable old peasant settlements of twenty or more years mix uneasily with an impetus of new migrants seeking the "coca rush." Cultural codes, values, political culture and alligiances become highly volatile and unstable under such conditions. In Putumayo, Guaviare, Middle Magdalena, Bolivar, and Meta, this instablity has allowed the political-military penetration of the paramilitary groups at the expense of the guerrillas. In Monterrey, San Pablo, Simiti, Puerto Asis, and Mapiripan, paramilitary forces were able to establish beach heads of local support from among deserters from the guerrillas, ex-soldiers, disgruntled peasants, and unemployed youths.

The "coca culture" lives in tension with revolutionary ideas based on self sacrifice for the cause of radical change. The coca culture is based on a crude form of capitalism where "easy money" is the goal, and the means are irrelevant because these practices by definition fall within the contours of the illegal and the amoral. Thus, the guerrillas confront their anti thesis—the coca culture—when they try to recruit their members and to expand their political base. The political economy of coca presents yet another challenge, which economists term the "opportunity cost and benefit." A potential recruit knows that as a coca wage picker *raspachin* could earn three hundred dollars a month (in a country where the minimum urban wage is less than $100) which far exceeds anything he/she can hope to make as a soldier with the guerrillas.[26] Of course, other factors influence individuals' decisions and choices, such as the political history of the family, family feuds and vendettas, guerrilla pressures, and the prestige and status that an association with the guerrillas provides, which neither the coca culture nor its economy can offer.

The illegal economy has provided risks and opportunities with which the guerrilla movement must contend in a dynamic interplay. A major outcome of this interplay was the ability of paramilitaries to consolidate their military presence in areas where a process of class differentiation, through land acquisition and concentration developed. In the 1980s and more so in the 1990s, narcotraffickers and their associates in organized crime, particularly the emerald barons, acquired more than 10 percent of the most fertile lands in the country.[27] The narcotraffickers and the coca economy accelerated the process of class differentiation, producing a propertied class (merchants, well-to-do peasantry, and cattle ranchers) in some regions such as Magdalena Medio, Bolivar, Antioquia, and Uraba, Casanare, and Cesar. The new class structures and the consolidation of the bourgeoisie in new regions led to a counteroffensive sponsored by segments of the bourgeoisie and rural middle class.[28] Chapter 5 discusses in greater detail the implications of such social change and its impact on the delicate balance between the guerrillas and the state.

FARC'S STATE-MAKING CAPABILITIES
AND ITS POLITICAL ECONOMY

FARC emerged in 1964, but it did reach its zenith in the late 1990s, although it might seem counterintuitive that a rebel force could grow stronger after the collapse of the Soviet Union and its demoralizing effects on Socialist thought. But although Colombia's conflict like many other intrastate wars coincided with the cold war years, it never fully corresponded to cold war politics, which explains why it did not end when the cold war did. Social conflicts such as those in Colombia, Angola, Sudan, Afghanistan, and Somalia outlived the end of the cold war, and some new ones emerged such as in Mexico, Rwanda, Burundi, Algeria, ex-Yugoslavia, and the ex-Soviet Union. They correspond to two phenomena: the shifts in the international political economy, which continually shapes their domestic markets, class structures, modes of political power contestation, and group identity, and the manner in which local actors articulate their responses to them.[29] In this mode, national political institutions become crucial in mitigating antagonistic articulations and negotiating so as to avoid violent social conflicts.[30] The historical record provides bountiful evidence of both institutional failures and successes, but here we focus on institutional failures. We focus now on the guerrillas' state-making response to the shifts in the international political economy (including the illicit economy) and to the state's institutional crises. Charles Tilly, who argued that state agents carry on four types of interrelated activities, introduced the concept of state-making capability:

1. War making: Eliminating or neutralizing their own rivals outside the territories in which they have clear and continuous priority as wielders of force.
2. State making: Eliminating or neutralizing their rivals inside those territories.
3. Protecting: Eliminating or neutralizing the enemies of their clients.
4. Extracting: Acquiring the means of carrying out the first three activities-war making, state making, and protecting.[31]

For the purpose of this research, war-making and state-making functions can be combined since we are dealing with an interstate conflict that involves the extraction of resources by providing protection to clients in order to eliminate their inside rivals. In our theoretical framework, the Colombian guerrillas' struggle with the state is a struggle for hegemony between two opposing state-making processes, and for that end both actors sought protection rents to cement their war-making capabilities.[32]

Any struggle for hegemony could terminate by one force prevailing over the other or by a compromise commensurate with the respective power of the belligerent actors, or protract becoming a war system. Our task here is to identify the conditions that determine the constitution of a war system. In this respect, the capability of extracting protection rents becomes a key indicator to the war system's prospect and to the political economy. The evaluation of the political economy includes the material (such as economic and military capabilities) and non material assets (such as political capabilities) and that each actor accumulates in a war system condition.

FARC'S ECONOMIC AND MILITARY ASSETS

FARC grew from a ragtag guerrilla group of 44 combatants in 1964 to a formidable army force of more than 18,000 combatants strong, whereas its largest counterpart in Guatemala claimed 6,000 during its peak in the early 1980s, the FMLN of El Salvador had 8,000 guerrillas, and Shining Path had 10,000 by 1989.[33] This growth makes FARC the largest guerrilla group ever in Latin America. This section provides the causes behind such success, starting with the most obvious explanations and then moving up the ladder of complexity.

The National Front regime (1958–74) was an exclusive political arrangement that left out the working class, middle class, and peasantry from the political process. Such exclusion was compounded by the state's failure to provide the protection to one of its own main clients: the large landowners. This failure can be attributed to the inability of any segment of the dominant class to establish its hegemony and the inability of state institutions to solve the conflicts between peasants and landowners. The peasantry, particularly the colonos, who needed to protect their newly acquired lots, found defense leagues and then the guerrilla groups a viable option for economic survival. This in turn was exacerbated by landowners' encroachments and the state's policy toward colonos, poor peasants, and sharecroppers. The degradation in the peasant economy provided fertile grounds for the guerrillas' recruitment strategy as a protector of the peasantry, particularly when it coincided with the failure of the peace process of the Betancur government.

From 1978 through 1995 period, the Gini index for the distribution of income among the rural poor remained stable at 0.34, whereas in the urban areas it declined from 0.30 to 0.25.[34] Coca plantations gradually became an important source for economic survival of more than 1 million poor peasants and colonos. The guerrillas in turn protected the peasants who worked in their areas of operations and influence. The interplay of these variables enabled the guerrillas to grow. The coca boom also presented FARC with an opportunity to strengthen its state-making capabilities, an important indicator for the positive political economy (PPE), which sustained the war system. FARC levied taxes on drug merchants and traffickers ranging from 7 percent to 10 percent of the market value of a kilo of coca paste. The market value fluctuates with changes in international markets, local market structures, quality, production risks, and transportation costs. As a result, estimates of FARC tax income from the illicit economy fluctuates accordingly between $60 and $100 million per year particularly by the early 1990s (see table 4.3).

According to a study conducted by the Departmemt of National Planning, a government institution, FARC and ELN extracted about $600 million in protection rents from narcotraffickers in 1996 and less than $200 million annually for 1997 and 1998, respectively.[35] Other sources of income include ransom money; taxes on large landowners, cattle ranchers, agribusiness, and multinationals; and bank robbery (especially the Agrarian Bank, Caja Agraria, defunct since 1999).[36] The guerrillas also have investments in transportation companies, housing projects, restaurants, services, gold mines, and others (see table 4.3). The total income of FARC could amount to $300 million per year. In fact, the government estimate is much higher. The FARC income is estimated to be around $500 million, of which about $200 million (40 percent) derived from taxing plantations and drug processing, and transportation operations.[37]

Between 1964 and 1980, FARC's military activities were concentrated in rural areas, particularly in areas of colonization and small property production where sharecropping dominates. But these activities were minimal during this phase since the war was of low intensity and did not involve major confrontations with the armed forces. Things started to change with the 1982 FARC conference that had far-reaching effects on the development and consolidation of the war system in Colombia. The conference came at a time when the country was witnessing an increasing penetration of crops of coca and poppies in what Thoumi calls the "coca boom" due to its price increase during 1982 and 1983.[38] As mentioned before, the interdiction policies applied in Peru and Bolivia made Colombia a substitute to compensate for the production loss in international market demands.[39]

The conference was held as the Betancur government was negotiating with the guerrillas. The conference resolutions focused on developing FARC's fighting capacity by upgrading its guerrilla forces into an irregular revolutionary army. Its military personnel were sent to the Soviet Union and Vietnam for training. And a military academy was established to prepare the guerrilla force for a command structure and a chain of command comparable to that of the regular army. The shift to an irregular army required that the FARC develop its armament, command, control, and communication systems (C3) which was not possible without increasing its protection rent. The FARC decided in its seventh conference to double its fronts and to move closer to middle-sized cities, and strategic areas of natural resources (oil, gold, emeralds, and coal).[40] The objective was to create a strong economic infrastucture for FARC. When the FARC Plenum was convened in 1989, FARC was up from 44 fronts, increasing from 27 in 1984, and planned to have 60 by 1992 with an estimated force of 18,000 combatants (300 fighters per front) and 80 by 1994 (400 fighters per front, for a total of 32,000).[41] It is unclear whether this last objective was achieved. What is almost certain, however, is that by the end of 1999 FARC had at least of 18,000 divided into about 60 fronts.

FARC's estimated budget for increasing its force from that of 13,200 in 1989 to that of 18,000 in 1992 was about $56 million (estimated at the 1989 exchange rate of 380 pesos per dollar), to be spent on arming, training, and upgrading the command, conrtrol, and communication system. In its 1989 plan, FARC contemplated the creation of a mobile strategic guerrilla unit (by 1994–1995) that would require the acquisition of 6 small airplanes, 2 ships, 10 speed boats, and a radio station and the construction of 4 airports, and 480 communication radios. The total costs were estimated to be $156 million.[42] By the mid

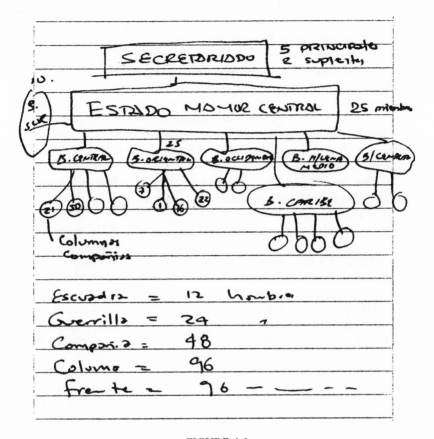

FIGURE 4.1

Yazid Arteta, Commander from the Eastern Bloc of the FARC, interview with author, Bogota, November 1998. Arteta drew this diagram in which appears the organizational structure of the FARC composed from above: the Secretariado (5 permanent members and two supplements); then Estado Mayor Central (25 members); then we have the Blocs distributed along the countries georgraphical divisions: south, center, east, west, Middle Magdalena, Caribbean, and Cesar. The blocs are in their turn made up of Fronts.

1990s, FARC demonstrated its newly gained military power in a series of large-scale operations involving between 300 and 600 combatants capturing key army positions in Las Delicias, Patascoy, San Miguel, and Puerres, among others (see chapter 3). Hence, FARC state-making capabilities reached higher levels in the 1990s, reinforcing and being reinforced by a balance of forces between the state and guerrillas, which had allowed this state of affairs in the first place.

The increase in the FARC state-making capabilities had a great impact in its areas of influence such as Putumayo, Guaviare, Meta, and

Caqueta. This impact can be assessed not only in terms of its role as a state with an almost undisputed territorial control and its monopoly control of the use of force, but also in terms of FARC's role in the expansion of commerce, providing means of transportation (such as speed boats), constructing landing strips, and adjudicating and arbitrating social and personal conflicts. This is in addition to providing health and education services. In many municipalities of these areas, the only authority, beyond the symbolic state police station in the capital centers of the municipalities, is that of the FARC, and it is the sole provider of essential public services.[43]

During the 1980s FARC decided to extend its radius of operations outside its traditional colonization zones such as those in Sarare, Aruaca, northeast Boyaca, North of Santander; Magdalena Medio Santnadereano, south Cesar, and the Catatumbo region. With the increase in the protection rent extracted from illicit drug trafficking, FARC consolidated its military force in Meta, Guaviare, and Caqueta, Putumayo, Cauca, Santander, and Sierra Nevada de Santa Marta. The major noticeable change during the late 1980s and the 1990s was FARC's movement toward areas characterized by large property structures and agribusiness economic activity. Such a shift corresponded to geostrategic considerations, and political and socioeconomic interests (see table 4.4).

The geopolitical consideration behind this expansion lies in the FARC strategy of encircling the capital, Bogota, and other key cities, by consolidating its power base in the Cordillera Oriental. For that objective, FARC expanded its military presence in nine municipalities in Cundinamarca, primarily those adjacent to the area of Meta, a FARC traditional stronghold, and Boyaca. This did not alter the strategic balance of power with the state's coercive forces, but it nonetheless generated systemic effects. The war system became less stable because FARC's expansion required extracting more protection rent from large landowners, cattle ranchers, multinational corporations, and narcotraffickers, who in turn responded by contracting private security and paramilitary groups. This unleashed a process with a set of new dynamics that contributed to the consolidation of the paramilitary groups in the second half of the 1990s, undermining the bi-polar structure of the war system. Thus, initial behaviors and outcomes influenced later ones, which led to systemic change over time, an issue explored in chapter 5.[44]

Table 4.4 demonstrates important trends in the guerrillas' military activity. The first notable trend is consolidating the guerrillas' military base in areas of internal colonization from 36 municipalities to 54. These areas are conflictive since colonization involved occupying private or public lands. This trend also confirms that the guerrillas' main social bases are the peasant colonos. In this context, the guerrillas increased their activity in areas of frontier colonization. The strong military presence of the guerrillas in areas of colonization reveals the increasing organic linkages between colonos and guerrillas.

Table 4.4 also shows new trends in guerrilla activism, particularly in areas of latifundios from 9 municipalities to 53 in the Caribbean coastal line, representing a 59 percent of this category total. This was a significant increase that brought with it an escalation of conflict in these municipalities. The guerrilla group also increased its military activity in rural areas where agribusiness enterprises developed (from 6 to 32 municipalities). This last reflects the guerrillas' relative success in penetrating areas where agro-industrial capital has established a base and where the peasant economy is being transformed. In these areas, the guerrillas have benefited from the labor-capital disputes, siding with labor unions to negotiate better salaries and benefits. The guerrillas pressure these enterprises to invest in these municipalities in an attempt to cushion the process of economic transformation. Finally, the guerrillas extract protection rent from agribusinesses. A similar case was that of the agribusinesses located in urban areas where the guerrillas increased their presence from 8 to 18 municipalities. Finally, another trend is the guerrillas increasing military presence in secondary cities (from 1 in 1985 to 26 in 1995). This leap is due to the guerrilla groups interest in breaking from its isolation in remote rural areas, and to its increasing organizational capabilities.[45]

FARC seeks to improve its negotiating leverage in the case of a settlement. Situating its forces close to Bogota and other major cities serves the purpose set in the Ten Points Program adopted at FARC's eighth conference for the resolution of the armed conflict, which included FARC's participation in a national reconciliation government. This FARC political strategy also generated an unwanted political consequence: increased support for the paramilitaries by large landowners and cattle raisers who feared that in the eventuality of a settlement a strengthened guerrilla force would impose land reform at their expense.[46]

FARC succeeded in building an urban base of support in the marginal barrios of Cartagena, Baranquilla, Medellin, Barancabermeja, Bogota, Bucaramanga, and Cali. Residents are either first-generation recent migrants from rural areas or their children. According to military sources, the number of these urban militia members in Bogota is estimated two thousand to twenty-five hundred.[47] The national figures could reach 4,000 to 6,000 urban militias members. The political-military roles of these urban structures are multiple: to facilitate the movement of the guerrillas from and to the cities; to provide logistical support, medical supplies, ammunitions, refuge for wounded combatants and weapons; and to extract protection rents (war tax) from merchants, including those in downtown Bogota.[48] Since 2000, FARC has used these urban networks to levy the 10 percent tax (FARC's law 002) on those individuals whose income exceeds 1 million dollars per year.

In the 1990s, FARC also expanded in key strategic areas which were outside its *despliegue estrategico* "strategic expansion" in the eastern slopes of the Andean Mountains. According to the above table, these areas are more urban, developed, latifundista with capitalist enterprises and rich with natural resources. This expansion was driven by two main considerations according to FARC officials: to move the war closer to urban centers and intermediate cities, and exert more political pressure on the state and the dominant class and increase its rent extraction.[49]

GUERRILLAS' CONSTRUCTION
OF LOCAL POLITICAL POWER

Although collecting taxes is the prerogative of governments, the guerrillas in many villages, municipalities, and regions assumed that governmental role.[50] The examples offered below demonstrate that the guerrillas crafted its state-making project by helping in channeling funds to public works. The guerrillas have two main sources of funds: private companies such as multinational corporations, national companies, and public enterprises; and state resources devoted to the municipalities. Most of these moneys end up in investments in public projects such as vocational schools, road paving, public health, and environmental protection. The taxation mechanisms of FARC, developed and enhanced in the 1990s, are complex because they involve intermediaries such as neighborhood councils (Juntas Acción Communal, JAC), subcontractors, and municipal councils.

The way this system works is best explained through an example. In Barrancabermeja, Westinghouse, Merielectric, and TPL (an Italian company) had a project to construct an electric plant in 1997. Through intermediaries from the sectors where the plant was being built, the guerrillas made a series of demands, which included the construction of a $2 million vocational school to train the youths of the popular barrios and a $150,000 project to generate 200 jobs. The guerrillas through JAC, the neighborhood council, which is a locally elected committee, carried out the negotiation. What is interesting is that the community actively participated in the wheeling and dealing of the negotiations between the guerrillas and the companies involved. In this case the guerrillas did not extract any direct protection tax, but rather gained the political support of a popular sector. Now the companies operate with the guerrillas' protection.

Events in Puerto Wilches, Magdalena Medio, provide another example. FARC kidnapped eight engineers who worked on palm production under the pretext that their firm is financing paramilitaries in Sabana de Torres and San Alberto (Middle Magdalena). FARC demanded protection rent from an oil-palm production but was rebuffed. A negotiation process ensued sponsored by a local NGO. The outcome of the negotiation was that instead of paying taxes to FARC, the firm promised to invest in the local development of the area and to allow small palm producers to have more participation and say in the local market.[51]

These examples represent modalities that are repeated elsewhere, such as Casanare and Aruaca, where oil and coal multinationals operate. British Petroleum, for example, was compelled to invest in local schools, vocational training, and local projects in order to avert guerrilla attacks. Negotiation was carried out through indirect channels in order to avoid state scrutiny and paramilitary reprisal attacks. FARC, as well as ELN, was acting in areas of their influence or where they could project their power as enforcers of income distribution and channel investment into public projects.

Bolivar in the Serrania de San Lucas provides an example of another modality of taxation. The targets are not corporation nor multinationals but small miners. According to the miners interviewed, guerrilla (mainly ELN) charges them $13 per gram monthly, and they also charge the intermediaries that sell the gold to the Central Bank. The ELN and FARC are rumored to have front companies that trade with gold. What the guerrillas do is organize the market relation between the miners and the traders and stabilize prices and ensure completion of contracts. This minimizes transaction costs and reduces risks by ensuring compliance with the agreements.

The guerrillas play another important role in areas where they exercise influence or can project its influence: they cite public officials for corruption and force them to reinvest in public work. Governors, local council members, alcaldes (mayors), and even senators have been subject to guerrilla justice, which might include (revolutionary execution) assassination of the person implicated. Citing public officials for corruption by the *muchachos* (as the guerrilla are amicably called) is generally well received in communities.[52] Nonetheless, such practices could also bring criticism if the case against the official is not well documented and publicized.

ELN GENESIS AND TRAJECTORY

The roots of ELN can be traced to San Vicente de Chucuri and Simacota in Santander in 1965. Unlike FARC, which is a Marxist-Leninist group,

ELN considers itself a national liberation movement inspired by the Cuban revolution and its ideology and draws on a hybrid of Marxism-Leninism and Christian Liberation Theology.[53] A good number of its founders were of working-class origins, peasants, and middle-class origins who participated in regional and national social struggles. The ELN class composition reflected the dominant class structures in Santander, North Santander, south Bolivar, and south Cesar, where the ELN drew its main support base.

The ELN focus of activity was urban centers, student movements and the labor unions. As early as 1987, ELN considered building its urban militias, a project later adopted by FARC and EPL. ELN manifested the praxis of the "revolutionary foco" advanced by Che Guevara and Regis Dubray that the revolution could be led and promoted by a political-military group (foco) without necessarily establishing a political party. Political organization could follow guerrilla warfare.[54] FARC did not follow that model, but rather believes in the centrality of a Communist Party in leading the struggle. ELN considered Magdalena Medio to be central to its state building project because of the region's geopolitical and economic importance. It included mountainous terrains, jungles, the most important rivers of the country (Magdalena, Sogamoso, Opon and bordering the Cauca River) and coastal highways. It bordered Venezuela and the natural resources of the region (oil, coal and gold). These features combined made Middle Magdalena the heart of Colombia. Hence, the control of this region is key to national and international politics.

CLASS AND GENDER COMPOSITION

The founding group of ELN was constituted of 16 members, all of them of urban middle-class origins with the exception of Jose Ayala, who was of small-propertied peasant origins from San Vicente de Chucuri.[55] What is notable is that ELN is more consistent in terms of its leadership class composition with the other guerrilla groups in the region and distinguished from the FARC. By the late 1990s, the leadership of the ELN was still predominantly of urban middle-class origins (see table 4.5).

The highest authority in the ELN organizational structure is the National Directorate. This is broken down into 80 percent of peasant origins and 20 percent of middle-class backgrounds. In the 1989 ELN conference, the average delegate was 33 years old, had nine years of militancy, and had a high school education; and only 8 percent were women.[56] About 80 percent of the ELN leadership is of urban middle-class origins with only 20 percent of peasant origins, such as its current leader Nicolas Bautista (Gabino), who is the son of a peasant leader.

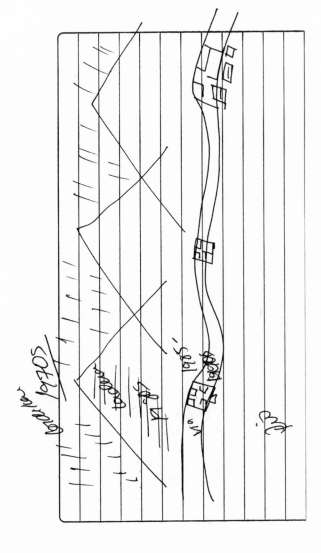

FIGURE 4.2

This sketch illustrates the ELN strategy which is divided into three phases reflecting the evolution of this guerrilla organization. The first phase (1965–1980) was when the ELN concentrated in the high mountains building its cadres and networks (cordillera). The second phase (1980–1985) was when the ELN started descending toward small population centers (ladera). The third phase (1990–present) started when the ELN reached the medium-sized population centers along critical highways (via carretera-rio). The sketch was drawn by ELN commander Felipe Torres.

TABLE 4.5
ELN Founding Group (circa 1965)

	Class origins	Profession/occupation
Fabio Vasquez Castaño	Lower middle class	Bank clerk
José Ayala	Small-propertied peasant	Peasant
Ricardo Lara Parada	Middle-class urban	University student
Heliodoro Ochoa	Middle-class urban	University student
Víctor Medina Morón	Middle-class urban	Engineer
Julio Cesar Cortes	Middle-class urban	Physician
Camillo Torres Restrepo	Upper-class urban (prominent family)	University Professor &priest
Pedro Vásquez Rendón	Middle-class urban	Student
Heriberto Espitia	Small-propertied peasant	Peasant
Julio Portocarrero	Middle-class urban	Student
Domingo Laín	Middle-class origins (Spain)	Priest
Luís Rovira	Middle-class urban	Student
Mario Hernández	Middle-class urban	Student
José Merchán	na	na

Source: Felipe Torres and Francisco Galan, ELN Commanders, interview with author, Itaqui, Antioquia November 28, 1998.

In the Direcion de Frente de Guerra (Directorate of the War Front) which is the second level in the organizational echelon, the peasant representation is about 50 percent and about 20 percent are women. The Regional Directorate, Directorate of Fronts, and Directorate of Fronts under Construction constitute the third level in the organizational structure. The members of the Regional Directorate are mostly of urban origins, whereas the members of the other directorates are almost all of peasant origins.[57] Most ELN members of urban backgrounds come from small and medium-size regional cities, such as Bucaramaga, Barancabermeja, Cucuta, Valledupar, and others (see table 4.6).

The urban-rural divide is reflected on views on ideological and political issues ranging from the role of the working class in peasant societies in the revolutionary process and the nature of revolution. ELN Commanders Felipe Torres and Francisco Galan explained that

during the 1964–1978 period, these differences assumed violent forms, leading to purges and liquidation of the "urban elements" that trans-

TABLE 4.6
ELN Class and Gender Composition of National Directorate (DN) 1998

Peasant origins	20%
Workers	None
Middle class	80%
Men	100%
Women	None

Source: Felipe Torres and Francisco Galan, ELN Commanders, interview with author, Itaqui's Maximun Security Prison, Antioquia, November 28, 1997.

ported bourgeois ideas and norms into the organization. As a result some of the best ELN leaders such as Heliodoro Ochoa, Victor Medina Moron, Julio Cezar Cortez, Ricardo Lara Parada and several others lost their lives in petty political disputes that under different circumstances could have been resolved without resorting to firing squads. The ideological disputes between urban/rural and working class/peasant leadership started to ease by the mid-1980s although traces of that conflict linger within the ELN.[58]

ELN RENT EXTRACTION AND CAPABILITIES

The ELN was practically defeated in 1973 in Anori (Antioquia) after the state delivered a series of strong blows that reduced the organization's military capabilities. However, the ELN recovered, from less than 500 guerrillas in 1979, and by 1998 had more than 5,000 combatants. This growth was facilitated by the resolution of the rural/urban political dispute and the organization's extraction of rent payments from oil companies in its areas of influence. The construction of the pipelines of Caño Limon-Coveñas provided a lifeline for the movement. Starting in 1983 with the reunion of the front of "Heroes and Martyrs of Anori" ELN strategized to double its fronts. By 1984, the north front was established in the Middle Magdalena (Serrania de San Lucas) and the southwest front in Cauca and south Huila, and a year later, the northeast front was operating in North Santander and north Boyaca. And in 1986, the northeast front was formed operating between Barrancabermeja and Bucaramanga in Santander. The southwest front in Antioquia was reinforced with the formation of another front in the area.

Oil production companies in Arauca provided the ELN with an excellent source of protection rent, particularly to its "Domingo Lain" unit, which became one of its financially and militarily strongest fronts. Both ELN and FARC negotiate the implementation of public works and projects funded by multinationals that generate employment funded in areas under their influence, such as in Arauca, Casanare, North Santander and Santander. Such practices consolidate the guerrillas' support and political power within the communities.

The northeast front covers a strategic corridor where the center communicates with the north of the country by railroads, and roads and has influence over the border area with Venezuela. The northwest front, which carries out more the 20 percent of the armed operations depends for its finances on the extraction of protection rent from the mining of gold in the area and corporations that use the Medellin-Bogota highway. It is estimated that this front extracts about 30 percent of the ELN rents.[59] The ELN now has an estimated force of five thousand to six thousand fighters and has an estimated annual income of $150 to 200 million (see table 4.3).[60] Like FARC, it controls a number of corporations and it invests some of its income domestically and in foreign markets. In this sense the political economy of the guerrillas has become intertwined with socioeconomic and political variables affecting the livelihood of thousands of families in their areas of influence. Companies established with guerrilla capital, subcontracting from state enterprises such Ecopetrol, and multinational companies provide a job market for local entrepreneurs and workers. In addition ELN protects two to three thousand of coca plants growers in the south Bolivar and North Santander, predominantly colonos and sharecroppers, and the subsistence peasant economy, which provides a vital source of income to over 300,000 families (more than a 1 million persons) at the national level.[61] In this sense, the war system becomes institutionalized as a modality for the allocation and distribution of economic resources, employment, and pattern of development and integration into the world market. The coca economy illustrates this last point: peasant coca growers supported by an armed resistance are capable of negotiating their re-incorporation into the legal global economy.

The protraction of the conflict and its low intensity allowed the guerrillas to establish their political and social control of vast areas where the only authority was their own. State incursions are seasonal and do not destabilize the guerrillas' hegemony. The ELN exercised authority virtually uninterrupted over Serrania de San Lucas, south Bolivar from the mid 1980s and until the late 1990s, when military and paramilitary incursions were launched. The same can be said about regions in North Santander such as Catatumbo.

Since the 1996 Third Conference of the ELN that covened in Simiti (south Bolivar), the organization decided to restructure its military organization by incorporating its columns of 40 to 50 fighters into Commandos de Area which could have as many as 600 combatants. Such restructuring came in response to two changes: the introduction of mobile brigades of the army, which started harassing the guerrillas in the North Santander, south Bolivar, and Cesar; and the increasing economic, material and human resources at the disposal of the ELN. By 1996, the ELN and FARC recorded high incomes allowing them to enhance their fire power as well as to enlist more fighters (see tables 4.3 and 4.7).

In military and economic terms, both the ELN and FARC built an impressive war machine that managed to permeate most of the country's municipalities and regions, and in this sense they accumulated a positive political economy. This condition allows the two insurgent movements to grow if other factors remain constant. However, this is never the case in systems; conflict dynamics and changes in the actors' environment produced either by their actions or by exogenous contingencies such as changes in international oil or coca prices can affect local peasants, narcotraffickers, and guerrilla rents. This, alters the overall dynamic and dialectic of conflict and destabilizes the war system.

An example for this new dynamic is the one ushered in 1997 when the ELN suffered some important setbacks. It lost in combat around 477 fighters (almost the size of a Commandos de Area, or a battalion in regular army structures) and several hundred were captured.[62] It lost strategic areas such as San Vicente de Chucurí (Santander), parts of the northeast Antioqueño and of south Bolívar, and the Serrania de San Lucas, a zone that the paramilitaries of Carlos Castano are trying to occupy.[63] Since the mid-1960s these areas were undisputed safe havens for the ELN. The dynamics of war are changing, and the ELN has yet to take the military initiative. These dynamics and the forces propelling them are discussed in chapter 5.

TABLE 4.7
ELN Fighters and Presence/Municipality, 1986–1996

	1986	*1990*	*1994*	*1996*
Fighters	800	1,800	2,800	4,000–5,000
Presense in municipalities	180	250	280	350 (out of 1,071 total municipalities)

Source: Consejaria de Seguridad de la Presidencia, Bogota, Colombia.

EJERCITO POPULAR DE LIBERACION (EPL)

The four hundred-strong Ejercito Popular de Liberacion (EPL), the smallest of the insurgent groups in Colombia, was established in 1967 as the armed branch of the Partido Commninista Marxista Leninista (PCML), a Maoist political party which had its origins in the Communist Party. In the 1980s, the EPL broke with the traditional Maoist doctrines of prolonged war and the leadership role of the peasantry and reestablished its links with intellectuals. EPL started its military activities on the borderlines between the departments of Cordoba and Antioquia, a traditional refuge area for the liberal guerrillas during La Violencia. In the 1970s, the organization managed to develop a support base within the working class in the banana plantations and among peasant colonos.

At its zenith, EPL enlisted about 2,000 fighters, a majority of which were peasants and students.[64] In terms of their regional concentration, EPL was predominantly from Antioquia, which led to the misperception that it was a regional guerrilla group.[65] EPL in 1984 accepted President Betancur's initiative of peace, and by 1994 the vast majority of EPL fighters abandoned the armed struggle, except for a splinter group led by Francisco Caraballo. Its military activity is concentrated in Antioquia, North Santander and Guajira mostly and is carried out in coordination with FARC. Some of its ex-members have become engaged in criminal activity and paramilitarism. EPL's contribution to the guerrillas' state-making process is very limited compared to FARC and the ELN, and it largely depends on kidnapping for ransom as its main source of financing. There is no information about the rent that this organization generates.

CONCLUSION

How far along is the guerrilla groups' state-making process? During the 1990s the guerrillas' power reached it zenith, stretching its influence into new strategic areas and population centers. This occurred because of the comfortable military balance between the guerrillas and state forces in effect since the 1980s. Neither the state nor the guerrillas have attempted to radically alter that condition. The occasional flares, such as the 1973 Anori (Antioquia) military operations against the ELN, or the army's 1990 attack against Casa Verde (FARC headquarters in the Meta) were anomalies to the condition of a low-intensity war and the rather stable equilibrium of the war system. Neither major operation led to any significant alteration in the balance of the war system.

FARC and ELN capitalized on the impasse by consolidating their political power at the municipal and village levels, practically playing the role of de facto state dispensing justice, regulating market relations and protecting the environment, by applying what FARC calls "Reglas de Convivencia." The rules stipulate laws and sanctions regarding issues such as carrying arms, fishing, hunting, working hours, liquor consumption, prostitution, interfamily violence, drug abuse, and cutting trees. The impasse provided stability to the war system and allowed the guerrilla groups and the state to coexist and accommodate their strategies to these conditions.

The guerrillas shifted their strategy to the short and mid-term. Rather than seize political power by assuming the state central apparatus and institutions, they deconstructed state power at the village and municipal levels and moved upward. The guerrillas are responding to the state's failures in mitigating rural conflicts and are filling a hegemonic void left by the state. The guerrillas managed with relative ease to establish its hegemony in parts of the country for almost two decades. In many instances, the guerrillas coexisted with a minimal state presence, such as a police station, with the understanding that the guerrillas hold the power.

In municipalities in North Santander, Casanare, south Bolivar, Caqueta, Putumayo, and Cesar, the guerrillas' power is exercised through the election of local municipal councils and mayors and the disbursement of public funds.[66] According to some testimonies, FARC does not impose its candidates but rather as in the cases of the 1998 municipal elections in Yondo, Cantagallo, and San Pablo (all in Middle Magdalena), town meetings were organized where candidates were chosen freely and then a general election is held.[67] In Yondo, FARC candidates did not win, whereas they did in the other two villages. In Mogotes (North Santander), ELN did something similar which they called a "constituent public assembly," in which candidates were chosen for general election.[68] It is ironic, that candidates could even have affiliation with the Conservative or Liberal Party, yet by accepting the rules of the game set by the guerrillas, they qualify for election. These are examples of how the guerrillas are constructing their hegemonic power at the local level by employing democratic means such as popular elections.

The guerrillas occasionally adopted a more obtrusive strategy to challenge the state's authority: they disrupted by launching military strikes against the candidates of the traditional parties and calling to boycotting a "meaningless process" since it reproduced the traditional elite and legitimate a corrupt system. This practice became a litmus test of limitations and strengths of each of the two contending hegemonic projects: guerrillas and the state. In 1985, the guerrillas had a presence in 437 (40 percent out of a total of 1,071) municipalities, but today they influence 622 (58 percent), out of which they exercise a great degree of authority in 255 (25 percent) municipalities according to the National Federation of Municipalities.[69] This is a good example of the increasing guerrillas' state-making capabilities complementing its military and economic power.[70] We can deduce, then, that the guerrillas were able to accumulate sufficient military power, political power, and economic resources to be interested in protracting the war given their inability thus far to defeat their enemies: the state and, as we will discuss later, organized crime.

By successfully consolidating their power in local areas, the guerrillas were able to achieve an important support base for armed struggle. These moves for local political power gained momentum in the 1990s and led to systemic reverberations perturbing the comfortable impasse of the war system, particularly when large landowners, the incipient narcobourgeoisie, and the emerald mafia led by Victor Carranza and Rodriquez Gacha were affected. During the same period, they had been amassing lands to launder their money, which collided with the guerrillas goals. In a complex system such as the war system, this created outcomes that none of the actors may have anticipated.

Two processes—guerrillas' attempt to build local power and organized crime's strategy of acquiring land—gained momentum in the 1990s, leading to a significant escalation in the war, destabilizing the dynamics of the war system and the comfortable impasse (détente) on which it had rested for almost a decade (1985–95). Both processes were generated by the same phenomenon: drug economy. This in turn led to a constant power struggle in the organization of market relations between the sellers and the buyers of illicit crops, that is between the peasants and the narcotraffickers. Narcotraffickers initially accepted the guerrillas' rules, including the taxes they imposed on them, but narco-paramilitary groups emerged in the late 1980s in many areas (Santander, Antioquia, North Santander, Cesar, Meta, Cauca, Casanare, Huila, Boyaca, Caqueta, Putumayo, Uraba, and Cordoba) that wanted to rid the business of guerrilla interference. This aspect is discussed in chapter 5.

Finally, the FARC success in obtaining a demilitarized area of 42,000 square kilometers from the state (double the size of El Salvador) inhabited with a population of about 100,000 people has put this group closer to achieving its proclaimed status of belligerency than ever before, hence, accelerating its state-making process. At the end of 1998, the state accepted demilitarizing this area to inaugurate peace negotiations with FARC. The FARC's incessant demand for a demilitarized zone since it lost Casa Verde (Uribe, Meta) in 1990 finally paid off. This is undoubtedly the highest point in the guerrillas' forty-year struggle, which confirms our analysis that FARC's struggle to consolidate its control in a number of departments lies within the state-making project of the FARC. The self-proclaimed status of belligerency is now de-facto but gaining international recognition such as the one implicitly offered by Venezuela, and the 1999 letter of petition signed by 25 European intellectuals, politicians and human rights activists asking President Pastrana to recognize FARC as a belligerent force.[71] Then, we can conclude that the comfortable impasse not only allowed the guerrillas to consolidate their political and economic gains achieving a positive political economy but helped also in protracting the war. The latter, however, must be analyzed in conjunction with the other war system actors' political economies, namely, the state and organized crime.

CHAPTER 5

Paramilitaries, Organized Crime, and the Dynamics of War

The main argument of this chapter is that one of the main outcomes of the comfortable impasse between the state and the guerrillas was the accelerated development of more than 110,000 hectares of illicit drug plantations in less than a decade, bringing into the war system new destabilizing, yet consolidating actors: the narcotraffickers and their paramilitary organizations. This chapter discusses the narcotraffickers' relatioship with the other actors of the war system, the state, and the guerrillas, and their impact on the war system dynamics and prospects.

SOCIO-HISTORICAL CONTEXT

Colombia's geographic position at the gate of South America was more of a curse than a blessing as the country's most recent history attests. Since the Spanish Conquest, the Colombian Carribbean Coasts served as a corridor for contraband and transit of slaves, gold, and merchandise. After the 1903 independence of Panama from Colombia, these routes were largely maintained by new generations of contrabandits and subsequently by narcotraffickers. Ample evidence indicates that between 1968 and 1970, the first contacts with U.S. traffickers to transport the marijuana from the Sierra Nevada of Santa Marta on the Atlantic Coast were Colombian contrabandists that knew the traditional routes from the free market in Colon (Panama) and the Antille.[1]

Contrabanding activity was largely a function of the tariffs the respective governments have on imported goods. When these tarriffs were high, then contraband increased accordingly, for example, during the government of Lleras Restrepo and then under Ayala Turbay. Both governments raised tarriffs on imported goods, contrabanding increased accordingly. The so-called San Andresitos markets where contraband products are sold flourished in the country's main cities. The merchandise ranged from electronics, whisky, cosmetics, and cigarettes to weapons. Contrabandits with their long experiences and well-established networks with international markets provided a logistical infrastructure for the export of marijuana in the 1970s and coca, and opium in the 1980s and 1990s.[2] This is an important factor that helped Colombia in becoming a major exporter of illicit drugs.

The steep and almost uninterrupted decline of the agricultural economy since the 1960s encouraged the development of alternative economic activity such as illicit drug plantations and contrabanding. Both activities corresponded to the different impulses and contradictions generated by the crisis of the economic model of development and socio economic dislocations that these crises created in a country where in 1960, 60 percent of its population was still living in rural areas and it was not until the 1970s when the 57 percent became urban. Cotton, which is largely cultivated in the Atlantic Coast region (La Guajira, Cesar, and Magdalena) was in a decline due to cheaper synthetic imported products. This in turn affected the main production center of Textiles in Antioquia. These areas later became centers for narcotrafficking organizations. Similarly, the exports of sugar were also facing the international quotas set by the United States, and this affected the sugar industry concentrated in the Valle del Cauca. The exports of emeralds' also witnessed decreasing productivity due to the needs of more sophisticated extraction equipment, decreasing international prices, and violence between competing Mafia groups for the control of emerald mines in Boyaca. The regions bordering Venezuela that depended on trade with it were affected by the devaluation of Venezualas'currency. This contributed to the increase of contrabanding and to the decrease in the commercial exchange between the two. These mentioned regions all became the grounds for marijuana, coca, and later in the 1990s, of opium poppy.

Marijuana became the main cash crop in the 1970s in what is referred to as the golden era marimbera which came in the wake of a crisis that hit cotton plantations and production due to cheaper synthetic imports, mostly contraband merchandise. Marijuana plantations were encouraged and supported by traffickers from the United States who appreciated the high value of the tropical marijuana. These plantations received technical support from U.S. agronomists and experts.[3] As a result of the rural economic crisis, some large farmers and cattle ranchers shifted to marijuana production in the Sierra Nevada De Santa Marta, Guajira, Cesar, and Middle Magdalena. By 1974, about 80 percent of the farmers in the Guajira planted marijuana. This economic boom was soon followed by a bust in the early 1980s when the prices of Colombia's marijuana started declining with the emergence of a more potent and cheaper marijuana variant in the United States and with the emergence of other competetors in world markets. This decline in the demand for Colombia's marijuana led to a shift to coca plantations in various areas suitable for its cultivation.

THE STATE HEGEMONIC CRISIS
AND NARCOTRAFFICKING

In light of the above, a central question begs for an answer, and that is why did Colombia provide fertile grounds for contrabanding and narcotrafficking? One can argue that many other countries in the world were subject to similar declines in their rural economies and neither became producers of illicit cash-crops nor were their markets invaded by illegal economic activity. The obvious answer to why Colombia became one of the main theaters for contraband and narcotrafficking was the inability of its state to extend its authority over the national territory. Hence my thesis is that the increase of illegal economic activity is a function not only of dire economic conditions, but result also from the state's hegemonic crisis exacerbated by an armed insurgency that has been trimming the state's authority since the 1960s.

A preliminary look at where coca plantations have been concentrated in Colombia supports my argument. The five departments listed in (table 5.1) with the highest coca production concentration have a very weak state presense, if any, beyond a small police force (sometimes less than fifteen officers) stationed in the department's main urban centers. In most of the cases the police officers do not even dare to step outside these centers. The control outside the municipal urban centers (cabezeras) of the departments of table 5.1 ocsilated between guerrillas and narcotraffickers from the 1980 through 2001. The only constant, however, has been the weak state presence. Coca producers from these departments, emphasized that the only authority (prior to the introduction of the coca) that they knew was that of the guerrillas. The advent of coca increased the need of an authority to control the problems gen-

TABLE 5.1
Coca Plantations 1999 by Department (hectares)

Putumayo	37,000
Caqueta	30,000
Guaviare	28,000
North Santander (Gabarra)	2,800
Bolivar (Serrania de San Lucas)	2,800
Total	100,600

Source: United States Department of State, 1999 Report. In 2000, the estimates were at about 110,000 hectares.

erated by the coca boom, such as conficts between growers and buyers, violations of contracts, prostitution, crime, alcoholism, and uncontrolled encroachments on the environment. That ready authority in those departments was welcomed by the local residents. Consequently, these areas became guerrillas' strongholds beginning in the 1970s

But the most revealing and relevant aspect to this chapter is the increasing trend in illicit plantations since the 1980s. Illicit plantations increased by 400 percent between 1978 and 1998 to cover an estimated area of 100,600 hectares (see table 5.2).[5] This dramatic increase in illicit plantations coincided with the changing military balance between the guerrillas and the state as evidenced in the decreasing fatality ratio rates favoring the guerrillas (from a ratio of 1:1.52 in 1988 to 1:1.35 in 1999) (see chapter 3). Moreover, if we consider the increasing number of municipalities under the guerrillas' control, then a better picture emerges that supports the argument. In 1983, the guerrillas controlled only 173 municipalities, which constituted 13 percent of the country's total; by 1998 the guerrillas expanded their control to 622 municipalities, a 61 percent of the total. In most of the municipalities with illicit drug plantations the guerrillas have military presence or control. For example, the oppium poppy seeds plantations, are noted in 174 municipalities and in 123 of them that is in 70 percent, the guerrillas have military presence and the right-wing paramilitary allied with narcotraffickers control 46 municipalities or about 26 percent.[6] All of these municipalities are practically off-limits to the state.

This observation supports my central thesis that the emergence of narcotrafficking and its consolidation was facilitated by the inability of the state to sustain its hegemony in vast areas of the countryside beyond occasional military incursions or expeditions. Notwithstanding the cri-

TABLE 5.2
Coca Plantations (hectares)

	1995	1999
Peru	115,300	38,700
Bolivia	48,600	21,800
Colombia	50,900	100,600

Source: U.S. Department of State, 1995 and 1999. In 1973, Colombia exported about six tons of cocaine to the United States, by 1999 it exported about five hundred tons. The 1973 figure is based on Colombia CASP Report 1974–1975, Airgran, American Embassy in Bogota, Department of State, National Archives, p. 4.

sis of the subsistence peasant economy, the absence of state authority, and its inability to produce a viable economic alternative to coca plantations, the guerrillas' stance made it easier for colonos and poor peasants to substitute their unprofitable legal cash crops to illegal ones.[7]

The comfortable impasse between the guerrillas and the state provided a window of opportunity for peasants (particularly squatters, "colonos") and even some commercial farms to shift to illicit plantations without fearing state's punitive action nor guerrillas' shifts in tactics. This latter observation is based on the guerrillas' policy toward illicit plantations which was consistent since these crops made their first appearance in the 1970s. The guerrillas' policy provided an institutional setting—given the unstable nature of illegal cash-crop markets operating within the context of a civil war—stable enough to encourage peasants to assume the risks.

In spite of fluctuating world prices, because illicit cash crops remain more profitable than traditional crops, approximately 400,000 to 500,000 peasants plant them and assume the risks that this economic decision entail.[8] The fluctuation in the prices of coca leave from 1978 through 2001 did not affect significantly the increase in cultivation of illicit crops since illicit cash-crops remained more profitable than traditional crops. The economic cycles of illicit crops production by themselves do not affect the decision of poor peasants to shift to alternative crops because very few cash crops can yield as much as three crops per year as coca does which increase the probability of off setting previous losses. Most likely, peasants are able to recoperate their investment costs in a year or two.[9] Very few cash crops offer such economic advantages to poor peasants. Then, the explanation of the changes in coca production and illicit crop production in general lies in the political coercive side of the equation to make it costlier.

This explains why the United States, and some other countries relied on a strategy combining of increasing the costs of production by increasing the risks: fumigation, eradication, persecution, and interdiction of transport routes, and alternative crops. This strategy relies mainly on policing and denying the peasants the leverage to renogotiate the terms of their re-incorporation into the legal world economy. In this sense, in Colombia, the military balance between the state and guerrillas carries more weight in explaining the exponential increase in drug production than the purely economic explanations since the state and its international backers were not successful in increasing the costs of production to the peasants making their business unprofitable. So far, the balance of power between the guerrillas and the state has prevented the curtailment of illicit drug production and consequently has opened the prospects for the illicit crops' growers to negotiate a settlement that takes into account their interests, particularly, if we consider that the peasants of Bolivia and Peru, where both states were able to project their hegemonies undeterred by insurgencies, were unable to extract enough consecions from their respective states and international actors (such as the United States and the United Nations) to assure the survival of their subsistence economy.

In Peru, after 1995, in the wake of the capture of its leader Abimael Guzman with main cadres a debilitated Sendero Luminoso was incapable of checking the state's policy in its tradtional areas of control in Ayacucho, which in turn facilitated the eradication efforts of the state paralleled with an air interdiction policy. These factors led to a decline of 60 percent between April 1995 and August 1995 in coca leaf price in Peru's market after the demand plummeted due to the difficulty of transporting coca paste to Colombia for processing into cocaine.[10] However, between 2000 and 2001, the prices of coca leaf increased to about two-third of its 1995 highs, and some farmers are shifting back to coca. But this shift was not substantial enough, as we have seen in the size of areas planted with coca (see table 5.2). The ability of narcotraffickers to reinvent new routes and methods of trafficking did affect demand for coca and its local price but the supply was checked by the state's policy and its ability to enforce. In this sense, Peru's state was capable to reduce coca plantations.

Bolivia represents a slightly different case, which largely supports our argument. Bolivia grows about 70,000 acres of coca, which yield about $300 million a year from the drug.[11] The increase in prices of coca and the market limitations in alternative crops led again to a slight resurgence of coca plantations from 1997 through 1999. Such development, nonetheless, confronted state repression supported by the United States. The peasants attempted to resist and formed "defense leagues" and carried out hit-and-run operations against the army, but soon their movement was suppressed, and the peasant leaders had to flee, perhaps to reorganize and fight another day. The peasants' resistance did, however, slow the eradication efforts during 1998 and 1999 and soon after the rebellion was suppressed, the state resumed the carrot and stick policy limiting the increase in plantations. As a result, the peasants were left with little political leverage to renegotiate the terms of the illicit crop substitution program, such as prices for their new cash crops, subsidies, marketing, and technical training, nor were they able to push the state to improve social, health, and education services in their areas.

Hence, the cases of Bolivia and Peru illustrate that the ability of the state in extending its hegemony and control is a critical variable in our study of the political economy of illicit crop plantation. These successes contrast sharply with the failure of the Colombia's state.

This is not to imply that guerrillas have encouraged illicit plantations because there is no evidence to support such contention, but simply to indicate that the guerrillas did not halt the process and neither was
the state able or willing to address the plight of poor peasants.[12] But
there is something that the guerrillas did offer according to testimonies
of cocaleros and experts on this issue, "security" and stability in some
areas of illicit production. The guerrillas projected power and controlled
the abuses of the narcotraffickers and their intermediaries. This condition reduced the costs of transactions, particularly the risks that a poor
peasant would incur in an uncertain economic environment. This condition provided an institutional setting encouraging the production of
illicit drugs and prohibiting capitalists from transferring the costs of production (including risk) to labor by reducing the costs of their product.
In 1990, for example, Colombia had only 40,100 hectares planted with
coca constituting 18.8 percent only of what the Andean countries
planted and producing 13.7 percent of the coca leaf and 1999, the area
was expanded to more 100,000 hectares.[13]

The increase in illicit plantations in Colombia in spite of the state's
aggressive fumigation policy is also attributed to the survival economic
strategies applied by the peasants to mitigate the negative effects of fumigation. One component of such a strategy is increasing the lands planted
with illicit cash crops by cooperating with one another to increase the
work force, cut production costs, and diminish the possible loss to fumigation. With an increase in planted areas, the colonos guarantee that at
least part of the crop will survive the fumigation, hence covering their
costs and allowing them with some surplus to sustain their existence.[14]
This peasant's survival strategy would not be feasible, however, without
the guerrillas' support (tacit or implicit) which inhibits the state from
development of a more aggressive sustainable coercive policy.

THE POLITICAL ECONOMY OF
NARCOTRAFFICKING AND THE STATE'S RETREAT

By the mid-1980s, a new social stratum was emerging in Colombia that
built its fortune on the marijuana boom and later capitalized on the coca
production. The consequences of this development were multifaceted.
At one level, it aggravated the hegemonic crisis of the state particularly
in controlling fiscal policies, money supply, interests rates, and taxation,
thus reducing the state's role in the economy. This was against, the backdrop of a relatively small public sector. In the 1990s, Colombia's public
sector expenditures ranked only nine out of twenty-six Latin American
countries, and the public sector constituted only 14 percent of the GDP,

while the general regional average was 28 percent of the GDP. The humble size of Colombia's public sector has been a pattern from 1987 through 1996.[15] In contrast, the money returns from illicit drugs was estimated to range between 4.2 pecent of the GDP in 1980 to a high of 10.9 percent in 1984 and 3.5 percent in 1995.[16] This substantial amount of money made the design and implementation of monetary and fiscal policies a very difficult task for the state.

Consequenly, the state was compelled not to impose a value added tax and to re-circulate drug money (mainly dollars), and transferring it into international reserves in order to prevent the dollarization of the economy. The government was also foced to devalue the peso in 1991, and since then, the peso has been devaluated several times. Moreover, the drug dollars and their conversion into local money increased the money supply and consequently increased the marginal demand for goods and services, which in turn increased the inflationary pressure on the economy.

Narcotrafficking impacted also the fiscal and monetary policy of the state through contrabanding of goods that became one of the most used mechanisms for money laundering. The latest evidence of the state's failure to curtail contraband that affected the country's balance-of-payment and taxation policies was presented by Fanny Kertzman, director of Customs Control (DIAN). Kertzman expressed the critical crisis of the state in revealing, "The authoritities are impotent and incapable of defeating contraband," she explained, "In Colombia there are criminal sectors protected by the custom authorities"; hence, as long there is narcotrafficking and the importation of illegal goods is the most effective money laundering mode, contraband will continue" Kertzman added,

" There are powerful groups that are protecting contraband which include members of congress who participate in this business and obstruct justice, politicians that import goods such the famous T-shirts used in electoral campaigns, business groups that ignore government pleads and finally and more importantly the multinational corporations chiefly, Korean and Japanese, that keep furnishing the goods for contraband."[17]

Kertzman illustrates a core aspect of the institutional crisis of the state: in containing the negative economic effects of narcotrafficking and contraband, which denies the state coffers billions of dollars in direct taxes. This in turn reduces the government capacity to govern since the governability and the capacity to implement an effective taxing system are intertwined, and the latter is one of the fundamental functions of a state. A question is in order here: what does the narcotrafficking challenge represent within the context of struggle for hegemony between guerrillas and the state? If state hegemony, as argued, has been in a state of "perpetual crises" since independence, impeding the state formation and consolidation, then what is the significance of this new moment?

If we take the two historical junctures under which guerrillas and narcotrafficking emerged, and we analyzed them in a dialectical mode rather than in juxtaposition or chronologically, we find that the guerrillas challenged the state hegemony in the political-military spheres, and narcotrafficking circumvented its interference in the economic spheres. In this dialectical mode we can develop a better appreciation of the dynamic relationships among these three actors and put the state's crisis in its proper historical context. More important, this mode will help in defining the main social antagonisms that this new dialectic (state, guerrillas, and narcotrafickers) brought to bear on the war system.

Narcotraffickers are economic liberals par excellence and agents of globalization because of their international clandestine business is against some states' rules (regarding narcotics) but not against the free enterprise system, open markets, or the cherished property rights laws, which ultimately protect their interests. Their economic activities during the 1980s in effect accelerated the famous "apertura" economic opening. Protectionisms and trade tarriffs became meaningless under the increasing onslaught of contraband, which by 1988 amounted to about $1 billion (on the eve of the apertura) and constituted about 22 percent of the country's total imports. Government tariffs became obsolete since the tax evasion became rampant among most importers through the decreasing billing and other evasive methods. Thus "la apertura" or economic opening was a "fait accompli" years before it was formally institutionalized by the Cesar Gaviria government (1990–94). What the government did however in addition to its acceptance of the fait accompli is to reform the archaic import-tax system that had more than twenty-three methods of taxation.[18]

However, the tax changes did not put a stop to contraband. It continued unchecked during the governments of Ernesto Samper (1994–98) and Andres Pastrana (1998–2001). In 1999, for example, the value of contraband goods increased to $2.2 billions (more than doubling in a decade), that is, about 25 percent of total imported goods and about 50 percent of Colombia's exports,[19] casting serious doubts about the ability/and or capability of the government in dealing with a problem of such magnitude without generating serious economic dislocations and political instability. The problem includes not only the owners of the narcotrafficking enterprises but also more than a 400,000 illicit plant producers, and thousands of small entrepreneus who operate in the San Adresitos. Thus, the issue is tied in with the larger question of the civil war upon which resolution rests the solution of contraband and narcotrafficking.

THE NARCOBOURGEOISIE
POLITICAL ROLE AND THE STATE

The trajectory of the relationship of the narcobourgeoisie with the state and the other sectors of the dominant social classes oscillated among coexistence, alliance, and conflict during the last two decades.[20] This oscillation has been a function of three interrelated factors. One is the tactical need of the state, particularly its armed forces, of narcoparamilitary groups to fight against the guerrillas, the working-class movement, and the political opposition by and large. In this manner we can explain the state's lack of determination to deal with the narcobourgeoisie and their armed militias. Two, the states' need for hard currency affected its policy towards narcotraffickers and their capital. "Repatraiting"—money laundering—narcodollars were crucial during the 1970s and 1980s when the Central Bank needed hard currency to support the Colombian peso and to provide liquidity to stimulate investment.[21] Such need increased during the banking system's crisis of 1982 and again in the late 1980s.[22] Finally the narcobourgeoisie's vast economic resources allowed the purchase of political influence through penetrating Congress by financing the campaigns of politicians, and bribing and intimidating judges and military officers. The epitomy of this corrupting/coopting phenomenon reached its zenith when Pablo Escobar the leader of the infamous Medellin Cartel became a member of Congress in 1982, and when the state and important political sectors accepted the "no extradition" demand by narcotraffickers in 1991.[23]

Political penetration of the state institutions paralleled the penetration of the financial sector through the famous "ventanilla seniestra"the "wicked window" of the Colombia's Central Bank (Banco de la Republica), which allowed narcotraffickers to "legalize" their drug money. This policy devised by the Lopez government in 1975 exempted narcotraffickers from paying taxes and protected them against punitive action. The oscillation of state-narcotraffickers relations can be divided into three main phases. The first was 1983–89, period when coca became the main cash crop supplantaing marijuana which dominated the 1970s. During this first phase, the narcotraffickers pursued the consololidation of their political base and control the areas where illicit drug production was concentrated. The control entailed establishing their hegemony over the coca production process. During this phase the narcobourgeisie also built a working relationship with the state, particularly its military institution in regions such as in Uraba, Middle Magdalena, and East Valleys. All of these were areas of coca productions.

The most notable manifestation of the alliances between narcotraffickers, large landowners, multinationals corporations, industrial groups

(Andi), and the state was in 1983 in Puerto Boyaca, in the Middle Magdalena, where a paramilitary organization (Autodefensas Campesinas) was formed and financed by the mentioned groups in an effort to fight the increasing influence of FARC in the region. As a result, FARC and the leftist groups were liquidated in Puerto Boyaca. This event inaugurated an unholy alliance that is still in effect in spite of the open war that took place in the second phase (1989–93) between the Medellin Cartel and the state, which ended with the death of Pablo Escobar, the most notorious drug trafficker.[24]

The war involving the state, sectors of the political elite, and the Medellin Cartel did not alter radically the state relationship with narcotrafficking organizations, nor did it affect the overlapping political and class interests between sectors of the narcobourgeoisie and sectors of the dominant class exhibited particularly in regions where peasants' resistance and guerrillas disputed their hegemony such as in Middle Magdalena, Uraba, North Santander, Bolivar, Putumayo, Antioquia, Cauca, and Caqueta. In these regions, if anything, the alliances among sectors of the political elite, army, cattle ranchers, and narcotraffickers were cemented.

The conflict between the state and narcotraffickers was not an all-out war so while it was fighting the Medellin Cartel, the state was complacent and collaborated with the Cali cartel. This latter was providing critical information about Pablo Escobar and his whereabouts at the time of his escape from prison in 1993. This was done in return for providing the Rodrigues brothers, leaders of the Cali Cartel, with leniency if they were to surrender. In this respect is worth mentioning "los Pepes" an acronym for those who broke with Pablo Escobar one of whom was Fidel Castaño which later became the founder of the United Self Defenses of Cordoba and Uraba (AUCU), which by the mid-1990s became the most important paramilitary organization in the country.

During the third phase (1993–present) the collaboration between the state coercive forces (army) and the paramilitary groups was an established fact. Many high-ranking military officers are collaborating and fomenting paramilitarism. One high-ranking officer explained to me the obvious rationale behind the army tacit and implicit collaboration with paramilitaries by saying "as long as they are fighting our enemy we have no interest in fighting them."[25] This view resonates within the highest circles of the military command.[26] Thus, the state-paramilitary groups relations are one of collaboration in the areas of conflict, that is on the ground, while maintaining an anti-paramilitary discourse at the level of the president. This analysis applies to the entire 1990s.

THE NARCOBOURGEOSIE-PARAMILITARY
NEXUS AND THEIR ALLIES

Chapters 2 and 3 established that violence as a method of conflict resolution has been applied in Colombia since the 19th century and that one
of the country's most chronic social conflicts was over property rights
and land titles. However, after 1920, violence became more pronounced
and reached new highs with the introduction of private armies who
became the defenders of the "social order." The evolution of violence
although unleashed by the ineffective state institutions embodying its
hegemonic crises took new forms over the years depending on the development of the dialectics of conflict, its actors, class interests, political
realignments and international political economy. That is why every single phase of violence is different from the other yet carries within it some
elements of the old. Our task is to discern continuities and ruptures in
the functions of violence within the sociohistorical context of this study.

The formal trajectory of paramilitary groups goes back to 1965
and 1968 respectively, when Decree 3398 and subsequently Law 48
provided the legal foundations for the creation of civil defense organizations through presidential order. These laws in turn stemmed from
the cold war counterinsurgency doctrines used by the United States in
its training programs in the Military School of the Americas, as the
Doctrine of National Security. The core of this program called for the
deployment of a combination of military, paramilitary, political, psy-
chological, and economic means in order to defeat insurgencies. The
Colombian military, as most of its Latin American counterparts,
incorporated this doctrine into its national strategies and political
socialization. In 1987, that is, almost two decades, after the introduction of the laws, then Minister of Defense, General Refael Samudio
affirmed the premises of National Security Doctrine in his defense of
the paramilitary groups by saying "that the civil committees of autodefense are legitimate if these communities are organized to defend
their property and lives."[27] When he made his statement there were
underway three different formations of paramilitarism: emeralds'
mafias, narcotraffickers-paramilitaries and cattle ranchers and landed-
elite-financed paramilitaries (usually refered to as "autodefenses").
Most of these paramilitary groups converged in the 1990s under a unified leadership and with a conservative political program to support
the state's armed forces.[28]

Thus when these measures were introduced in 1965–68 they came
after the emergence of FARC (1964) and the ELN in 1965. Since then,
paramilitary groups have assumed different incarnations in different
regions of the country.[29] Law 48 opened the door for the emergence of

private armies and consequently became an inherent part of the security of the social order and hence an integral part of the state counterinsurgency strategy. These groups as their history attests were built first and foremost to defend the interests of a core group of landed classes, emerald mafias, and narcotraffickers which inevitably became an integral part of the state's counterinsurgency strategy.

The emerald mafia and the autodefense of Boyaca are illustrative examples. In 1973, with the privatization of the mine exploitation of emeralds in Boyacá, came the confirmation of private armies or militias, which were tolerated by the state. The cause of state tolerance in Boyaca mining areas was partially due to its incapacity to deal with then predominantly small-scale mining operations carried out on part-time bases by peasants, which made it difficult to organize or control. Moreover, these small-scale operations were characterized by strong competition in an environment without clearly defined property rights, mine titles, and questionable state mining concessions. This was compounded by the lack of state institutions to adjudicate, arbitrate, and solve conflicts between these groups. Miners were left to solve their disputes by their own means, mostly through turf wars.

The zones of major emerald production were on the Minero River, which passes by emerald mining centers such as Buena Vista, Maripi, Muzo, Pauna, San Pablo de Barbour. This latter was located in the municipality of Puerto Boyaca, where ten years later became the show-case of paramilitarism. The miners of Barbour were in conflict with the miners of Coscuez who cut the market routes through Pauna to Chiquinquira, consequently forcing the miners of Barbour to find an alternative routes through the port of Boyaca on the country's main river, the Magdalena.This laid the foundation of a relationship between the miners of Barbour and busisness groups' elites, Henry de Jesus Perez and his paramilitary groups financed by Gilberto Molina, Pablo Escobar, and Gonzalo Rodriguez Gacha in Puerto Boyaca and in the Middle Magdalena.

The mining business was run on a clan-family base structure largely reproducing the "hacienda system," where allegiance to the boss is absolute yet is based on wage labor. It is a hybrid of production relations of precapitalists and capitalists constructed in a predominantly rural setting where minifundios uneasily coexist with extensive farming with all the social antagonisms that these could generate without conflict resolution mechanisms other than violence. The Carranzas' and Gachas families are two well-known emerald mafiosos in addition to the Molinas, Silvas, and Murcias clans. The first became the most important emerald business men in the country.

One of the factors most relevant to our investigation is that the formation of emeralds paramiliatry groups is grounded on the state's inability to produce and enforce a mining law. In 1947, the state attempted to do so by giving the Central Bank the only right to mine in the emerald-rich areas of Boyaca. But this did stop the development of clandestine mining in areas such as in Penas and Blancas. From 1947 through 1969, social conflicts increased in these areas, and the state was forced to revise its policy. In 1969, the mines were transferred to private investors, which in effect tranfered a public resource into a private property.

The privatization of the emerald sector without the proper institutional tools to mediate conflicts and adjudicate the distribution of mine resources was compounded with a polarized national environment resulting from La Violencia (1949–1958) and the insurgency (1964–). In the following years war became the main mechanism through which areas were divided and in defining leadership and hegemony over the sphere of emerald production.[30] Since its start, the process of granting the state concessions to private groups was marred with judicial problems and irregularities. This condition culminated in the "Green War" between the powerful emerald groups in 1988 whose main objective was the control of the mining areas.

As result of emerald wars, Victor Carranza emerged as the victor. Carranza maintained a standing paramilitary group with stretched relations with the narcoparamilitary groups. Carranza in the 1990s became one of the wealthiest national figures, with vast land properties in Middle Magdalena, Cesar, and other places. The power struggle between emerald clans converged with another struggle that was taking shape between guerrillas and its allies, the emerging narcobourgoisie and its large landowners and cattle ranchers in Puerto Boyaca. The two struggles intersected in this area, in the years that followed, when these social groups started disputing the territorial control of the guerrillas in areas where they acquired land properties and cattle ranchers. The emergence of Muerto al Los Secuestradores in 1982 was a watershed in the evolution of the conflict in Colombia, bringing social antagonism to higher levels of violence.

In November 1981, the M-19 (a defunct guerrilla organization since 1990) kidnapped Martha Nieves Ochoa, the sister of the Ochoas' Medellin narcotraffickers and asked for a ransom. A few months later, the Ochoa family called for a meeting in Medellin attended by a number of people (the real number is not known). The meeting was attended by narcotraffickers mostly from the Medellin Cartel.[31] In another version presented by FARC in a document presented to the Pastrana's government in 1999:

"On the 1 4 of February of 1983, the Attorney General, Carlos Jiménez Gómez, denounced before the Congress that in creation of MAS participated 163 personas, 59 of which were the army in active duty, representatives from Texas Petroleum Company, cattle ranchers and politicians, whose activity was in Puerto Boyacá, Middle Magdalena. It is being extended the vicious habit of the military of using private groups to achieve their counterinsurgency strategy."

Two important notes are in order. One is that narcotraffickers, large landowners, and cattle ranchers and local political bosses plus the military started putting in place a counterinsurgency strategy when the government of Belisario Betancur started negotiating a peaceful solution with the guerrillas. This event also demonstrated the new incarnations of the state hegemonic crisis and the level of its institutional fragmentation, particularly between the executive civilian authority and the military institution.

The military initiated a new phase in their political-military strategy which we can easily contextualize within the regional military doctrines and counterinsurgency strategies used in the Military School of the Americas more than with the government's policy. Such a divorce between the government policy and what the military was exercising on the ground contributed to the failure of hammering out an accord with FARC and the ELN. The other three groups (M-19, EPL, and Quintin Lame) that signed a peace accord were practically defeated by the paramilitary-military alliance.

Moreover, not only did paramilitary groups enjoy the support and training of the armed forces and international mercenaries from Israel and United States, but more important they relied on the vast economic resources of the narcotraffickers. The narcotraffickers supported paramilitaries enjoyed more autonomy in drawing their strategies since they had financial independence from the state. In the late 1990s this condition was present in areas such as Cordoba, Uraba, Middle Magdalena, Cesar, and Putumayo. In all these cases several military personnel, police officers, and local officials worked in tandem with narco-paramilitary groups and some became listed on their payrolls.[32]

In 1981, in Segovia, Antioquia, another paramilitary group, was under formation by Fidel and Carlos Castaño, whose father was kidnapped for ransom and later killed by FARC. The incident led the two brothers and some of their relatives to establish an armed group with a clear antiinsurgency vendetta.[33] The Castaños, who were upper-middle class landowners, offered their services to the military batallion Bombona that operated in Segovia, particularly in the area of intelligence service. Gradually they started to operate jointly with the army and later started building some organizational autonomy. The army was also instrumental in linking them with the paramilitaries of Puerto Boyaca represented by Gonzalo Gacha and Henry Perez. This was at the time when some military high-ranking officers in Puerto Boyaca and its surroundings started to have a stake in the economic returns of a successful counterinsurgency strategy, particularly by bying lands at a depreciated price especially when the guerrillas were present, and appreciating in value after the paramilitaries-military alliance managed to liquidate its suppport base.[34]

By 1988, the brothers Castaño started buying land in Cordoba, Uraba, southeast Antioquia, and the Viejo Caldas, and amassed a fortune mostly through extortion and narcotrafficking. Their links first with the Medellin Cartel and then with that of Cali consolidated their linkages with narco-traffickers. Today the paramilitary groups operate at the national level with a coordinated leadership with Carlos Castaño as its maximum leader. The Autodefensas Unidas de Colombia, (AUC) the United Autodefenses of Colombia is made up of the Occidental bloc, which includes Chocó and Urabá; the north bloc which has three fronts in Sucre, Bolívar, Magdalena, Cesar y la serranía de San Lucas; the bloc of the plains, with fronts in Ari-ari, Guaviare and Piedemonte; and the bloc metro which includes fronts from southeast, west, east and northeast of Antioquia. Its main strongholds are in the Nexus of Paramillo (Nudo del Parmillo, Antioquia) and the department of Córdoba, and from where the Autodefensas Campesinas de Córdoba and Urabá (ACCU) emerged in the 1980s.

The leadership of the AUC is a loose coalition of different private armies with common class and political interests in defending the socio-economic order in their fight against not only the armed insurgency but the leftist political groups and by and large the democratic forces and human rights groups. It is estimated that the AUC amounts to eight thousand fighters.[35] Most of which are: ex-military (about one thousand) and ex-military officers (hundred fifty) and the remaining are ex-guerrillas and small-time criminals drawn from intermediary and large cities and belong to the lumpen sectors of the petty bourgeoisie.[36]

Paramilitaries rely on two sources of financing: taxes on small businesses, contractors, subcontractors, and multinational corporations which they are hired to protect; contributions of large landowners and cattle ranchers. Since the 1980s, however, the paramilitary has increasingly relied on narcotrafficking to finance its army. In mid-1999, the government forces discovered one of the largest cocaine processing complexes near Puerto Boyaca, an important paramilitary stronghold, which makes the case that these groups depend primarily on narcotrafficking for their survival. This complex operated by the AUC has the capacity of producing eight tons of cocaine per month and occupied an area of ten square kilometers.[37] According to police estimates, the costs of constructing such a plant was about $5 million and could employ more than one hundred people.[38]

This discovery confirms the thesis that the AUC is becoming a narco-trafficking organization with its involvement in the processing, packaging, and marketing of cocaine.[39] And more important, the AUC is filling the vacuum left by the infamous narcotrafficker Rodriguez Gacha, who once led a powerful paramilitary group in the same areas where the AUC now operates and in the Meta. Gacha was killed in 1989. Ramon Isaza, who is a member of the AUC leadership and in charge of the Middle Magdalena, operated jointly this complex with members of the Medellin and Cali cartels. The AUC controls also the strategic corridor from Santander passing by Middle Magdalena reaching the Panama border on the Gulf of Uraba allowing trafficking with relative ease through the porous borders with Panama. In fact, in an interview conducted in early 2000, Carlos Castaño confirmed his organization's dependence on narcotrafficking, by revealing that the coca profits from the Catatumbo region (North Santander) alone, finance almost 40 percent of his 8,000-strong army. It is estimated that the AUC's annual income from narcotrafficking is about $75 million, which is approximately 80 percent of the group total income.[40] (See also footnote 85.)

THE GUERRILLAS AND PARAMILITARIES: ANATOMY OF THE CONFLICT

The industry of illegal drugs like most agribusinesses' raw material is carried on by a substantial number of peasants and agricultural workers in a very competitive market. In each phase of the production process, the number of participants is reduced due to a strong oligopolistic tendency which increases as one goes up in the production process.[41] At the wholesale level of the final product there are fewer sellers. At the distribution phase, the markets become more competitive. Our focus here is on the producers of the prime material, the colonos, poor peasants, and agricultural workers and their corresponding relationship with the guerrillas and consequently how the guerrilla-peasant relationship impacted the guerrilla-narcotraffickers relationship. In very simple terms, the conflict between narcotraffickers and guerrillas is analyzed here as part of the social antagonisms stemming from the production process taking place within the institutional contours of the war system. This conflict, however, at a general level constitutes part of the contradictions generated by capital and labor. Francisco Thoumi, a leading specialist on narcotrafficking, eloquently defined the nature of the antagonism by writing that narcotraffickers represent a raw form of capitalism, whereas the guerrillas originated from and are part of the struggle against capitalism, thus their interests are irreconcilable on the long term.[42]

   In defining the root causes of the narcotraffickers conflict with the guerrillas, the first that comes to mind is the primordial interest of narcotraffickers in controlling the market. Narcotraffickers act as a monopoly attempting to determine the price of coca leaves, coca paste, and wages. This monopolistic tendency inclusively led to severe conflicts between the major narcotrafficking organizations of Medellin and Cali. These conflicts assumed a violent nature since this is one of the main conflict resolution mechanisms available to groups operating outside the law when they cannot amicably organize their market shares. However, the nature of the conflict between the narcotrafficking organizations is qualitatively different than the one between narcotraffickers and the guerrillas who represent diametrically opposed class interests. The first is between members of the same class faction and its resolution does not necessarily require a change in socio-economic order but just a market adjustment to accommodate their interests as happened after the collapse of the Medellin Cartel and its replacement by the Cali's Cartel in the late 1980s. The case of the second is a manifestation of capital and labor antagonism, where the guerrillas objectively represent the interests of the producers widely defined, and thus the resolution of this type of conflict requires fundamental changes in the socioeconomic spheres as Thoumi argued. The nature and direction of these changes are decided by the correlation of forces between the two contending forces and their abilities to translate their military power into social, economic, and political gains.

Three main defining factors have determined the course of conflict between the guerrillas and the narcotraffickers. One was the presence of the guerrillas in areas of illicit drug production, which constituted a countervailing force in the market place where the price of labor was not solely decided by market forces or narcotraffickers' monopoly.[43] In areas in which the guerrillas' presence is weak or nonexistent, the price of labor is lower than in areas where it has strong military presence. The second factor was the taxes that guerrillas imposed on nacrotraffickers and merchant intermediaries, the introduction of taxation on illicit drug products which ranges between seven to ten percent per kilo of the local market value of illicit drugs. These taxes affected negatively capital accumulation and increased the costs of productions. Third, the surplus capital accumulated by narcotraffickers was invested in land leading to an unprecendented rapid concentration of property largely at the expense of small peasants and colonos. South Bolivar represents a case that is typical to the other regions, and thus discussing it in some detail will help in illustrating these three factors and the political economy of the war system with its different actors and complexities.

The production of coca in South Bolivar is mainly based on small properties of three and fewer hectares, but there are also large properties of 10 hectares and more, but these are not the dominant ones. In the early 1990s it was estimated that the total area of coca production occupied about 2,200 hectares, which could be roughly divided into 2.5

hectares as an average for each family. Consequently, there were about a thousand producers of coca with a relatively good level of technical development. By 2000, the government sources put the total area cultivated with coca at 6,500 to 10,000 hectares, which increases significantly the number of peasants involved in its production.[44]

Predominantly the peasants are colonos (squatters) in several cases they rent their lands in return for money or sharing the production. This type of relationship is called in the region as accompañamiento "companionship." In this context, the coca producers are of two types, those that produce and sell the leaves to be processed into paste in the same zone, and those that both produce and process the leaves. The traders buy the processed coca. The daily wage is six thousand Colombian pesos ($ three on an exchange rate of one dollar equaling two thousand pesos). This does not include food. The daily wage in other economic activities in the region is three thousand pesos; that is half of that of coca workers.

Some coca collectors "raspachines," chose to determine their wage price by amount of production, which could range between 6 to 8 arrobas (1 arroba=11.34 kilos) per day which could make his daily wage of 15,000 pesos ($7.5) with free food and a place to sleep. One season generates about 1,100 jobs in the South Bolivar or about 300,000 working days. The producers average 150 to 200 arrobas per hectare per season (four per year) extract 3 kilograms with a market value of 1,200,000 pesos ($600) discounting the production costs. The average monthly net income of a peasant constitutes about three to four times of the minimum wage.

It is calculated that the coca generated about $350,000 per week in south Bolivar, of which only 40 percent stayed in the area. Paradoxically, however, such income, according to a study, did not lead to any significant improvement in the population's standards of living or housing. This same study concludes that in the final analysis what is spent in the region is in bars, and discotheques and on sexual workers and not in factors of production. Most of the capital that is generated from coca production is invested in real estate in places such as Piedecuasta, Bucaramanga, Aguachica, and others.[45]

San Pablo, as most of south Bolivar, was until mid-1998 under the control of the ELN, but in October of that same year, paramilitary groups under the command of Carlos Castaño gained control of the area. A change in control led to a change in coca relations of production. Under the guerrillas, coca paste was bought by merchants, who in turn transported it to the drug cartels located in major cities where it was processed and exported to international markets. The paramilitaries, however, buy the product and transport it without intermediaries into international markets in collaboration with the new less centralized cartels, which came to replace the traditional and disarticulated cartels of

Medellin and Cali. Cutting down in the chain from producers to distributers meant reducing the costs and risks involved in the operation. But reducing the costs did not translate into better prices or better wages for the colonos, poor peasants and seasonal workers but allowed narcotraffickers to accumulate additional surpluses.

One of the main consequences of the paramilitary takeover and the elemination of the intermediary merchants in south Bolivar was a sharp decline in the price of coca paste. In May 1999, a few months before the paramilitary occupation, the coca paste was selling at 2,200,000 pesos per kilo (about$ 1100 based on an exchange value of 2000 pesos per U.S. dollar). By February 2000, the price of coca paste declined sharply to 1,400,000 pesos, that is decreasing by more than 60 percent in less that five months.[46] This steep decline in coca paste price occurred because the paramilitary became the only market, distorting the relationship between supply and demand. Under a "buyer monopoly" sanctioned by force, the coca growers were left with no negotiating leverage in the market place.

Coca growers felt intimidated by narcotraffickers after they lost important support with the displacement of the guerrillas who until recently prevented the narcotraffickers' monopoly.[47] In probing this issue further, peasants (mostly colonos) expressed few days after the paramilitary occupation that this power change could transfer disproportionately the risk of production to them if the prices of coca were to decline, which did happen a few months later. Arguably, this transfer of costs would not have been possible if the guerrillas were still in the region. When the insurgency controlled these areas, it enforced compliance of merchants and intermediaries with the terms of agreements, payments to peasants of market value, and reducing the transfer of costs in times of bust.[48]

The other side of the coin is the capital accumulated by the paramilitary bosses is in turn invested in real estate in other areas, fueling the inflationary prices of land, which in turn aggravate the struggle for land. This trend of buying land with narco dollars started in the 1980s, and by 1994, the lands bought by this emerging class amounted to 4.4 million hectares and are concentrated in the most productive areas of Middle Magdalena, Uraba, Cordoba, and the East Valleys (Llanos Orientales).[49] According to some estimates, this amounts to about 10 percent of Colombia's most fertile lands.[50] Such rapid accumulation of land in a decade generated a process of "counterreform," and most of these lands were bought in contested areas where land titles were dubious, bringing the conflict with colonos and poor peasant to a new highs.

The coca plantations are lucrative for the peasants for simple economic reasons, as one peasant from Monterrey explains. He said, "the costs of producing and transporting a load of plantain or yuca average $1.5 to $2.5 and is sold at $7 or $8 whereas coca paste is sold at 1,500,000 pesos ($750).[51] Clearly, therefore, peasants see coca as a logical alternative crop since they do not have to worry obout transporting their produce to regional markets from areas that lack basic road infrastructures or transportation systems. In this manner, global markets either legal or illegal help in articulating the rural economy and increasingly integrating it and exacerbating social conflicts. The most salient social conflict is the struggle to appropriate the surplus of illicit drug economy among guerrillas, dominant classes, the state, and norcotraffickers.

The adaptability of segments of the subsistence economy to the changes in the global economy in regions such as Middle Magdalena, Putumayo, Guaviare, and North Santander was due to the availability of virgin lands in the Amazonias, plains and high lands. Colonization of new lands became a safety valve to the subsistence peasant economy, supplemented with illicit drug plantations serving as a life support system. The second important factor that has helped the subsistence economy was the inability of the state to project its authority in areas under guerrillas' authority. Hence, the survival of the subsistence economy has depended on two intertwined factors: insurgency and illicit drug plantations. In more precise terms, the fortunes of the subsistence peasant economy depend on the balance of forces between the guerrillas and the state which paradoxically created its own dialectical antithesis: the narcobourgeoisie, an objective ally to the dominant class at large and the state. In this tapestry, the relations of production and one of the main social contradictions in the rural economy is becoming between a rentier-based capitalist mode of production championed by large cattle ranchers, land speculators (including narcotraffickers), commercial-coca plantations,[52] and mining and oil companies and a subsistence peasant economy supported by the guerrillas.[53] The subsistence economy, however, is fully integrated with global markets and cannot be characterized as precapitalist because peasants are mostly landless wage laborers producing for international markets. Hence, the contradiction between these two modes of production can be better understood and defined as a product of the interplay between a capitalist development and the social and political forces that oppose it.

MULTINATIONAL CORPORATIONS, NATIONAL COMPANIES, AND PARAMILITARIES

Thus far, the analysis has concentrated on the interplay of the three factors that fueled the conflict between guerrillas and narcotraffickers, namely: (a) the guerrilla threat to the narcotraffickers' monopoly of the illicit drug market particularly in determining the price of labor in illicit plantations; (b) Taxes that the guerrillas levied from narcotraffickers and their intermediaries; and (c) the narcotraffickers' surplus capital was mainly invested in land intensifying the concentration of land at the expense of poor peasants and colonos.

Another and more complex variant conflict is present also in south Bolivar, an important gold mining area, involving guerrillas, paramilitary groups, and multinational and national corporations. According to the Ministry of Mining and Energy, south Bolivar is the country's principal gold mining potential where more than 32,000 subsistence miners extract 42.01 percent of the gold that Colombia produces. Some claim that south Bolivar is the second most important gold reserve in Latin America. The amount extracted from south Bolivar was about eighteen tons in 1998. Most of the miners are peasant colonos from Boyaca and Santander that shifted to mining since the early 1980s, when gold appeared to be a viable alternative to their cash crops. This activity did not liberate those new miners from the subsistence mode of existence, since their economic activity is family based, and the possibility of accumulation has been very limited. The rudimentary modes of extraction and the primitive methods used have helped in maintainig that condition of subsistence.

The gold mining potential and the good quality of the gold attracted local and international companies. This is an interesting dimension of the war system, since it involves a number of national and international actors influencing the local dynamics of the conflict. It is very difficult to assess the role do multinational corportaions play in the conflict in south Bolivar, but from the information available and through interviews with local miners, there is evidence that there are some multinational corporations (such as Corona Goldfields SA) with mining interests in the region, particularly in areas of conflict such as Serrania de San Lucas. Since 1998 all municipalities where gold production is concentrated such as Rioviejo (195,783.10 onzes troy per year); Santa Rosa (34,729.29 onzes troy); San Pablo (5,676 onzes troy); Pinillos (3,880.24 onzes troy); Tiquicio-Puerto Rico (1,111.17 onzes troy); Montecristo (75.48 onzes troy); and Achi (63.67 onzes troy),[54] have been under attack by the paramilitaries and the armed forces, which made local peasants and miners suspect the link between the paramilitary's sudden interest in this area and the possiblity of the governments giving mining concesions to foreign and or local companies at their expense since they lack titles over the land.[55] An onze troy equals 31.103 grams.

In Simiti, an area that became under the control of paramilitaries in 1998, Compaqia Minera Archangel SA, a Canadian-based company, has the major contract in this area with a concesion of 13,764 hectares. In Santa Rosa del Sur, the Sociedad Ordinararia de Minas Cali (SOM) with three different licensing applications with a total amount of 2903.5192 hectare, followed by Mineros de Antioquia SA applied for a concessions of 2,624 hectares.[56] In Achi, Mineros de Antioquia has the main share of the granted concesions with more than 14,828 hectares. Keep in mind that all these are just licenses waiting the phase of exploitation, which will depend on how the conflict transpires in the future.[57] Most of these applications were presented in the second part of the 1990s, coinciding with an increase in the AUC activity in the region. It is difficult to make a conclusive assertion in this respect, but simply to suggest a plausible correlation between the two.

The absense of mining laws that protect the interests of subsistence miners and safeguard their future, and the encroachement of foreign and national capital have only generated social insecurity bringing into the forefront again the issue of the struggle for land rights, particularly since the AUC has declared this area as its prime military objective and consequently, hundreds of miners and colonos have been massacred and expelled from their villages, problematizing their claim to their untitled lots. The counterinsurgency strategy in this context is intricately related to the interests of rentier capital seeking raw material extraction and land speculation.

The bottom line here is if the paramilitary groups were successful in pushing out the guerrillas and establishing their hegemony in south Bolivar, that could translate into more investments from the companies that were granted mining rights. It is noteworthy that in my review of the number of concessions granted between 1996 and 1998, a substantial number of the companies are from Antioquia and Cali, which raises the possibility that at least some of them may be tied in with narcotraffickers' capital.[58]

The mobilization of miners during 1998 in protest of government mining policy and their mass exodus during the same year caused and propelled by the paramilitary groups of Castaño are telling in this respect. The objective of the paramilitary group has been to subjugate the entire region and make it succumb to the "modernizing" project of local and international capital in an effort to consolidate the developing rentier economy.[59] This paramilitary objective clashed with the subsitence mode of production sustained by small producers, miners, poor pesants, and fishermen (particularly in areas close to the Magdalena River). Such clash has been unmitigated by institutions designed to negotiate, arbitrate, and adjudicate social disputes caused by economic dislocation caused by such transformation. The outcome of the absence of state institutions in south Bolivar was the creation of the institution of the war system that determines the allocation of resources, their distribution, and the articulation of a rentier mode of production. The most interesting aspect of the south Bolivar case is the interplay between local and international capital, legal and illegal exports, narcotraffickers, the state, and guerrillas, a myriad that captures aspects of the complex operation and function of the war system.

Other cases of multinational corporations' involvement in the war system are British Petroleum and a host of other companies such as the French company,Total and the American company, Triton who are associated with the building and maintanance of the oil pipelines run from the oil fields of Cusiana and Cupiaqua in the department of Casanare to Coveñas on the Atlantic Coast.

The paramilitaries of Victor Carranza and Carlos Castaño (AUC) control an important sector through which the pipelines pass. For the last few years, the prime objective of both Carranza's and Castaño's forces has been establishing and consolidating a buffer zone that could diminish the guerrillas' influence in the surroundings of the pipelines. The most obvious goal of this strategy is to push the guerrillas from villages located in the pipeline areas and deny the guerrillas the extraction of protection rent that they obtained from the oil companies.

This paramilitary strategy coincided with BP contracting Defense Systems Limited, a British based security company, and Silver Shadow, an Isreali company.[60] Defense Systems Limited and Silver Shadow (owned by Asaf Nadel Israel's ex-military attache to Colombia) divised a security strategy in order to protect a strech of 115 Kilometers between Segovia and Remedio in Antioquia.[61] Their plan included military and "phsychological and intelligence operations" in the villages of Segovia and Remedios against the social base of the guerrillas. This at the time when massacres were committed by paramilitaries in both places, which raised important questions about the nature of the relationship among BP, its security companies, the army, and the AUC.

The army has a brigade and two batallions in the area, and number of their officers were implicated in massacres perpetrated against "guerrillas symphathizers" in collaboration with pamilitaries.[62] The above represents a case of how the concerns of multinational corporations intersect with the local actors of the war system and in their areas of operations. Multinational corporations provide an opportunity for the extraction of protection rent exacerbating a competition between multinational security companies and the local actors of the war system. Such a condition consolidate the war system as a modality for the distribution of protection rent among the contending forces.[63] The relationship between BP and the army is governed by agreements under which BP is commmitted to pick up the bill for maintaining the forces protecting its installations[64] (see chapter 3).

CONCENTRATION OF LANDS IN THE 1990S

In the 1980s and 1990s the narcotraffickers of Medellin and Cali bought significant properties in the Middle Magdalena region. Similarly, the emerald baron Victor Carranza who discovered the profits that real estate could bring has bought lands in the Middle Magdalena, Putumayo, and Meta. It is interesting to note that Carranza, for example, has bought lands in the municipalities of La Gloria and Aguachica using the paramilitary group Los Masetos to liquidate peasant resistance and force them to sell their properties. In south Cesar, the marijuana traffickers have bought land properties in Aguachica, San Alberto and San Martin during the 1970s.

In the Antioquia part of the Middle Magdalena, the Cali narcotraffickers have bought lands in Puerto Berrio, Caceres, and Caucasia in the latter, the price of hectare increased from 700.000 colombian pesos (about $350) to a 1,700,000 ($850) in a very short time. In areas close to the Pan American highway that links local markets with the Americas, prices of land appreciated even more from a mere a $10 per hectare to $1,000 per hectare in the last few years.[65] Currently in the midst of the most violent confrontations, the buying of lands goes uninterrupted. Between three thousand and four thousand hectares near Simiti were bought with capitals originating from coffee regions. Some of these investments are diverted into cattle ranching and improvements of pastoral land.

There have been changes in the sociopolitical configurations of the paramilitaries in Puerto Boyaca after the demise of Pablo Escobar and Rodriquez Gacha. Alejandro Reyes, a sociologist, argues that the control has transferred to large landowners, including emerald barons and retired military in addition to Victor Carranza, who is expanding his land acquisitions from Playon in the north toward south of Cesar helped by his paramilitary groups which provide security and hence help in the appreciation of land rents.[66] In my opinion the change did not alter the class nor the political character of the alliance but rather added an 'old group,' which acquired a new class status: the retired military with land possessions. It is an old group because high-ranking military has been involved since the late 1970s, with auto defense groups and paramilitaries in terms of training and logistical support in their capacities as officers in active duty. Now, we see more retired military with land acquisition in areas of conflict.[67]

Moreover, in the Santander part of the Middle Magdalena, the narcotraffickers, paramilitaries (MAS) and los Masetos of Carranza, and Gacha's remaining asscociates, collaborate in the land acquisitions process in each of the following municipalities: Rionegro, Barrancabermeja,

Cimitarra, Puerto wilches, Puerto Parra, El Carmen, and Sabana de Tor-res. This trend of land acquisition in Middle Magdalena demonstrates how the process of land concentration propelled by the narcotraffickers intertwined with the military counterinsurgency strategy is transforming vast lands from agricultural production to speculation, consolidating the base of a rentier capitalist development in which capital is mainly formed through land speculation.

In the other regions, the concentration of land is consistent with our findings in the Middle Magdalena. This trend in land acquisitions is spreading with the influx of the narcotraffickers surpluses. In a span of less than ten years (1980–88), from a total of 4 billion dollars, 45 percent were invested in land properties, especially cattle ranches (mainly used for speculation in land prices), and the rest was invested as follows: 20 percent in commerce, 15 percent in construction, 10 percent in the service sector, and 10 percent in recreation businesses.[68] The total amount of lands acquired by narcotraffickers in the country is difficult to assess, but building on Incora's and experts estimates, we can establish a bench mark range between 3 million and 4.4 million hectares. Alejandro Reyes calculated that by 1995, 4 million hectares were bought by narcotraffickers distributed in 409 municipalities constituting about 37 percent of Colombia's total.[69]

Antioquia occupies the favorite place in narcotraffickers' land acquisitions since it was the headquarters of the now defunct Medellin Cartel. Narcoctraffickers bought lands in 66 of the 124 municipalities of this department. Other regions of major land acquisitions by narcotraffickers are lower Cauca, Uraba, the northeast plains, and the coffee areas in the south.[70]

The increase in narcotraffickers' landownership in areas where there has been conflict over land since the 1920s and 1930s such as in Middle Magdalena, Bolivar, Cesar, Meta, and North Santander is not a mere coincidence. These lands are the most fertile in the country and are in prime geographic locations close to regional and national highways, which adds the speculative dimension that narcotraffickers brought into play. Nonetheless, the narcobourgeoisie land acquisition process has to be analyzed within the context of the long struggle over land between peasants and landlords, in which the latter resorted to building their own private armies, their autodefenses. Similarly, the narcobourgeoisie drew on that old pattern of building private armies to disposess small peasants, squatters, and their guerrilla supporters and then "protecting" their new land acquisitions since the state institutions were unable to do so.

By 1994 the guerrillas and narcoparamilitary groups coincided in the departments of Antioquia, Boyaca, Santander, Huila, Caqueta, Valle, Putumayo, Casanare, Cesar and Choco, among others. The guerrillas have a presence in about 48 percent of municipalities on the Caribbean Coast where there is a concentration of latifundios, and the paramilitary groups in 43.9 percent of those.[71] This is consistent with a broader trend: the guerrilla and paramilitary groups coincide in about two hundred municipalities (out of a total of 1,071). From these two hundred, 25 percent are areas of colonization, 47 percent are underdeveloped with predominance of latifundios and large cattle ranchers, 10 percent are in areas of developed agribusinesses, 13 percent are in areas of predominantly middle-sized farming, and finally 5 percent coincide in urban municipal centers.

The highest percentage of municipalilties where the actors of the war system coincide is in the areas where latifundios and large cattle ranchers domininate and where a rentier economy is flourishing. This finding validates the argument that there is a continuity in the history of land struggle and that narcotrafficking did not represent a rupture but rather an aggravation of the crisis. The crisis is exacerbated by continuous expansion of large properties propelled by an influx of narco dollars at the expense of colonos and small-property peasants (see table 5.1). The second highest (25 percent) where the actors coincide is in areas of colonization. This can be explained by the traditional mode of capitalist development in Colombia since the 1920s. That is, colonos come and prepare the land for cultivation. This raises its value, and then investors and land speculators will follow either by buying them out or by forcing them out. In this mode, colonos have been spearheading the capitalist development by opening new frontiers with grave environmental consequence. In this manner, the areas of latifundios and colonization represent the main default axis of social conflict, invoking Barrington Moore's phrase.

THE POLITICAL ECONOMY OF MASSACRES

It is important to analyze the political economy of expulsion and massacres, which has made Colombia one of the most violent countries in the world. Since land titles are disputed in the areas where the conflict is concentrated, the expulsion of poor peasants and the colonos meant a transfer of the claim over the land. The expelled peasants had no legal right to return to the land before the introduction of the Law 387 in 1997. In this manner, property could change hands, and violence became a profitable vehicle as a means to this end. Against the institutional loopholes regarding property rights, massacres became an effective tool in the process of concentration of land. Massacres (defined as crimes that cause the loss of life of three or more persons) are employed also to eleminate the support base of the guerrillas. These two objectives underlined the political economy of this phenomenon.

According to the 1999 report of the Jurist Commission on Human Rights, the paramilitaries are responsible for about 40 percent of the massacres and 78.69 percent of the reported violations of international human rights recorded in 1999, whereas the guerrillas were faulted with only 16 percent of the massacres, and 17 cases of the cases committed against international human rights, the remaining were attributed to the armed forces and unidentified actors.[72] According to this same study, the paramilitaries are noted to be advancing in the north west of the country (Antioquia) and in areas of the Valle del Cauca.

In addition, it is noted that in 1999, most of the massacres were committed in areas where land concentration was taking place, such as northwest Antioquia and its vicinities where Castaño is based (108 massacres), followed by North Santander (30), Valle del Cauca (28), and south Bolívar (25). Breaking down the departments into municipalities, these areas indeed witnessed a process of land concentration spearheaded by narcotraffickers, large cattle ranchers, and other types of investments, such as mining in the area of south Bolivar.

In northwest Antioquia, particularly in the Nudo del Paramillo, where Castaño has established his main base, a significant amount of property was appropiated by his forces, which caused the expulsion of large numbers of peasants under the pretext of being guerrilla sympathizers. Nudo del Paramillo was part of FARC land until 1998 and is a strategic corredor to Uraba on the coast. In North Santander particularly in the municipality of Gabarra a strategic area in the Catatumbo region where it was estimated about 40,000 hectares of coca were grown and a stronghold of the ELN, paramilitaries killed 250 people during 1999 and expelled hundreds of peasants frome their homes.[73] Again the objectives of these massacres could be summed up as follows: (1) to control the coca region and eliminate the guerrillas' interference with the coca market as discussed in the previous section; (2) deny the tax income that the guerrillas' (particularly ELN and also FARC, whose forces operate in the region since the 1990s) generate from narcotraffickers' intermediaries and coca merchants;[74] (3) control the territory where the oil pipelines are located, which in turn could deny the ELN a source of income and more important weaken the ELN potential political leverage in influencing the state's oil policy toward the multinationals oil corporations;[75] and finally, facilitate the concentration of land in narcotraffickers' hands.

The municipalities of San Pablo and Simiti are cases in point where large areas bought by real estate speculators were part of the highest concentration of land among the 27 municipalities of the Middle Magdalena. In the north and center of the Valle (Buga, San Pedro, Andalucía, Tuluá y Bugalagrande) there is evidence that narcotraffickers did buy lands.[76] In all these same municipalities peasants were forced out, and massacres were committed between 1997 and 1999, which confirms an overall national trend.

The statistics of Consultoría para los Desplazados (Codhes), a human rights organization, demonstrate that 65 percent of the persons that were forced to abandon their lands and homes as a direct result of the massacres and death threats lost their rights to the land. Prior to 1997, there was no law that protected the rights of the displaced peasant, particularly when their lots are occupied by paramilitary groups or by their sympathizers. During the 1990s, about 1,700,000 hectares were abandoned by about 2,500,000 poor peasants which are currently occupied either by armed actors or by their clients.[77] The manner in which this process takes place is best described by one displaced peasant:

> first comes the paramilitary incursion which recommends that peasants leave the area within a certain period of time. If they do not respond, then a number of the targeted population are killed in view of the inhabitants to force the population to leave. Then paramilitary sympathizers, mostly from other regions, are brought in as sharecroppers or tenants and at the same time serving in paramilatry force to occupy the abandoned lots. In the meantime, the land becomes in dispute with the previous colonos, since the only right to the land that exists is the physical occupation of the place at the time of adjudication. In case there is land tiltle peasants are forced to sell.[78]

This description roughly captures an ongoing process that has characterized several areas, such as Nudo de Paramillo, south Bolivar, Putumayo, Cesar, and Valle. The psycological impact of the massacres has been enormous achieving one of the prime objectives of the paramilitaries and the military. A study found that most of the displaced left their villages and towns because of threats (39 percent) and fear (23 percent) of paramilitaries' punitive actions.[79]

The Law 387 of 1997 attempts to regulate the consequences of the forced displacement by obligating INCORA to register the parcels that were abandoned by the displaced in order to deny the forced expropriation. This same law provides INCORA with legal instruments to provide those peasant with land titles to adjudicate to them land in other places. This law, however, does not address the plight of those that were displaced prior to 1997 and whose lands were expropriated, nor does it stop the process of forced displacement, leaving thousands of peasants in limbo. It is estimated that 1.7 million people were forced out of their homes between 1985 and 1999.[80] Law 387's application and effectiveness from 1998 through 2001 remains at best a shy attempt to redress the injustices committed. The big question remains: how can the state guarantee the returns of peasants without land titles when it cannot even guarantee the return of those that have a land title?

PARAMILITARIES AND THE WAR SYSTEM

So far, the central arguments advanced are that the two main actors of the war system, the state and the guerrillas, have contributed to the generation of a third actor: organized crime and its paramilitary organization. I discussed the dynamics of this process, particularly the guerrillas' tacit and implicit support of the poor peasants and colonos shift to illicit cash crops. I analyzed how sectors of the state (military) and the landed oligarchy in their turn supported these groups in order to respond to the guerrillas' challenge. This interaction between the mentioned actors took place under a military impasse between the initial contending forces (state-guerrillas) that facilitated in the first place the introduction and then the propagation of illicit drug plantations in the 1980s and 1990s, a condition that in turn led to the emergence of a new social force: organized crime (narcotraffickers and emerald mafia) and their paramilitary organizations.

In this mode of analysis we can capture the systemic effects (balance of power, which in our case is a military impasse) on actors and the systemic outcomes produced by actors' behavior and strategies, such as the guerrillas' support of peasants; or, the military, landed oligarchy, and organized crime support of the paramilitary. Morover, in system analysis outcomes, as the impact of the emergence of narcobourgoeisie-paramilitaries on the war system, can neither be explained nor predicted nor assessed by exploring the individual inputs of the war system actors taken separetely. But rather on the ways the behavior of one actor's strategy depends on those of others and how actors and their environment shape one another.[81] Finally how all these impact the system.

In the discussion above I have demonstrated the actor's behavior and interaction during the 1980s and 1990s. The rest of this chapter assesses the impact of the paramilitaries on the war system. For this purpose, I will divide the development of the paramilitary groups into two main phases. The first phase is the 1984–94 period (December 1994 was the date when the first paramilitary national summit was held) under which the paras acted at the local level and largely in response to regional and localized needs of the large landowners and narcobour-goeisie to protect their investments. This was the formative phase during which the paramilitaries lacked a unified command structure and an articulated antisubversive national strategy. Their main areas of operations were in the north of Antioquia (Segovia and later in Cordoba and Uraba) Puerto Boyaca, and Meta.

During this phase an alliance among narcotraffickers, landed oligarchy, agribusiness groups, cattle ranchers, consevative political leaders and sectors of the military was forged, laying the groundwork for the second phase in the development of this group. The paramilitaries counted only several hundreds (according to the Ministry of Defense, the ACCU counted 93 men in 1986) during their first phase and largely depended on the logistical support of the army in terms of armament and training. Their mission was simply to carry out assassinations of leftist leaders and union activists, and peasant organizers, in other words, carry out the "dirty war" that the armed forces did not want to do in avoidance of international and national human rights' groups' scrutiny.

In terms of the groups' finances, they mostly relied on narcotraffickers and the donations of the landed oligarchy in their areas of operations. The paramilitary credentials as a counterrevolutionary force were also enhanced considerably by their success in subduing the workers' unions in the banana plantations of Uraba and by uprooting the peasants' leftist organizations from the latifundios on the Caribbean Coast such as that of Sincelejo. These successes ushered in the beginning of the second phase (1995–) under which the paramiliatry groups became a force of about 4000–5000 well-armed and trained men operating in various fronts. By 2000, the Ministry of Defense estimated that the number of the AUC force increased to 8,000 fighters.[82]

Their armament also increased during this second phase, adding to their arsenal heavy armament such as mortars, anti-aircraft missiles, and U.S. made-helicopters-it is rumored that this include Apache helicopters-.[83] Their radius of military operations started to move toward the south of the country (Putumayo, Meta and Guaviare); north (Santander, North Santander), and east (Casanare, Arauca). In this form, Castaño took concrete steps toward the formation of a national strategy for which the Puerto Boyaca and Uraba models served as the prototypes. What is the driving power behind this exponential increase in paramlitary power in the span of a few years?

A number of factors helped the AUC to become a major political and military force. One was the political vacuum left on the armed political right resulting from the death of Rodriguez Gacha in 1989 and the demise of the cartels of Medellin and Cali respectively in the 1990s. The second factor was the brother Castaños (Rafael—killed in the 1990s— and Carlos) successes in Uraba and Cordoba enabled them to play focal point in any counterinsurgency national strategy. Finally, the Castaños control of Uraba and other areas close to the borders with Panama, a main contraband route, gave them a comparative advantage to play such a leading role. This in turn made them capable of inheriting the narcotrafficking network and contacts in the interior of the country and international markets. The control of the narcotrafficking business and other contraband activity has contributed substantial amounts of money to build an army of mercenaries.[84]

Hiring foreign trainers from Israel and the United States allowed AUC to professionalize their forces from a group of hired-to-kill assassins to a more professional force that is able to sustain combating the insurgency. By the late 1990s, the AUC acquired about thirty aircrafts, eleven of which are cessna, four shipping planes, fourteen helicopters with military equipment (including Black Hawk), and one sophisticated military helicopter equipped with the state-of-the-art emergency operations. This is in addition to several boats to be used for water transportation. The total costs are difficult to assess, but an educated guess could put the AUC operational costs per year at $80 to $100 million. This is a substatial amount of money that the AUC needs to extract in order to maintain its operations.[85]

PARAMILITARIES AND RENT SEEKING

Notwithsatnding its strong dependence on narcotrafficking, the AUC counts also on the protection rents it extracts from cattle ranchers, large landowners, agribusiness enterprises, and merchants. It has developed a taxation system parallel to the one of the guerrillas and the state. There are some notable differences, however, between the taxation system of the paramilitary and that of the guerrillas. While the guerrillas target the middle-income to upper-income groups in its areas of operations (applying a progressive tax system depending on income) the paramilitary groups are not that discrimimantory. The paramilitary groups in the Middle Magdalena, for example, tax the poor street vendors (25 cents/ each case of soda) as well as small contractors and large subcontractors.[86]

Landowners with properties of seventy hectares with hundred to two hundred head of cattle are taxed $150 per month (based on an exchange value of 2000 pesos per dollar); in contrast, the guerrillas, would have charged about $500.[87] This is a significant difference that could explain why middle and large owners found in the paramilitary a more rational, cheaper way to safeguard their class interests. However, according to one peasant testimony poor peasants in the areas where the paramilitary operates are forced once a week to dedicate a day to work in planting or in cleaning weapons. It is a form of "part time slavery" where labor power is appropiated without any wage remuneration.

Agribusinesess in the Middle Magdalena, such as the African palm sector, a thriving industry in the region, are taxed by the paramilitary about $4 per hectare per month. There are about fifty-four thousand hectares planted with African palm that could generate $210,000 monthly, and about $2,520,000 per year.[88] If we look at the municipal distribution of the plantations, they are in San Pablo, Aguachica, Río de Oro, San Alberto, San Martín, Barrancabermeja, El Carmen, Puerto Wilches, Rionegro, Sabana de Torres, San Vicente de Chucurí y Simacota.[89] Since most of these municipalities became under the control of the paramilitares in the 1990s, one can infer that the paramilitaries are taxing most of the African palm industry. This inference is supported by a number of experts working in the region.[90]

The paramilitaries also levy protection rent from the multinational corporations, but the amount of money generated is very difficult to estimate. In the words of Castaño he said "We tax the multinationals as the guerrillas do."[91] He gave the following case as an example "we discovered that one multinational corporation that has business in one Caribbean island was giving the guerrrillas $15 million so we asked the multinational to be given also money."[92] Castaño did not reveal the figures. This example illustrates how some foreign companies are subject to pay protection rent similar to local businesses that are in areas not touched directly by the civil war. It also demonstrates how the war system contributes to the redistribution of income between diverse groups.[93] Oil and mining corporations, their intricate relations with the war system's actors are more complex since most of the oil fields and mines are located in areas either dominated by the insurgency or disputed by the state's forces and the paramilitary, as was discussed before.

In Cordoba, the AUC levies about $144,000 per year, according to Castaño.[94] He explained that this amount is considerably low because Cordoba is "a liberated area" and there are no significant military costs there.[95] Castaño added that this is not the case in zones affected by the guerrillas; there the protection rent is significantly higher and the local groups affected by the insurgency are expected to shoulder the financial responsibility. The rent-seeking behavior of the paramiliatry assumed various ingenious modalities depending largely on the socioeconomic structures and conditions in their regions of operations. One of the modalities is subcontracting from private or government enterprises. In this form they employ their sympathizers and consolidate their social support base, generating at the same time income by also charging protection rent.[96] This dual purpose is becoming common and is applied also by the guerrillas. In fact, the paramilitary acquired it from the guerrillas.

The paramilitary groups in the 1990s reinvented themselves from a mere satellite to the army and its inteligence services to forces with their own momentum and needs for expansion and a political agenda. This is a qualitatively new condition that is affecting the war system constitution and dynamics. The rising cost nof maintaining a combating force is an important consideration in the paramilitary strategy in controlling vital economic areas such as south Bolivar, Middle Magdalena, Casanare, Putumayo, Arauca, and Uraba, which are rich in coca, oil, gold, silver, and emeralds. Rent extraction in these areas is vital to accommodate the paramilitary needs of consolidating their military power and economic interests.

The paramilitary groups of Castaño and of the East Valleys (narco-traffickers and the emerald mafia) carried military operations and massacres in Mapiripán (Puerto Alvira 1997), San José del Guaviare, San Carlos de Guaroa, Miraflores y Puerto Trujillo, areas which until 1996 were under the hegemony of FARC. Two main objectives underline the paramilitary strategies: (a) control the strategic corridors used in contrabands of arms to undercut the FARC's supply routes from Ecuador and Peru; (b) control the strategic economic areas of oil, gold, emeralds, coca, oppium poppies, and cattle ranching in order to deny the guerrillas protection rent extraction. The paramilitary groups aspire to gain strategic advantage over the guerrillas by their control of key economic areas and deny or dispute with the guerrillas's rent extraction in order to diminish the insurgency "war making capacity" and its "state-making potential," borrowing Charles Tilly's phrases.

On the ground, the paramilitary groups have managed to curtail the protection rent that the guerrillas (ELN) enjoyed in some areas such as South Bolivar (generated from taxing gold merchants, about $9 million per year)[97] and in parts of Cesar, Putumayo, and Guaviare. This paramilitary action has in turn led to fierce confrontations in various areas between them and the guerrillas and between army and the guerrillas. Thus, the paramilitary's actions generated new conflict dynamics leading to more aggressive military tactics applied by both the guerrillas and the state's armed forces. Consequently, larger resources are committed to the war as manifested in an increase in military spending and more important, the increased involvement of the United States in the conflict either through a substantial increase in its military aid (from $289 millions to a $1.3 billion to be spent during the fiscal years 2000–3).

What I argue, however, is that the comfortable impasse upon which the war system rested from the 1980s was eroding by the end of the 1990s. The conflict has incrementally become more intense, involving larger forces and hardware raising substantially the costs of the war and creating a new phase in the life cycle of the war system. Two core questions emerge in this respect: (a) What are the characteristics of this new phase? (b) Would this new condition enhance the possibililty of breaking the war system, opening the possibility of a negotiated settlement?

Three indicators are taken to validate my central thesis that the emergence of the paramiltary groups did destabilize the comfortable impasse of the bipolar war system. These indicators are: (a) number of violent deaths and massacres; (b) number of war related fatalaties; and (c) economic costs of the war. The trends in changes in these indicators are examined for 1988 to 2000 (see table 5.5).

Figure 5.1 shows a clear trend in the increase of homicides which took hold after 1985 coinciding with the emergence of narcotrafficking and growth of paramilitaries such MAS (Muertos a los Secustradores) and the autodefenses in Boyaca and Codoba and Uraba. By the mid-1990s, when these groups became more unified and grew to an organized army, the homicide rate in the country witnessed a significant increase. It is difficult to attribute the increase in the homicide rates solely to the impact of paramilitary groups on the dynamics of the civil war, but when we look at how the homicides are distributed at the municipal level, a clear pattern emerges. In the 297 of municipalities in which the homicide rates exceeded the national level rate, 80 percent of those municipalities are concentrated in ten departments: in Antioquia (70); Cundimarca (31), Valle (28), Boyaca (21), Santander (18), Meta (17), Caqueta (14), Caldas (13), Risaralda (12), and Quindio(10). Ninethy-three percent of these municipalities belong to rural and 7 percent to urban areas.

In terms of the class structure, 72 percent of the most violent municipalities belong to the middle peasant of the coffee region, and 56 percent are municipalities of frontier colonos. In this manner we can observe that homicide rates increased in the 1980s and 1990s and increased in municipalities with clear class differentiations (coffee region). In these municipalities the income distribution is highly unequal, undepinned by the lack of institutions for resolving conflicts.[98] Labor disputes over wages, contract violations, personal disputes, and private property rights are often adjudicated by violent means. During the 1990s, the coffee region suffered important economic setbacks affected by the declining returns of coffee and an increase in unemployment in this region exacerbated by an increase in guerrilla and paramilitary presence leading to a rise in the rate of homicides as well as politically motivated crimes.

In Antioquia, the municiplaities most affected by homicides high rates are in the regions of Montana and Middle Magdalena, in which both the paramilitaries and the guerrillas are active, such as the municipalities of Argelia, Caracoli, Puerto Berrio, Puerto Nare, and Remedios in the Antioquian part of Middle Magdalena. In Uraba, again the most violent municipalities are where paramilitaries and the guerrillas coincide such as in Apartado, Carepa, Turbo, Chigorodo, Mutata, Dabeiba, and Necocli, and the north of Uraba.[99]

In the municipalities belonging to areas of frontier colonization, the high rates of homicides, such as in the Plains, Caqueta, Putumayo, Meta, Guaviare, and Casanare, are attributed to the economic risks and opportunities created by the illicit drug plantations and the social decomposition that this type of rentier economy generate. Nonetheless, these conditions have been compounded by the paramilitaries' attempt to control the process of production by mainly using violence. Thus, it is possible to infer that paramilitaries in the mentioned municipalities have contributed to the increase rates of homicides.

The number of massacres committed has also increased at the national level which reveals a consistent trend. In 1994, 505 persons were victims of massacres, 531 in 1995, 370 in 1996, 660 in 1997, 899 in 1998, and 847 in 1999. In 2000, the number of massacres increased by 22 percent from the previous year, reaching 205 mass killings in which 1,226 died (see figure 5.1 and table 5.5). Since 1996 the number of massacres increased significantly reaching its highest levels since 1988. This should not be a surprise. As was discussed in the section on massacres, most of killings were committed by the paramilitaries.

The third indicator of a new phase of the war system is the increasing resources committed to war as indicated in military and the guerril-

FIGURE 5.1
Number of Victims of Massacres, 1988–2000

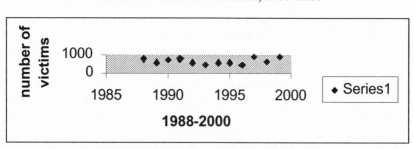

Source: Policia Nacional, Bogota, Colombia.

las defense budgets. The defense expenditures increased significantly during the 1990s at a 15 percent rate reaching 3.5 of the GNP, the highest ever recorded. In 1998 the military expendintures were 335,000 million pesos (about $186 million at an exchange rate of 1,800 pesos per dollar) and in 1999 it increased by 37 percent to 485,000 millions of pesos ($269 million).[100] These increases reinforced the escalation in the conflict, which again coincided with the new dynmics of war precipitated by the increased activity of the AUC in the second part of the 1990s (see table 5.3).

The fast increase in defense expenditures especialy after 1996, is a clear response to the changing dynamics of the war system. This dynamics increased the costs at a faster rate. The dynamics of war is accelerating at a rate that is excceedinly straining the resources available to the state in times of economic crisis and eroding the positive political economy that the military accumulated in phase of comfortable impasse. Case in point: the military faced a budget deficit in the year 2000 that caused a drop in its operation.[101] Thus, the increase in military budgets coincided with the consolidation of the paramilitary, suggesting that this is ushering in a new phase in the war system.

The guerrillas also responded and contributed to the new dynamics of the war system. FARC for example launched its largest military operations ever against the army. In the 1996–1999 FARC forces ranging

TABLE 5.3
Military Expenditures 1988–1999 in Thousand Million of Pesos

1988	714	1.8
1989	801	2.0
1990	836	2.3
1991	790	2.6
1992	850	2.3
1993	1069	2.5
1994	1160	1.8
1995	1272	2.6
1996	1846	3.0
1997	2000	3.2
1998	3350	3.5
1999	4580	3.7

Source: Ministry of Defense, Bogota Colombia.

TABLE 5.4

Year	Place	No. of fighters	(FARC)	(Army)
1996	Puerres	300 FARC fighters	na	31 dead
1996	Caquan	1000 FARC fighters	na	62 dead and 43 prisoners
1997	Delicias	400 FARC fighters	na	27 dead and 60 prisoners
1997	San Juanito	300	12	16 dead
1997	Patascoy	400	na	17 dead and 18 prisoners
1998	Juan Jose	300	15	35 dead
1999	Gutierrez	500	35	37 dead
1999	Casanare	300	50	No casualties

Source: Ministry of Defense various years and Informes de Paz, Oficina del Alto Comisionado para la Paz, 1997 and 1998.

between three hundred and a thousand combatants staged well-coordinated attacks and scored important military victories.

The Puerres (1996), Caguan(1996), Delicias (1997), Patascoy (1997), San Juanito (1997) San Jose (1998) and Guteirrez in 1999 attacks launched by FARC were unprecedented since the beginning of the armed insurgency in the early 1960s in terms of their magnitude, the number of forces involved, armament and coordination of forces. The cost such attacks in terms of training, equipments, armaments, and ammunitions were no less than a million dollars per attack which is a substantial cost for an insurgency. The total annual costs incurred by the FARC with an average of four or more attacks against main military bases without counting the attaks against police stations in villages and cities would be around $4 to 5 million. The operational costs of maintaining an army of eighteen thousand combatants with the ammu-

TABLE 5.5
Indicators of Rising Violence 1988–1999

	1988	*1990*	*1994*	*1999*
Civil war Fatalities	NA	3,871	2,384*	4,014***
*Number of people killed in Massacres*****	700	400	504	847
Military Expenditures % GNP	1.8	1.3	1.8	3.7
*Number of combats between guerrillas and the armed forces***	866	690	1,374	1,252

* Camilo Granada and Leonardo Rojas, "Los Costos del Conflicto Armado 1990–94," *Planeacion & Desarrollo*, Vol. XXVI, No. 4 (October–December 1995), p. 143.

** Source: Jesus Bejarano Avila, Camilo Echandia, Redolfo Escobedo, and Enrique Querez (eds.), *Colombia: Inseguridad, Violencia y Desempeno Economico en las Aread Rurales* (Bogota: Universidad Externado de Colombia & FONADE, 1997), p. 52.

*** Comisión Colombiana de Juristas, *Panorama de los derechos humanos y del derecho humanitario en Colombia 1999* (Bogota: Comision Colombiana de Juristas, 1999).

**** In 2000, 1,226 people died in massacres, the highest record since 1988.

nitions, armament, C3, and logistical support would be at about $80 to $100 million per year.[102] It was estimated that FARC's annual income was in the range of $300 million.[103] It is highly unlikely that FARC will be able to maintain the momentum of war due to its increasing economic costs as well as the political costs that it might incurr in terms of its fatalities, civilian casualties, and desertions from its ranks (see chapter 6). In 1999, the FARC lost about 775 fighters, the highest figure since the beginning of the armed struggle in 1964.[104] Civilian casualties are also rising rapidly, in 1999 alone 24,358 people died violent deaths at an average of 2,029 per month.[105] This figure is one of the highest recorded in the 1990s. In 2000, the number of violent deaths increased by 5 percent from 1999 to 25,660 people, averaging 2,135 per month.[106] War related fatalities also increased significantly from 2,384 to 4,024 in 1999. In 1990, war related fatalities reached a high of 3,871 killings. That was due to the escalation of the war resulting from the army attack on FARC's headquarters in Casa Verde and the escaltion of in narcotrafficking terrorism. The number of war related fatalities decreased after 1990, and started increasing again after 1995 reaching a peak in 1999.

In economic terms, the country is in its worse economic crisis since the Great Depression of the 1930s. These factors are creating a malaise with the war which will have a negative toll on the guerrillas' public appeal and recruitment strategies. All of the above suggest that the conflict in the late 1990s has entered a new phase where homicides, massacres, war related fatalities, and the costs of the war are increasing, which make my thesis that the paramilitary groups enduced a new dynamics of conflict valid.

The paramilitary groups' strategy supported by the narcotraffickers, reactionary sectors of the landed oligharchy, military, and the political elite collided with that of the guerrillas, particularly in economically strategic areas generating a cascading chain reaction that none of the actors is able to control. In light of such escalation, the army also was forced to respond to the new dynamics by pressuring for more rents to upgrade and restructure its forces in order to preserve its priviliges. The paramilitary groups as a third force are also seeking political spaces and rents and thus undermined the bipolar war system, ushering in the beginning of a multipolar system. The multipolar war system is so far unstable, and its instability is increasing the costs of war, deminishing the positive political economy for its actors and hence offering a window of opportunity for peace. Perhaps the actors and the international community will capture this opportunity.

CHAPTER 6

The Dominant Classes
and the Prospects of Peace

The previous chapter discussed the new dynamics of the war system precipitated by the emergence of organized crime and paramilitary groups. I also demonstrated in the chapter's last section the main indicators of this new dynamics, namely, the sharp increase in state's defense expenditures, and the increasing guerrilla and paramilitary costs (human and material) and the increase in the number of massacres and homicides. This chapter presents the macroeconomic impact of the new dynamics of the war system. The chapter sheds light on how the war system economy in the 1990s began taxing the country's economic growth, saving rates, and raising the costs of private investments. I evaluate how these negative economic indicators led to a shift within important sectors of the dominant class—particularly its internationalized faction—regarding negotiating peace with the guerrillas. My central argument is that since the late 1990 there has been a shift in the political attitude among an important segment of the dominant class in favor of a negotiated settlement for the conflict mainly because of the increasing costs of war, which are jeopardizing the country's economic growth and its incorporation into global markets.

THE COSTS OF WAR VERSUS THE COSTS OF REFORMS

Rates of Investments and Violence

In the late 1990s the effects of the war system initiated in the mid-1960s started taking their full economic effects. Obviously that was because the actors involved became stronger and their radius of operations wider, and new actors emerged and were incorporated into the war system. It has been argued throughout this book that the war system was not the optimal choice of the actors, but rather was dictated by conflict strategies adopted by actors under a condition of military impasse. Keep in mind that the origins of the war system lie in the instability of property rights in rural areas, and that the resort to violence was the mechanism to settle land disputes, to accelerate the concentration of land properties and rentier capitalism. Two important questions are important to consider in our analysis of the 1990s: What are the political implications of the declining weight of the landed oligarchy—as one of the main propellors of the war system—in the country's economic configuration? And, how long are the other segments of the dominant class willing to subsidize the continuation of a low-intensity war with a clear escalating tendency since the second part of the 1990s?

The analysis of the interaction of the war system with its environment is important to complete the assessment of the functioning of such a system. One of the macro economic effects-or costs of the civil war—was the decrease in private investments. It was estimated that violence, political and non-political, affected the private investments in Colombia with coefficients 0.2 and 0.3 which are not very high, yet if the country's homicides rate per 100,000 was brought down by 75 percent of its (63.7 per100,000) current rate to match Latin American averages, the private investments could increase from 9.45 percent to about 13.5 percent of the GDP.[1] According to a study of the Ministry of Justice, every increase of ten homicides per 100,000 can affect the investment as high as 4 percent of its value.[2] Some even claimed that if homicide rates in Colombia had remained at their 1960 level, total annual investment in Colombia today would have been 20 percent higher.[3] Decisions to invest are affected negatively by an insecure political environment with a precarious institutional setting compounded with high rates of homicides, ransom-kidnappings, and robberies, all of which have been notoriously high in Colombia since the 1990s. In the 21st century, more than any time before, capital needs stable institutions to reduce what Oliver Williamson called the "transaction costs" incurred by monitoring and enforcing contracts. The expansion of global markets, finance capital, copy rights laws, and patent markets needs mechanism to enforce compliance. In this regard violence increases the risks of contracts compliance and the costs of economic transactions, discouraging capital investments, which fetch more stable and secure markets.

Chronic violence is a symptom of chronic institutional crises revealed by the inability of the state's institutions to enforce the rules of capital,"legal" capital. In this same vein, a consensus is emerging among some social scientists about the critical role of "social trust" as an integral part of "social capital" in enhancing economic growth. Social capital refers to social organizations such as norms, trust, and networks, which can improve the economic performance in a given society by facilitating coordinated transactions. Violence with its political and criminal expressions debilitates the evolution of social capital (that is the subsuming process of social relations to the needs of global capital) and increases the uncertain environment of market transactions.[4]

Mancur Olson, on his part, brought to a sharper focus the risks implied in economic transactions in Third World countries. In Olson's opinion, markets in the poorest countries generally conduct self-enforc-ing transactions with goods exchanged for other goods or for money instantly. Transactions that involve time and distances with promises to pay the next week for goods received this week is a risky contract for the seller. If such contracts cannot be made with trust, then an entire mar-ket will be missing, a feature that most underdeveloped countries share, this is in addition to unreliable contracts and weakly enforced property rights which according to Olson are essential for capitalist development. Olson attributed this failure, in part, to the lack of "encompassing democratic systems."[5] Olson's claims are not far-fetched in light of our study of Colombia, since both precarious property rights and a weak state are two of the country's main features.

Furthermore, some estimate that in societies where laws and property rights are respected, economies grow in an average of 1 percent to 2 per-cent faster than those where land properties and laws are not protected.[6] In Colombia, where the state is unable to enforce the law and protect pri-vate property, private investments declined from 12.5 percent of the GDP recorded in 1994 to a low 5.7 percent in 1997.[7] This sharp decrease can-not be attributed only to the increasing levels of violence recorded in the post-1995 period, but certainly this was the major contributing factor.[8]

Foreign capital investments in Colombia have been negatively affected by the increasing costs of capital investments such as the ones incurred by the multinational oil corporations. They pay an increasing war tax which was 37 cents per barrel (or 1.8 percent of a $20 barrel), and by 1998 it was raised to 7 perecent for a barrel of light oil. To these we must add the security costs and the rent sought by the guerrillas, the state, and paramilitary groups. This is not to say that the multinationals are losing in Colombia, but only to demonstrate that their profit mar-gins are less than in other markets with no civil war. It is estimated that multinational companies' security costs average 4 percent of the compa-nies' operating costs in the developing world. In Colombia the costs are substantially higher, 10 percent. The overall figures of foreign direct investments did reflect a significant increase between 1990 and 1997 from a $345 million to $4.5 billion in 1998; but it declined in 1999 to $4.2 billion.[9] Most of these investments were made in the oil, mineral, services, financial, private security and insurance sectors. But this increase in foreign direct investments did not reverse the shrinking cap-ital account, which showed a decline in investment inflows, from $4.6 billion in 1998 to $1.8 billion in 1999.[10]

The increasing levels of violence have also impacted the rates and the structure of foreign investments in the country. A survey of 134 foreign companies operating in Colombia conducted by the Ministry of Foreign Trade found that 32.9 percent considered insecurity and violence as the main disadvantage for investing in Colombia; 19.4 percent of the total respondents considered political and economic instability as the main disincentive; 14.5 percent considered the high tariffs as the barrier for investments; and 8.1 percent viewed the bureaucratic red tape as the culprit.[11] The multinational exporting companies were asked what factors that hindered them from increasing their sales in outside markets. Their responses were: the high costs and the insecurity of transportation, 21.8 percent; high tariffs 20 percent; the complex system of export licensing, 14 percent; insecurity, 13.9 percent.[12] Thus, insecurity is among the highest concerns of foreign companies affecting negatively their investments in local market and their sales in international markets because it raises the costs of opportunities, transactions, transportation, and hence, production.

ECONOMIC GROWTH

The cost of the civil war is calculated in this study as the expenses that private and public sectors incur in property damages caused by the armed conflict, human capital lost, medical expenses of treating civil-war—related injuries, loss of productivity of the victims, and refugees, military outlays, extortion, and robberies.[13] The costs increased significantly since 1994 and tripled between 1996 and 1997, from $1 billion to more than $3 billion. This jump is attributed in part to the significant increase in defense expenditures (from.2.6% of the GDP in 1995 to 3.5 % in 1998) and to the increase in the number of robberies, extortion, and kidnap ransoms notably after 1993 (see figure 6.1).

Extortions, robberies, and ransoms are transfer of capital from one group to another, mostly from the haves to the have-nots.[14] It is argued that about 15 percent of the GDP is the amount transferred annually from the productive sector to guerrillas and organized crime.[15]

State officials estimate that the direct and indirect costs of war affected negatively the country's economic growth by at least three points in 1998.[16] The estimates for the previous years were two or fewer percentage points. The annual costs of war as the percentage of the GDP has changed from a 1.61 percent in 1991, decreasing to 0.97 percent in 1994, rising again to 1.64 percent in 1995, 2.08 percent in 1996, and to 3.1 percent in 1997. Such estimates prove again the validity of my thesis that after 1995, the war system in Colombia entered a new phase unprecedented in the history of the conflict.

FIGURE 6.1
Total Costs of the Civil War, 1992–1998

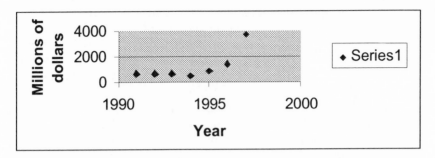

Source: Based on data obtained from Planeacion Nacional and the reports Racionalizacion del Gasto Y de Las Finanzas Publicas, 1996, 1997, and 1998, Bogota, Colombia.

Montenegro and Posada noted that the increased levels of homicide affects the levels of economic growth after a certain point. Although that the relationship is not linear is more parabolic that it is to say when economic growth increases, homicides tend to increase, but when homicides increase after a certain point, economic growth tends to decrease.[17] By the late 1990s Colombia reached that point where negative economic growth was recorded in 1998,1999, and 2000, respectively for the first time since the Great Depression of the 1930s. It would be an exaggeration to claim that the negative economic growth is caused only by violence, but certainly what has been ascertained by economists is that in 1998, the 3–point economic decline was caused by the war system related costs, which were roughly equivalent to the negative growth recorded. The GDP in 1999 was about $88 billion declining from $91 billion in 1998. This translated into a per capita decline from $2,465 in 1998 to $2,192 in 1999, that is, the per capita decreased in only one year by 11 percent. In 2000 the GDP declining trend continued, reaching $82 billion. This is to be added to significant decline in property values by 30 percent discounting the increase in prices.[18]

What is of significant implication on the dialectics of war and peace is the change in the fortunes of the largest Colombian conglomerates in the late 1990s. In 1998, Julio Mario Santo Domingo, Lius Carlos Sarmiento and Carlos Ardila Lulle, who were traditional members of the Forbes 200 list lost their place. The explanation was the devaluation of the Colombian pesos and the fall in the Colombian stock market prices, which led to a 30 percent loss on their value. Forbes estimates that during 1998, the fortune of Sarmiento decreased by 36 percent from $2.5

billion to $1.6 billion; Ardila Lulle by 38 percent, from $2.1 billion to $1.3 billion; and Santo Domingo by 27 percent, from 1.5 billion to $1.1 billion. All of these conglomerates have significant investments in Colombia. These losses are significant given that Colombia for the most part since the 1940s has a record of steady economic growth with no significant downturns. This growth took place while the rest of Latin America suffered from the debt crisis, Colombia's economy maintained a steady growth.

Against this backdrop we appreciate more the impact of violence "real and perceived" on the economic decline of the dominant classes, particularly its conglomerates. Nicanor Restrepo, the representative of the Antioquian Sindicate, an important member of *cacaos*, as this group, is referred to colloquially, explained eloquently the causes behind the conglomerates' current interest in finding a negotiated settlement with the guerrillas. He said " The civil war is costing about $3 billion (about 5.4 billions de pesos) in activities directly related to the war that we could use in consolidating the state security, the justice system, the prison system, finance the police forces, and increase our expenditures on education and in health sector." Then he added: "If Colombia were in peace its economic growth would have been 10% annually." Finally, Restrepo concluded " Let us think what is the impact of the civil war on the opportunity costs that we are losing in terms of foreign and national capital investments, our inability of developing the tourist sector and our agribusiness."[19]

Restrepo's views provide good insights into the motivations of the conglomerates in seeking a peaceful settlement of the war. Such a mind-set coupled with meetings between the representatives of the cacaos with the guerrillas in 1998, 1999, and 2000 are unprecedented in this respect.[20] The conglomerates took the initiative in meeting with the guerrilla representative in Costa Rica and then in San Vicente del Caguan known colloquially as "FARC landia," where the peace negotiations are taking place. Subsequently, Restrepo became a representative of the conglomerates in the government negotiating team. The political behavior of the cacaos constitutes a qualitative leap that brings Colombia closer to peace than any time before. Certainly, the economic costs of war and the decline in the conglomerate fortunes are forcing the conglomerates to redefine their political role with equal force as they adjust their economic strategies to accommodate the forces of global capitalism. This latter is virtually impossible to accomplish without reducing the levels of violence, stabilizing property rights, and putting in place effective state institutions. In order to achieve those, the guerrilla groups is the port of entry for the establishment of a "more encompassing" political system.[21] This is as a prerequisite to effective state institutions based on a new hegemony. The success of the conglomerates and their allies depends on the "leader-group" abilities to transcend their own corporate interest and project a moral authority widely accepted by the other factions of the dominant classes and the subordinate groups.[22]

The consolidation of economic conglomerates in Colombia is something relatively new within the dominant class. The formation of these groups took several decades, benefiting from the state's economic protectionism, and was not until the 1980s that these groups reached the level of maturity and strength preparing them to engage with global capitalism. During the last two decades their business ventures included the crucial areas of information technology, mass media, telecommunications, insurance, and banking. There are fourteen main conglomerates (companies and groups), which have a share of 25 percent of the GDP.[23] These businesses put them on the forefront as globalizing agents within Colombia and helping in integrating Colombia with global markets. Such strategic position as the gatekeepers with global capital certainly equips them with political leverage within the dominant class and the political elite alike.

If we take the stock market capitalization, which is the sum of the market capitalizations of all firms listed on the domestic stock exchanges, as an indicator of Colombias' integration process into global financial markets, we will find that there is a notable increase during the 1990s, from $1,416 million in 1990 to $13,356 million in 1998. In regional terms, Colombia is fourth in stock market capitalization after Brazil, Chile, and Argentina which means that the country is integrating fast with global financial markets.[24] Of course, that the Colombian conglomerates own the lion's share of the stock market companies.

Another key indicator of Colombia's integration into world markets is the volume of its global trade. The country's merchandise exports increased from $3,001 million in 1983 to $10,890 million in 1998; and merchandise imports from $4,963 million to $15,840 million for the same period.[25] In regional standards, Colombia comes fifth in imports after Mexico, Brazil, Chile, and Argentina, and sixth after these same countries plus Venezuela.[26] Again it is evident the trend in the country's global integration increased at very significant pace, tripling its exports and quintupling its imports. The political consequence of such a trend is the rising stakes of the more "integrated segments" of the dominant class in maintaining the momentum.

There are a number of core questions, such as: What is the significance of the consolidation of the conglomerates? What is its impact on the sustainability of the war system given the economic negative effects discussed above? Does the consolidation of the conglomerates mark a political rupture with the landed and cattle rancher elite, the staunchest opponents of land reform? And finally, do the conglomerates have the necessary political elements for constructing a new hegemony?

Economic weight and position in the market structure by themselves are insufficient if not complemented with agency and the articulation of a set of ideas attractive enough to other segments of the dominant class as well as the subordinate groups. In this respect, the conglomerates decided to have their own "think tank," Foundacion Ideas Para La Paz (Foundation of Ideas for Peace) to articulate their ideas and appropriate those of others. This is a remarkable development since it can provide the conglomerates with an intellectual advantage over its opponents within the dominant class as well as within the subordinate groups. Thus it is noteworthy that the first activity was to present the Foundation of Ideas For Peace to the FARC leader, Manuel Marulanda, only one month after its inception.[27] This new "think tank" is to be added to the arsenal of mass communication outlets owned by them. The majority of the country's most important television networks, radio stations, and newspapers are owned by these conglomerates. Certainly this allows the "massification' of their ideas, values, and project a sense of political, economic and moral unity. In the distant past, the "massification process" of rulers' ideas was relatively easier since emperors, kings, khalifas, and sultans constituted their authority in the name of God, and their rule was divine.[28] Such ideology was cost-effective at the times when the people accepted the "will of God" because it required less states expenditure on the coercive apparatus and/or mass media. In more recent times, however, the establishment of hegemony is a complex process negotiated and mediated by institutions, political parties, social classes, and interest groups facilitated by mass communication and information technology. It remains to be seen whether the conglomerates will be able to bring about a consensus and work their way through the state institutions, particularly the military, and persuade the cattle ranchers and the landed oligarchy to follow suit. What is certain is that the executive branch of government is synchronizing its peace strategy with that of the conglomerates.[29]

What is working to the advantage of the conglomerates is the changing mood within the remaining commercial and industrial middle-sized industries and businesses represented by the Consejo Gremial Nacional (National Business Council) which includes the country's most important industrial groups, agribusinesses, commercial groups, landowners, and banking sector. This Business Council founded in 1991 constituted a watershed in the history of the Colombian bourgeoisie in terms of its composition and interest articulation. The council serves as an important vehicle for interest aggregation of the different segments of the bourgeoisie and middle sectors through which their views are hammered and reconciled. Since its inception, the council has set its priority in finding a peaceful solution to the civil war.[30] Needless to say, the council success is the litmus test for the conglomerates ability to lead and chart a new political path for Colombia.

In the same context, a recent opinion poll revealed the changing attitudes of the economic elite indicating its members' concerns over the continuation of the war as an ever-increasing drain on the country's resources and decreasing chances for the state's military victory.[31] In February 1999, El Tiempo and Revista Semana, the two most important publications in Colombia, jointly surveyed the opinions of 538 executives of the five thousand largest commercial, financial and industrial companies. The poll indicated that 84 percent favored a negotiated settlement with the guerrillas, and 86 percent preferred paying the costs of peace rather than financing the war. Only 11 percent of those surveyed favored the continuation of the war.[32] However, of those favoring peace, 28 percent were not willing to pay from their own personal income, 25 percent were ready to pay only 1 percent, and 5 percent were willing to pay 20 percent of their income to finance the peace process.[33]

What is noteworthy is that only 16 percent of those surveyed objected to a land distribution of large estates of 200 and more hectares. Such an attitude of course is rejected by the landed elite and validates their suspicion that the costs of final settlement might mainly come at their expense, as the FEDEGAN president expressed.[34] The survey also found that the majority do not oppose the guerrillas' participation in Congress and ministries, nor they oppose reforming the military to allow the incorporation of the guerrilla forces.[35] Then, the remaining challenge for the conglomerates is to extend their leadership beyond the financial, industrial, service, and merchant sectors in order to persuade a peasant-based insurgency and the agrarian elite to join the peace process.[36]

The Agrarian Elite Decline and Resistance

In a stark contrast with the growing power of the conglomerates, the economic decline of the agrarian elite represented by the coffee growers, cattle ranchers, agribusiness groups, and large landowners is reflected in their decreasing share of the GDP during the 1980s and 1990s. While the service sector share increased from 43 percent in 1980 to 49 percent in 1998, the agricultural sector declined from a 22 percent of the GDP to 13 percent in 1998. The industrial sector registered an increase from 35 percent of the GDP to 38 percent during the same period.[37] These figures complemented with those of the financial market, reveal an emerging economic structure and a new social configuration of the dominant class. This configuration is clearly tilted toward the internationalist segment represented by fourteen companies and groups, mostly in the service sector.

To what extent is this new class configuration inclined to dismantle the war system and replace it with a conflict resolution mechanism more responsive to the requirements of e-capitalism? The answer lies in the ability of the conglomerates and the industrial bourgeoisie to break away successfully from the traditional and conservative sectors of the landed class, cattle ranchers, agribusiness, and their narcotrafficker allies.

In this respect, it is imperative to assess the political stance, and relative economic-political weight of three of the most conservative groups that represent the interests of the cattle ranchers, agribusinesses, and large coffee growers. The Federation of Cattle Ranchers (FEDEGAN), the Farmers Association of Colombia (SAC), and the Federation of Coffee Growers respectively.

The cattle ranchers' and agribusiness groups' positions did not differ much when it comes to how the state should deal with the insurgency. The presidents of FEDEGAN, FEDECAFE, and SAC were of the opinion that the state has to strengthen its military capabilities to force the guerrillas to negotiate. They differed; however, on the tactics. While SAC's president supported the Pastrana strategy, FEDEGAN's president was more critical.[38]

But before addressing these questions, some background information is pertinent in this respect. According to FEDEGAN, there were 300,000 cattle ranchers by the end of 1998, and of those about 41,689 are being taxed ($1,500 per year) by the guerrillas.[39] Those are mainly large and middle cattle ranchers that have their ranches in areas of guerrilla influence.[40] In return the guerrillas provide protection against cattle robberies. The guerrillas cannot extend this protection service to those outside their direct influence where they also sought levying tax-protection. This second group of cattle ranchers and large landowners tends to defect to the side of paramilitary groups and the state forces.

During 1998 alone, about 472 cattle ranchers paid kidnap ransoms of about $150,000 per person. This is to be added to the cattle lost to the guerrillas or to crime. The total capital loss of cattle ranchers is mainly a transfer of capital (in the form of taxes, ransom, and confiscation of cattle) was estimated at $650 million per year.[41] The above provides a flavor of some aspects of the cattle ranchers' conflict with the guerrillas and its peasant social base. The two main choices of this sector have been either to pay protection rents to the guerrillas or to build their own paramilitary groups. They chose the second. The paramilitary option was driven by a cost-benefit analysis in their attempt to recover grounds lost to the insurgency. In this area they scored some success in recovering territories from the guerrillas (at a very high human loss to the guerrillas and their peasants' support base) and hence reducing the transfer of rents, or at least save some of the transfers, since they have to finance the paramilitary. Second, paramilitary groups managed to safeguard their disputed property rights and their political power.

In that effort, the large landlords and cattle ranchers were aided by the emerging narcobourgeoisie, which helped in making the paramilitary option viable and economically sustainable, keeping in mind that narco-traffickers favorite investments were in land properties, ranches, and resorts in rural areas.[42] Real estate has been an effective money launder-ing mechanism, as a result, four point four million hectares became owned by narcotraffickers, with an estimated value of $2.4 billion.[43] The local branches of FEDEGAN in the Middle Magdalena, Cesar, Bolivar, Santander, and Cordoba among others are penetrated heavily by narco-traffickers, and this translates into more money to paramilitary groups as "stabilizers" of property rights, minimizing the transfer of rents to colonos and guerrillas.[44]

The $650 million lost (transfer) by cattle ranchers per year did not alter the stance of this sector for a number of reasons, which are impor-tant for my evaluation of the prospects of peace if this sector determines to oppose it.[45] First, the cattle ranchers as well as large land lords are the net losers of Colombian economic integration into world markets. Thus their transfer of rents to the guerrillas is entangled with a larger process of economic transformation propelled by the economic opening com-mencing in the 1990s. In this context we can understand these sectors: heightened insecurity in the face of president Pastrana's peace plan sup-ported by the conglomerates. Their common fear is that a historic com-promise is being hashed at their own expense, that is land reform.

In this light we might understand better Visbal's concerns that a "peace at our expense is no peace." This statement demonstrate the inse-curity of this sector as well as the tension that exists between cattle ranchers and the conglomerates. He continued, "why are the monopo-lies [the conglomerates] planning a land reform. Why don't they envis-age a plan to redistribute Avianca, or Banco de Bogota [both owned by the conglomrerates]."[46] Thus the cattle ranchers' support of paramilitary groups is not only responding to immediate interests (in securing their rents and properties) but is also tied to renegotiating their position within the country's economic structures in a more globalized economy. This sector as well as the agribusiness sector (with few exceptions such as exporters of flowers, bananas, and coffee) were affected negatively by the open market policy, and they in fact are in favor of protecting their products and some gradualism in the process, which could allow them to adjust.[47] What adds insult to injury is that both sectors feel that they did not reap any economic benefit from the economic "apertura" of the

1990s. Now they have to contend also with the prospects of a historic compromise among the state, conglomerates, and peasant-based guerrillas at their expense.[48]

Finally, it is important to note that cattle ranchers' and large landowners' properties are appreciating, particularly because most of their lands are concentrated in nodal trade points (Bolivar, Middle Magdalena, Cordoba, Cesar, Antioquia, Riseralda just to mention a few). Thus, relinquishing parts of these properties to landless peasants depends on a tradeoff that is difficult to assess at this point. But what matters for our study is to highlight that the economic predominance of the conglomerates given their international and domestic power does not automatically translate into political hegemony. The cattle ranchers and large landlords are posed to resist. And in this posture, they are supported by sectors of the military, retired military with land possessions, and conservative political forces such the one led by Alvaro Uribe Velez (the ex-governor of Antioquia), Harold Bedoya (ex-general commander of the armed forces) and sectors of the narcotraffickers and paramilitaries.

Land property rights remain the main stumbling block, as was true almost eighty years ago because land properties remain a source of wealth even with the changes in the global political economy. The change in this new phase of capitalism is that a good part of the capital could be formed and accumulated without the direct appropriation of the surplus values of peasants' labor but rather through land speculation and land appreciation (an integral aspect of rentier capitalism) enticed by a more globalized economy. Yet this land-owning class still constitutes an integral part of the capital or as Karl Marx contended, it is part of objectified social labour. "In the sense that capital for the capitalist is a perpetual pumping machine for surplus labour, land for the land owner is a permanent magnet for attracting a part of the surplus-value pumped out of capital."[49] Then the issue is whether Marx's 140 years-old analysis on ground rent as part of capital formation and a generator of class conflict remains relevant in the e-global economy. Defining the current political economy of land conflict in Colombia could help us in finding an answer.

To elucidate, in Colombia the expected increase in ground rents and values raise the stakes of the conflict and also complicate its possible solution. In this connection it is important to mention some of those state's projects that are triggering a spiral speculation in land values (and conflict) in areas mostly affected by them such as the following:

• The dry canal Atlantic-Pacific (Atrato-Truandó) and its interconnections with train tracks of Medellín-Buenaventura and the roads linking the Pacific with Medellín and Pereira.

- The high way Urabá-Maracaibo (Venezuela).

- The river interconnection between Orinoco-río Meta-Buenaventura;

- The interconnection of River La Plata-Amazonas-Napo-Putumayo-Tumaco, with ports in Puerto Asís.

- The highway system in the Middle Magdalena and other major projects.

These roads and communication systems connecting Colombian local markets with those of Ecuador, Venezuela, Peru and Panama will form the veins through which globalization is expanded and consolidated. In this manner, conflict over land and property rights is not a remnant of the precapitalist mode of production, but rather is about capturing nodal points in the economy of the future. And in this same vein, the strategic lands located near areas of oil wells, coal, emeralds, silver, copper, and gold mines as we have discussed earlier in chapter 5, form part of this diagram of land conflict where landlords are trying to expand and consolidate their property rights with the protection and help of paramilitary groups and the military.[50] As a consequence of this reality, in less than a decade almost 1.7 million people—mostly peasants—were displaced from lands that are chiefly located in these areas.

The agribusiness stratum is represented by SAC, although its enterprises are more integrated with global markets than FEDEGAN—particularly SAC's leading exporting businesses such as flowers, bananas, palm-oil, and sugar—but remains politically conservative in its ideological orientation. This is attributed to the heavy weight of banana, palm and sugar agribusiness, all of which have a nexus with right-wing political groups, the military, and the paramilitary groups.[51] Keep in mind that most of these enterprises are located in areas of land conflicts and guerrillas' military presence such as Uraba, Cauca, Cesar, Bolivar, Sucre, and Middle Magdalena.

A few months after I interviewed Jesus Bejarano, the SAC board of directors forced him to resign the presidency because of their irreconcilable positions toward Pastrana's peace strategy. Jesus Bejarano, in opposition to the board, supported the process. Jesus Bejarano was replaced by Fernando Devis, representing one of the most conservative sectors of SAC—the banana plantations of Uraba (president of Augura)—opposes Pastrana's peace initiative.[52] Fernando Devis political views were closer to the one espoused by FEDEGAN than were those of Bejarano.[53]

Coffee, once constituted the mainstay of the economy. In 1996 coffee production, contributed about 3 percent of the GNP and 16.2 percent from the country's total exports. In the agrarian economy, coffee production shared only 10 percent of the rural GDP.[54] The declining economic weight of coffee in the Colombian economy has left the coffee stratum of the rural elite with less political leverage. The declining fortunes of coffee exports have been three-decade process. Jorge Cardenas, president of FEDECAFE, explained eloquently this process and its wider implications on the large coffee growers, by saying that the "declining size of coffee in the economy has reduced the coffee elite political role in general and diminished its capacity in influencing public policy."[55] He added "Other sectors, such as the financial and industrial, have in contrast gained more power and political leverage in the 1980s and 1990s."[56] Cardenas emphasized also the role of cacaos and their easier "accessibility" to the president of the republic than the one they have.

At another level, and in contrast with the other sectors of the agrarian elite, the main centers of coffee production remained relatively untouched by land conflicts and concomitantly by the guerrillas' military activities and taxation until the 1990s. In coffee plantation areas, property rights were more consolidated and stable that those in areas of colonization. Nonetheless, the guerrillas increased presence in the "Coffee Axis" (Eje Cafetero) coincided with the increasing crisis of small coffee producers, higher levels of unemployment, and with the insurgency political and military expansion strategy. Such changes put the coffee growers closer to their counterparts, the cattle ranchers and agribusiness affected negatively by the guerrillas' expansionism.

At the ideological-political level, FEDECAFE's president shared with the remaining agrarian elite of SAC and FEDEGAN, common ideological grounds such as his support of a "strong army" and a "military solution to the conflict."[57] This ideological affinity shared by the three most important groups that represent the interests of the agrarian elite is just another hurdle confronting the constitution of hegemony. Then it is reasonable to conclude that the success of the cacaos and their allies in bringing a negotiated end to the war will depend on a compromise that does not overlook the interests of the main sectors of the agrarian elite and provides the peasants with the sufficient economic means to subsist in the e-global economy.

HEGEMONY AND COUNTER HEGEMONY: INCENTIVES AND DISINCENTIVES OF THE GUERRILLAS

By 1999, the guerrillas reached a point of diminishing returns on the application of violence as a mean to obtain political gains. The marginal utility of the armed struggle has reached its limits because of the growing power of paramilitary groups and the increasing U.S. military involvement in the conflict, which are making the continuation of war more costly. The U.S. military aid to Colombia increased from $66 million in 1996 to $287 million in 1998 and jumped to $860.3 million of a $1.3 billion package in 2000.[58] Such a significant increase in the U.S. military assistance is poised to exacerbate the civil war augmenting the costs of its continuation.

Although the death ratio did improve in the guerrillas' favor in the 1990s as demonstrated in chapter 3, the peasant base of the guerrillas has suffered tremendous loss of lives via massacres committed by the armed forces and the paramilitary groups.[59] Entire villages are being destroyed in strategic areas to deny the guerrillas refuge, sources of recruitment, and information gathering on enemy movements and economic resources. These losses are important considerations that will have significant bearing on the guerrillas' decision to seek a negotiated settlement.

At another level, in the last two decades, the FARC and ELN have built considerable fighting forces but are facing the costs of maintaining the momentum given the scarce resources on which both forces could draw. The potential of extracting resources from the narcobourgeoisie and its networks (middle-men traders), cattle ranchers, landlords, and other business groups is diminishing because of the rise of powerful paramilitary organizations whose raison d'être is defending these sectors. In this respect, the paramilitaries have been successful in diminishing the size of potential "tax payers" to the guerrillas, hence denying the guerrillas critical income to maintain the momentum of their growth and to compensate for the increasing costs of the conflict.

Levying "revolutionary taxes" from the upper and middle classes is also becoming costly, affecting the guerrillas' prestige and political appeal among these sectors and among progressive forces as well.[60] Particularly criticized is its kidnap-ransom method, which brings between 20 percent to 30 percent of the FARC's and ELN's annual incomes.[61] The political costs of kidnap-ransom is outweighing its economic benefits, particularly that this method is being increasingly criticized by human rights groups and international organizations, which make the guerrillas' position even more indefensible.[62]

At another level, the guerrillas as a revolutionary project face the enormous task of socializing and politically educating recruits in an environment increasingly loaded with the ideological effects of consumerism and the immediate gains that a deserter might obtain by defecting to the other side. Since the guerrillas apply the death sentence to those wishing to abandon their ranks, these individuals are compelled to desert, and when they do, they can either join the government forces as informers or guides or join the paramilitary groups. The government did not offer deserters other options, making them recyclable among the war system's actors.

The AUC is increasingly becoming a magnet for those willing to desert since it offers protection and better salaries than the guerrillas and the army. According to Felipe Torres, the ELN commander, the guerrillas do not offer salaries to combatants, but rather "irregular" compensation to help the guerrillas' family. FARC and the ELN provides about $90 (based on an exchange value of 2000 pesos per dollar) monthly in compensation, while the paramilitary is a paid army, and its salaries are even higher than the minimum wage of a worker in the industrial sector ($150). The AUC paramilitary wages range between $250 and $1,000 depending on rank supplemented by a $10 bonus for each "guerrilla" killed.[63] It is obvious that the higher paramilitary salaries increase the incentives to desert. In fact, paramilitary in its propaganda offers the would be guerrilla deserter higher salaries (ranging from $500 to $1,500 depending on rank) than those of the regular AUC paramilitary soldiers.

According to military intelligence sources during 1997 and 1999, the guerrillas' desertion increased by 47 percent. If this figure is accurate, then this is an important factor to be considered in the discussion of the incentives and disincentives of the guerrillas for peaceful resolution of the conflict. It is plausible to argue that the economic crisis in the country is also affecting the incentive of some of the guerrilla members to desert who find themselves obliged to support their families' decreasing meager incomes.[64] Furthermore, desertion in this context becomes a function of the economic crisis and the availability of protection and higher wages. The paramilitary provides both.

In evaluating the military balance in early 2000, there is no doubt that the paramilitary-military axis has at least for the moment stopped the advance and consolidation of the guerrillas' authority in regions such as south Bolivar, North Santander (Catatumbo region), Putumayo, Casanare, Cesar, Uraba, and Choco. Between November 1998 and October 1999, the FARC lost 775 combatants according to military sources. If this figure is correct, this is the highest ever since the FARC inception in 1964.[65] The paramilitary groups have made military incursions in regions that for years have been guerrillas' safe-heaven. South Bolivar, Putumayo and Catatumbo are cases in points. These areas are important areas for strategic military purposes (trafficking of arms to guerrillas through Venezuela, Ecuador, and Peru) and for the tax extraction from gold merchants and narcotraffickers.

The above depicts the overall conditions acting upon the guerrillas and hence their incentives to find a peaceful exit from the armed conflict. These conditions suggest that the economic, political, and military assets accumulated during the comfortable impasse of the 1980s and 1990s are being progressively taxed by an escalating conflict, presenting the guerrillas with an option to negotiate now or wait and risk serious losses. In my opinion, Colombia's guerrillas have a historic chance to renegotiate the re-integration of the coca growers into the "legal" international capitalist economy, having in hand two important negotiating cards: guns and illicit drug plantations. Needless to say, the guerrillas are capitalizing on these two bargaining chips and are also realizing that the current situation is the best and is unlikely to improve in the future.[66] This can explain why FARC proposed its Ten Points for a National Reconciliation Government program and was also keen in supporting the candidacy of Pastrana who based his presidential campaign on a peace platform. The paradox is that both FARC and the conglomerates supported Pastrana. This coincidence of political interests supports my central argument that the guerrillas as well as important sectors of the dominant class and the political elite are realizing that the costs (political, economic, and social) of the war system have become unsustainable by the late 1990s.[67]

Moreover, the illicit drug plantations, which allowed the colonos, poor and small peasants to subsist during the last three decades in spite of capitalist development coupled with a violent process of land concentration, also constitute an important arrow in the guerrillas'quiver. The insurgency may finally help in bringing about a "peasant path" of development after the failure of the National Association of Peasant Users (ANUC) to do so in the 1970s.[68] According to Leon Zamosc, the peasant path is "characterized by the distribution of land among large numbers of smallholders, which leads to peasant farming based upon family labor."[69]

I will venture to hypothesize that in Colombia, in contrast with Nicaragua and El Salvador, the neo-liberal model most likely will be curtailed and the political system will be more inclusive. In this context, it is relevant to invoke Jeffery Paige, who argues that in the 1980s, Central America found a new route to the transition to democracy through socialist revolution from below. In the spirit of Barrington Moore, Paige contends that breaking the power of the landlords was necessary for the triumph of democracy. In distinction from Moore, Paige argues that the agro-industrial bourgeoisie could not carry out this task itself: they and the landlords were two fractions of the same elite.[70] The actions of the armed left in El Salvador and Nicaragua were necessary to break the alliance and weaken the power of the landlords. However, Paige concludes that the irony is that the outcome of their efforts was the triumph of the agro-industrial bourgeoisie and neoliberalism. How do these Paige-Barrington theoretical conclusions apply to Colombia?

Moore's thesis based on his study of the peasant revolutions in France (18th century) and Russia and China (20th century) largely holds in Colombia. He contends that "a revolutionary movement is much more likely to develop and become a serious threat where the landed aristocracy fails to develop a really powerful commercial impulse within its own ranks. Then it may leave beneath it a peasant society damaged but intact, with which it has few connecting links. Meanwhile it is likely to maintaining its style of life in a changing world by extracting a larger surplus out of the peasantry."[71] The only departure from Moore's thesis is that for the last four decades, Colombia's agrarian economy has been undergoing a type of capitalist transformation based on land speculation (rentier-capitalism) rather than productivity, a process propelled by intensive ranching, hydrocarbon extraction, and the illicit drug economy, creating an important segment of the landed class that while it extracts surplus out of the peasantry in one region, it also seeks the peasants' lands (in economically strategic areas), whose value is decided by global markets and not by productivity.[72]

This new landowning bourgeois faction's efforts to capture prime lands, however, have faced the resistance of peasants whose social and economic bases are damaged by the capitalist transformation but not enough to affect their ability to produce organized responses.[73] The new landed speculators (narcobourgeoisie and other wealthy individuals), the agro-industrialists, the traditional landlords, and the cattle ranchers are factions of the same social class, and their political interests (particularly of those that have their lands and businesses in areas of guerrilla activity and influence) coincide in their opposition to cede to the peasantry and to the guerrillas' political and social demands. Moreover, the land speculators like the traditional landed faction have preferred the use of violence as a mechanism for political control and land concentration, since land speculation and ground-rent remain their main source of wealth accumulation. In this mode, the change in the class configuration of the landed elite did not lead to a political alteration in its behavior as a collectivity. All landed elite factions with some variations remain allied ideologically with conservative political forces, the military, and paramilitary groups, all of whom were instrumental in creating and maintaining the war system as a cost-effective mechanism for defending their interests.

Similar to Nicaragua and El Salvador, Colombia's guerrillas have incrementally helped in dismantling the conservative grip of the landed class on the political system, thus giving other sectors of the bourgeoisie whose global vision and class interests (not tied to ground-rent or land speculation) a historic chance to break away and search for an institutional alternative to the war system.[74] Given that in early 2001, the war system became a "high-maintenance job" given its costs and the urgent impulses of global economic integration and the institutional changes needed (such as securing property rights) that correspond to this process can not be fulfilled in a violent environment, violence, then, has exhausted its utility, or so it seems.

If violence has exhausted itself as a conflict resolution mechanism this does not automatically translate into building a new political system with effective institutions that could arbitrate and adjudicate social conflicts. The building of such a new system and institutions in Colombia will depend on class collaboration between the peasants and the bourgeoisie and their ability to hammer out an accord that could consolidate the state authority and legitimacy. Moreover, the success of their class collaboration also depends on incorporating landowners (including narcotraffickers) who are debilitated and fractured (in terms of organization), but not defeated. For those latter forces, the inertia of the war system and the vested interests of multiple social groups (such as city gangs, sectors of the military, and organized crime) are on their side. Hence, signing a peace agreement does not automatically dismantle the war system.[75] But rather, it might take a number of years to lower the levels of violence to international levels. Nonetheless, these are the contours of a settlement if hashed out under the current balance of power, class configuration, and international conditions.

HEGEMONY VERSUS THE WAR SYSTEM

To recap, a successful hegemony depends on measuring coercion with persuasion, as Gramsci noted. The adaptation to the new methods of work cannot come about solely through coercion: the apparatus of state coercion needed to obtain such a result would certainly be more costly than high wages. The key is to combine coercion with persuasion in forms that are suitable to the society in question.[76] In this vein, democracies' political survival depends on how to strike the right balance between coercion and persuasion given the class, race, regional, and gender divisions. In Colombia, the business conglomerates, as discussed, are questioning whether the price of coercion, that is the costs of maintaining the war system as mechanism of conflict resolution, is becoming more costly than high wages, that is, land reform and a more equitable distribution of income and political power.[77] In other words, sectors of the dominant class are contemplating the deconstruction of the default hegemony, the war system, and reconstructing in its place a more "encompassing hegemony" by persuading the peasant-based guerrillas by granting them some concession as a price to accept a new basis of their authority and stabilizing property rights. The price of maintaining the war system has become too high and does not measure up to the opportunities that peace could offer to important sectors of the dominant class. Stabilizing property rights and reducing transaction costs, primordial elements for the advancement of capitalism, cannot be achieved under a war system that destabilizes the first and increases the costs of the second.[78]

FINAL THOUGHTS

The previous chapters have found that the three main causes that lead to the formation and consolidation of the war system were present in Colombia. Chapter two demonstrated that the failures of the state institutions in adjudicating, arbitrating, and mediating social antagonisms stemming from land conflicts since the turn of the twentieth century provided the groundwork for the subsequent evolution of the war system. This first condition was supplemented by the abilities of antagonistic social actors—peasants and large landowners—to adjust to a condition of violent conflict under which they were better off than their status ante. I have shown also that the military, guerrillas, and organized crime (as representatives and as mutations of the peasants-landlords conflict) invariably accumulated political and economic assets (a positive political economy) which were not possible to obtain prior to the initiation of hostilities or under a high-intensity conflict.

One of my main findings in this research is that the protraction of the civil war in Colombia for about forty years cannot possibly be understood without exploring the interconnection among its main actors—the state, guerrillas and organized crime—and without evaluating variables such as contingencies, social structures, and agencies that shape the actors environments and in turn affect their behavior. The sum total of all these variables is the war system, which exhibits properties that are different from those of its parts. The war system is an outcome of actors' behavior and is not necessarily their optimal goal, given that the guerrillas and the state's optimal choice is to prevail over the other and establish hegemony. But since the balance of power did not allow this to happen, actors adjusted their goals and strategies.

For example, the unintended outcome of the guerrillas' support or indecisiveness in dealing with the colonos and poor peasants shifting to drug plantations brought into the conflict new actors—narcotraffickers and their paramilitary groups. The narco economy provided the guerrillas with risks and opportunities. One of the risks involved was the possible generation of a new social actor with diametrically opposing class and political interests than those of the guerrillas. Drug plantations offered an opportunity for increasing the financial resource of the guerrillas by taxing narcotraffickers. On the state side, the narcoeconomy offered also risks and opportunities. The risks were the possible erosion of the state' authority, corruption of its institutions, and the threat of an international backlash. The narcotraffickers offered also an opportunity as an ally in the state's fight against the insurgency. Narcotraffickers constituted a valuable source of badly needed liquidity in the financial markets, at least for a while, before exerting inflationary pressures in the 1990s.[79] The effects of the guerrillas and the state actions regarding narcotrafficking generated an unforseen outcome, such as changing the conflict from a low-intensity into a higher-intensity one, causing an erosion in the positive political economy they developed earlier.[80]

But the central question that begs for an answer is this: Is the war system an unintended consequence of actors' behavior? The answer is positive, but only in part. Actors responded to a balance of forces that is beyond their control, since it reflects a power relationship with an adversary, and consequently actors developed alternative strategies that helped them in adjusting and capitalizing on the prevailing balance of forces. The military, for example, developed a containment military strategy instead of seeking the elimination of the guerrillas' threat, and the guerrillas decided on consolidating their political power at the local municipal levels instead of seeking an outright military victory. In this mode, the fundamental units of social analysis—structure and agency— are incorporated in the war system analysis.

In systems analysis, as Jervis argues, one cannot infer from the desires or expectations of actors and vice versa because actors seek advantage and try to outstrategize one another, some of them if not all must be surprised. The most obvious reason is competition, since my main concern is the system of violence that is constructed during a civil war competition acquires even more weight in determining the stability of an inherently unstable system. The state, the guerrillas, and organized crime competed violently in the protection-rent market. That is because whoever captures the largest piece of the protection-money pie has more resources to pour into his/her war-making and state-making capabilities. Competition is taking place in the context of an unregulated anarchic system, because if competition were regulated, then this could entail either the partition of a country (de facto or de jury) or devising a power-sharing formula, thus transforming a war system to a peace system.

Actors' competition for resources then is one of the main sources that predicate the instability of the war system. In game theory, the actors in the Colombian war system are mainly engaged in a Prisoners Dilemma game where defection rather than cooperation has been the ordering principle of the actors. Since the mid-1990s, the actors in Colombia's war system's non-cooperative and aggressive military strategies (particularly the strategies of narco-paramilitary groups) affected negatively the comfortable impasse and the system's environment: that is to say affecting economic performance of the country, the class interests of important sectors of the dominant class, and the lives of the majority of the subordinate classes, particularly the peasants.[81]

If my analysis is valid, then Colombia's civil war is most likely to follow the Lebanese path discussed in the following chapter. In Lebanon, the exorbitant costs of the civil war eroded the positive political economy, whose coincidence with favorable international conditions helped in bringing the Taif Accord of 1989 which ended the war (see chapter7). Similarly in Colombia, we are witnessing an increasing costs of the civil war and a spill-over effect onto Venezuela, Ecuador, Panama, Peru, and Brazil, which is making these countries more nervous and interested than ever before in seeing a peaceful end to the conflict. In few words, the conflict is becoming a destabilizing factor in the region and also due to its narcotrafficking component has become an international concern. Europe and Japan with vital interests in the region are also showing more assertiveness in pushing for a peaceful accord. All of the above demonstrate that the elements of a new system (hopefully a more peaceful one) and its social forces are being fomented by the decaying system of war. The question is, will the main social and political actors capitalize on this "ripe" moment? Or would the increasing military intervention of the United States create new conditions for the prolongation of an agonizing war system?

The most obvious consequence of the current U.S. policy to commit more resources and personnel to support the military ($1.3 billion, 80 percent of which is for military purposes) is to further disturb the war system exacerbating the civil war. In effect, the U.S. policy driven by the "war on drugs" might delay, if not derail, and prolong the collapse of the war system. This is because this mainly military aid subsidizes the costs of war (that the local elites otherwise would have to pay) and subsequently strengthens the most conservative sectors within the dominant classes, the army and the political elite at the expense of the other sectors (such as the economic conglomerates) that believe that this is the most opportune time to settle the conflict. Negotiation in the midst of an armed conflict is a complex process, particularly when it has formidable opponents, as the one discussed. The least that this process needs is an intrusion of the magnitude that the U.S. military aid brings to bear. A better approach by the United States would be to encourage the belligerent forces to reach a peaceful settlement by extending the carrot of its willingness to commit resources for alternative crop development sufficient to safeguard the livelihood of the peasants (that are farming illicit plants) if a compromise is reached.

In this respect it is instructive to highlight the pilot project that the State of Maryland is applying to entice its tobacco farmers to substitute their traditional cash crop with strawberries, hothouse flowers, and other crops. Under this alternative crop development plan, Maryland offers guaranteed income for a decade based on each farmer's crop volume for 1998, at a three-year average of recent market prices (one dollar per pound.) Maryland will also provide the support and the technical assistance to make the transition possible and sustainable.[82] I think executing a similar project in Colombia (and in Peru and Bolivia) could be more fruitful in the long run than the current "militaristic approach" that has proven its futility and myopia in the past. Such an alternative crop program could provide serious incentives to the guerrillas, and peasants and could also be cost effective to the Colombian state and the U.S. government in the long run. More important, however, such a plan gives the peasants' illicit plants growers a guaranteed income of ten years, which equals their current earnings, stabilizes the subsistence peasant economy, and defuses social and political conflicts. During the ten-year period proposed in the plan, the peasants will have more time to experiment with other crops, learn about them, command new marketing strategies, and obtain the technical support needed for a sustainable development with a more humane face.

The previous alternative plans implemented in Bolivia, Peru and Colombia failed because they were designed for short-term ad-hoc bases and without any serious efforts to consider a longer-term plan (say ten years) that gives the peasants a better opportunity to acquire new skills and technical expertise and to find stable markets. That is why ex-coca growers who experimented for a few years (on an average of less than five years) with coffee, cacao, rice, African palm, and pineapples soon found that their incomes were not only much less than what they used to obtain from their coca crops but were worsening with price declines in global markets. Under these precarious economic circumstances, some peasants in Bolivia and Peru are shifting back to coca in spite of their respective states' punitive actions since the costs of the risks are becoming much less than the opportunity that coca could offer given its current price upward swing.[83] Finally, the costs of the recommended (Maryland proto-plan) will be considerably lower than the $23 billion that the U.S. government and the local states are spending on the "drug war's" law enforcement and without counting the medical costs of addiction, loss of social capital, costs of criminality, costs of prisons, and other related costs incurred in a battle with an imaginary and elusive enemy.[84]

The next and final chapter of this book shifts gear and focuses on placing the Colombian war system within a wider context by analyzing the three experiences of Italy, Lebanon, and Angola in an attempt to capture nodal points in the problematic of protracted violence.

CHAPTER 7

Colombia's Civil War
in Comparative Perspective

In comparative analysis, the method of agreement and difference is
employed by identifying similarities in the dependent variables associated with a common outcome, such as a war system, and by identifying
the independent variables that produce different outcomes: In other
words, political and criminal violence that do not lead to war systems.
This chapter considers three different cases: Italy, Lebanon, and Angola.
Italy was chosen because in spite of its violent 19th and early 20th century history a war system did not develop. The goal here is to explain
why this outcome was possible in Italy and not in Lebanon, Angola, and
Colombia. In Lebanon, violence became institutionalized in a war system that collapsed after a fifteen-year life cycle. The Angolan war system continues three decades after the Angolan war of independence.

For the most part, the literature on Colombian violence has focused
on the historical peculiarity of its sectarian struggles between the Liberal
and Conservative Parties. Such interpretation is based on the numerous
civil wars that erupted in Colombia during the 19th century: 1830–31,
1839–42, 1851, 1854, 1860–62, 1876–77,1895–1902, and thirty-four
rebellions (according to Malcom Deas).[1] This chapter discusses cases of
violence that demonstrate that Colombia's political and criminal violence is not unique if seen in comparative terms, as Deas has argued.

ITALY: AN ABORTED WAR SYSTEM

Italy in the 19th and early 20th centuries suffered from the typical problems of state building that most of the Third World nations are still contending with in the 21st century. Italy's weak state, Mafias, and hired
assassins were notorious, which gave some grounds to comparative
analysis with Colombia such as the one advanced by Malcom Deas. The
importance of this comparative exercise is to dispel the notion that
countries are locked into their own histories and are thus doomed to a
perpetual cycle of violence as some of the studies of violence suggest. I
concur with Deas's view that Colombia was not a particularly violent

country in the 19th century by regional or international standards. The case of Italy is particularly useful because it does not fit the mold of comparative analyses that limit the exercise to either regional schemes or to an overarching underdevelopment concept. In the 19th and early 20th centuries, the Italian state was "weak" in the sense that the elite was unable to produce a hegemon, in Antonio Gramsci's terms, and persuade its subjects to accept the logic on which the political system is based. The Italian elite in the late 19th century did not yet satisfy Gramsci's most advanced condition of hegemony, which he labeled the "third moment" (see chapter 3).

John Davis's study of 19th century Italy describes a state whose weakness manifested itself in an inefficient judicial system, corrupt and ill-equipped police, and private armed vigilante groups and paramilitarism.[2] By the late 19th century, the outcome was a high level of violence whose toll was more than 4,000 homicides a year (sixteen times more than in Britain), and more than 40 percent of all crimes remained unsolved.[3] In many parts of the country the state's legitimacy was uncertain. Many notables were alienated, disliked the state's intentions from the start, and obstructed its officials. The influence of those notables, however, was at the same time being eroded by economic change. The impression was that even if such notables had been the class base of the new state, they would have been weak pillars.[4] When the state took repressive measures, such as the military occupation of Milan (whose toll was 80 killed and 450 wounded) or repressive measures under Crispi, inspired by the anarchist menace and almost ending in the elimination of the opposition, the resulting backlash forced the state to abandon these measures.[5]

The Italian police apparatus was corrupt; it did not enjoy the confidence of the dominant classes and even less the subordinate groups, the main subject of their repression. The weakness of the state stemmed from the lack of a hegemon as a leader-group that transcended its own corporate interest and projected a moral authority widely acceptable to the other factions of the dominant classes and the subordinate groups. For such an objective, hegemony would need effective and functional political and judicial apparatuses to allow the mediation, arbitration and adjudication of social conflicts, thereby averting the necessity of violent resolution. Against this background, political and nonpolitical violence flourished in Italy.

One of the most important parallels with Colombia is the failure of Italy's Risorgimento liberalism, especially in the years after 1878, to resolve the agrarian question when it reached its peak crisis. In fact, political and criminal violence converged in Sicily and the Mezzogiorno due to the types of agrarian structures (absentee large landowners) and a weak state presence. The Sicilian landlords formed a compact force, which according to Davis was not easily resisted or divided, making it difficult for the state to arbitrate or adjudicate conflict with peasants.[6] Davis noted that one of the key variables, in addition to economic structures that determined different forms of rural violence in Sicily and the Mezzogiorno, was the relative weakness of the state.[7] Increasingly, large landowners relied on mafia paramilitaries to maintain social control and to safeguard their large estates. Peasant revolts and criminal violence came about because of the relative weakness of the state in resolving social conflicts.

The Mafioso, according to Anton Blok, was a violent entrepreneur specializing in economic and political mediation between traditional social classes and between the countryside and the outside world.[8] The Mafioso played a key role in managing the processes of conflict and accomodation among the state, the landowning elite, and the peasants, as it monopolized the central political, coercive, and economic junctures between the countryside and the larger economic and political systems. Thus, in 19th century Italy the Mafia performed the role of economic mediation. The most remarkable similarity between the paramilitary groups in Colombia and the Mafia in Italy (up until 1922) is the relationship they maintained with political institutions and the legitimacy that both acquired through that relationship.

In Italy, the unification of the country was based upon a tacit alliance between the northern industrial bourgeoisie and the southern landed elite, which shaped the political system until 1922 when the Fascists took over. The terms of the alliance were the perpetuation of the social and economic order in the South, complete freedom of action for the dominant elites at the local level, and access to government resources by southern deputies in return for their unquestioning support in Parliament for any government majority, regardless of its program. Hence, the state delegated to local elites the power to govern in its name, and those in turn assumed the functions of maintaining order and social stability in the countryside. In the absence of the state's central authority and of much of the propertied class (mostly living in urban centers), as Judith Chubb argues, the local elite became in many cases either identical with the Mafia, or at the very least, protectors of it. The Mafia also served as an armed agent of the state in the task of repressing political opposition.[9] This was noted from 1943 through 1950 in Sicily, a period that was marked by peasant revolts and mass occupations of large estates, led by Communist and Socialist parties demanding land reform. During this period, the Mafia allied itself initially with the Sicilian Separatist Movement (dominated by large landowners fearing the growing influence of the left) and recruited many bandits into the Separatist movement to form a countermilitary force against the peasant and the leftist parties.[10] The threat of large-scale peasant movement combined with increasing cold war tensions cemented the ties between Christian Democrats and the Mafia, both notoriously anticommunist.[11]

It is interesting to note that the Mafia in Sicily also collaborated with Allied forces. American intelligence services had established contacts with American Mafia bosses and through them with counterparts in Italy to facilitate the invasion. Subsequently, many noted Mafiosi were rewarded with political positions in local administrations. After 1947, the cold war was taking shape, leading to the ejection of the leftist groups from the national government. The right-wing leaning of the Christian Democrats (CD) persuaded the landowners and the Mafia who championed the Separatist movement to close ranks against the left.[12] Since then, the CD on its part increasingly relied on the Mafia at the local level.

In 1950 land reform was introduced under which 20 percent of agricultural land in Sicily and two-thirds of the land occupied by latifundios passed to small peasants. Consequently the Mafia as an armed guardian of the landed class and the "the privileged intermediary" between the peasants and the landed elite underwent a transformation.[13] The Mafia adjusted to new market conditions inside Sicily and at the national and international level, making itself a more formidable force living in a symbiotic relationship with the state and its institutions. This process of transformation was best described by the sociologist Pino Arlacchi a specialist on organized crime. He argued, that during the 1960s and 1970s "availing themselves of the altered economic and institutional climate of the 1970s, Mafiosi of the gangster type developed their economic activities to such a spectacular degree that they now have to be included among the most powerful enterprises.' He added, "The state managed to establish a monopoly of force during the preceding two decades [1960 and 1970s] and thus contributed, by way of denying them any other option, to the conversion of the Mafiosi to criminal activities." He concluded that the state has been allowed to place the entire repertoire of violent and aggressive behavior typifying the day-to-day component of the man of honor during the 1930s at the service of the accumulation of wealth by illegal and legal means.[14] The result of this complex state-Mafia relationship and its mutations corresponding to political, social, cultural, and economic changes was a symbiosis in which the Mafia acted as a hegemon in the crime market controlling the levels of violent crimes largely complementing the state functions. This can in part explain the decrease in organized crime-related homicides since the 1950s.

Another important factor contributing to the reduction of violence was the Communist Party's renunciation of the use of political violence as a vehicle to seize political power and its acceptance of the rules of the political game. This position of the CP denied smaller revolutionary groups such as the Red Brigades, in spite of their violent tactics, the opportunity to become a serious challenge to the state hegemony and to draw any significant support among the working class and the peasants. This proved that the instruments of class collaboration institutionalized under the welfare state expanded the social base of the state and consolidated its social hegemonic position.[15] In this way, violence in Italy became less entrenched than in Colombia and did not develop into a war system. The counter-hegemonic force opposing the state (the left) was not strong enough to constitute a match in politicomilitary terms, and the dominant classes and political elites managed to build a new hegemonic consensus that included a modus vivendi with organized crime. The cozy relationship between the CD Party, which dominated the political scene for most of the 20th century, and the Mafia supports this argument.[16] In fact, prominent CD leaders, including Giulio Andreotti, have had links with organized crime since 1947. Ernesto Savona's study of the Camera dei Deputati (Congress) provides evidence of organized crime's manipulation of the system of public contracts affecting the allocation of resources and public policy.[17] The Savona study and the Andreotti case are examples of the symbiosis between organized crime and the state that emerged since 1947.[18]

Italy's earlier violent history did not shape its history after World War II, partly because the Italian Communist Party, the most important political force of the left, abandoned armed struggle tactics as a means to seize political power, and partly because of the state-mafia symbiosis. Italy's homicide rate of 4.7 per 100,000 recorded in 1994 was among the lowest in the industrial world.[19] The intermittent confrontations among the Mafia, the Italian police force, and the judiciary between 1983 and 1993 did not affect their links with the political establishment.[20] Mutual economic and political interests have cemented this relationship as the Savona study of public contracts demonstrates. Mafia leaders with huge economic resources at their disposal are capable of financing political campaigns and providing the logistical support for political aspirants, and politicians reap obvious economic gains from their relationship with the Mafia.

The exercise of violence by organized crime has been selective, targeting only its opponents within the state organizations, particularly the judiciary and the police. It adopted the carrot-and-stick strategy where violence is used only as a last resort and only with non-collaborating state officials, to eliminate crime-market competition, and to secure compliance in the market. This being said, the relatively low rates of violent crime in Italy in the 1990s attest to the state social base of support and the effectiveness of the 1948 political formulae in mitigating violent crimes without destroying the symbiosis with a "pacified" and more globalized criminal organizations. It remains to be seen when and how the state-Mafia symbiosis will be transformed or dismantled and whether this will affect the levels of violent crimes.

LEBANON'S WAR SYSTEM CYCLE

Historical parallels can also be drawn among Lebanon, Colombia, and Italy. In the 19th century Lebanon, several peasant revolts and sectarian conflicts erupted (1820, 1830, 1845, 1860), led by conflicting feudal chieftains.[21] After gaining its independence in 1943, the country's government was based on a consociational arrangement dividing political power between sect leaders (the functional equivalent of Liberals and Conservatives in Colombia). The political distribution of political power was based on the 1932 population census (the only official census since), in which the ratio of Muslims to Christians was 5:6.

In 1975 the civil war started in earnest, caused in part by the inability of the state consociational political structure to accommodate change. The emergence of new social forces, increased class polarization, income distribution gaps, and regional disparities exacerbated the pressing need for a more egalitarian political representation between Muslims and Christians after the demographic shift in favor of the first. Another important catalyst was the spillover effect of the Arab-Israeli conflict, which came into play in Lebanon's domestic conflicts, particularly its sectarian divide. Israel and the United States sided with the right-wing Christian political parties, and the then Soviet Union and some Arab states sided with the leftist Muslim alliance.

On the eve of the civil of 1975, Lebanon had a fragmented political elite and a polarized society along overlapping political, class, and sectarian lines. The state's social base was deeply shaken by intra-elite conflict and the emergence of a counter hegemonic force strong enough to challenge the state authority in most of the national territory supported by the Palestinian guerrillas. The armed opposition was able to establish control over vast parts of the country and was strong enough to prevail had it not been for the regional and international conditions that prevented an outright military victory. The 1976 Syrian military intervention, with the support of the United States and the acquiescence of Israel, defeated the leftist-Palestinian alliance and prevented the left from overrunning the last bastions of the state' army and its rightist militia allies.

Such international conditions and the realignment of forces that followed precipitated a military impasse that lasted more than fifteen years, during which warring parties did change in terms of leadership, class make-up, and political programs. But more important, they managed to adjust to a low-intensity war condition and establish a positive political economy in terms of the economic and political gains that this impasse allowed them to accumulate. In contrast to Italy, Lebanon's violence evolved into a war system where the armed opposition was able to sustain a war for more than fifteen years. This was the case in Lebanon and not in Italy, because the Italian state was able to work out a base of class and political collaboration manifested in corporatism under Mussolini, later expanding under the CD Welfare State. In contrast, Lebanon's political elite and dominant classes were unable to reengineer accepted political formulae that could serve as a base to rebuild hegemony. Thus, the mere existence of high indices of violence is not an indicator that we have a war system in operation. What is more important for our purposes here is the violence stemming from the hegemonic crisis of the state exacerbated by a credible armed opposition, producing an impasse.

Lebanon's warring parties started adapting to a low-intensity warfare interspersed with occasional flareups allowing them to accumulate political, economic, and cultural assets that exceeded the costs of the war. Hence, a condition of "comfortable impasse" settled in for the most part between 1977 and 1990. War was institutionalized, and some ground rules were established, such as the creation of the Cease Fire Committee to regulate the war. Tacit and implicit deals were made to coordinate taxation of imported goods passing from one area of domination to another, transfer of capital and land titles, and protection of private property. Deals (both tacit and implicit) were stricken between militia leaders in their own localities. The total amount of money circulating in the war economy was about $900 million per year (about 25 percent of the GNP) between 1978 and 1982.[22] These sums were distributed as follows: the PLO circulated $400 millions, foreign forces donated $300 million to the different militias, and $200 million came from internal Lebanese sources levied as protection rents.[23]

The war system produced new social and political forces. A new class of war entrepreneur emerged who capitalized on importing contraband goods, arms, and narcotrafficking.[24] This new class accumulated significant economic resources and soon was making a bid to be reincorporated into the dominant class. This is very similar to the Colombian narcobourgeiosie and paramilitary leaders (such as Pablo Escobar, the Rodriguez brothers, and Carlos Castano) attempt to be assimilated into the traditional bourgeoisie and political elite. In Lebanon, militia leaders sought political power and in 1990 became part of the new ruling elite such as Nabih Berri, leader of the Shiite Amal militia; Ily

Hubaika, a leader of a faction of the Lebanese Forces, a Maronite-rightist group; and Samir Jaja' leader of the Lebanese Forces. Most of the new members of the political elite came from petty bourgeois class origins and from rural areas.

Therefore, even though the war system was a product of a military impasse, the system dynamics generated new social forces that became part of the peace system established since 1990. Leaders of the war system became part of the constituting elements of the restored hegemony on the basis of the Taif Accord. The Lebanese and the Colombian cases call for a revision of the often quoted Clausewitzian dictum that war is a continuation of politics by other means. A more accurate description might be that politics is the continuation of war by other means. This may be more suitable to societies characterized by sharp political, sectarian, ethnic, racial, and class divisions and chronic crises of state hegemony. War in such cases is not conceived or analyzed as an anomaly or an aberration of historical processes, but rather as an integral part of them.

An important question comes to mind: How can a war system be transformed to a peace system? Drawing on the Lebanese experience could be insightful. The war system in Lebanon reached a high level of institutionalization, and its economy outstripped the traditional sectors of the economy and in effect absorbed them. The financial-banking sector, for example, flourished through the influx and circulation of the war economy money.[25] It was not a surprise that this sector suffered an economic setback when the war ended. Sectors of the commercial class were also incorporated into the war economy, helped by the decentralization of war-propelled commerce. Beirut's commercial district was a major theater of war, which forced old merchants and new ones to move their activities to new areas. Then how could such an institutionalized and dominant system break down?

System dynamics give us the answer. Systems are generally unpredictable because causes and effects are not unilinear in the sense that X inputs will invariably produce an equal amount of Y outputs. But as complex systems teach us, X inputs could produce unpredictable outcomes Z. In Lebanon, the war system generated new political forces and elites, but this process was coupled with violent inter and intra groups conflicts. One of these conflicts, which was critical in causing a systemic dynamic that led to the war system collapse in 1990, was the emergence of a new army chief, Michel Oun, who, in his pursuit of supremacy, changed the working rules of the war system by attempting to redraw the battle lines institutionalized since 1977.

This attempt generated a chain reaction leading to an escalation of war to unprecedented levels. The cost and damage caused by this new phase (which lasted less than two years) of the war was estimated at $2 billion of damages in properties that was about 8 percent of $25 billions that Lebanon lost during the civil war in infrastructure and production facilities. The military cost of Oun's "Liberation War" against the Syrian peace-keeping forces and their Lebanese allies was estimated at $150 million per month, with a total of $1 billion. These costs include salaries of soldiers, the price of arms and ammunitions, supplies, and medical expenses.[26] In effect, this phase of the war destroyed the economic bases of the war system. The cost of war became exorbitant, outweighing by far the capabilities of local actors' rent-extraction capacities. The war economy simply could not be sustained, especially when the cold war was winding down, further diminishing the chances of foreign military assistance to the warring actors.

In systems theory parlance, the Lebanese war system was chiefly bipolar until 1988; there was one hegemonic force on the Christian-rightist camp and a hegemonic coalition on the Muslim-leftist side. The Lebanese army splintered into different factions, but the core of the fighting force remained under the Maronite-right hegemonic umbrella until the emergence of General Michel Oun as chief of the armed forces and then as interim prime minister from 1988 through 1990. Oun tried to monopolize the leadership of the Maronite Christian coalition and to use it to "liberate" all Lebanon. Oun tried to change the rules of the comfortable impasse in his "Liberation War" against the Syrian forces and its allies and the "Cancellation War" against the rightist militias—the Lebanese Forces—which sought to change the battle lines and conquer territories occupied by other armed actors. General Oun's "new game" was never institutionalized because it coincided with regional and international changes (the Gulf War, Perestroika, and the eventual collapse of the U.S.S.R.) both, inconsistent with the rule of the new game, which required escalating the conflict in Lebanon. The then evolving regional and international environment led to a rapprochement between Syria and the United States and between Russia and the US both developments changed the contours of the Lebanese conflict.

The 1989–1990 war between Michel Oun and the Lebanese Forces (LF) led to the weakening of the latter militarily and politically. The war also denied the LF about 55 percent of its monthly income due to the loss of important sectors to Oun's forces, such as Beirut Port ($200,000); Land Registries ($800,000); and the taxes on residential areas, casinos, restaurants, and commercial districts ($250,000).[27] More devastating was the extent of destruction in this confrontation. The UN estimated that in four months (January to March 1990), about 1,500 people were killed; 3,500 were injured; 100,000 emigrated; and more than 32,000 became refugees. The material damage to the country's infrastructure was about $500 million, and the per capita income declined from $1,150 in 1987 to $800 in 1989.[28]

The rapid decline in GDP per capita and the 100 percent inflation that accompanied it affected not only the middle and poor classes but also important segments of the industrial and commercial bourgeoisie. Segments of this latter group that were instrumental in financing the rightist militias paid a further price when conflict ensued among the rightist political groups themselves. Many of their industries and commercial centers were damaged during that fight. The fighting brought to light the gravity of the political fractures within the rightist groups underlined by a power struggle between ambitious leaders and uncovered the deep rifts within the sectors of the bourgeoisie that supported them. Some members of this class sided with General Oun, others remained loyal to LF, another sector supported a splinter LF group, and some assumed a neutral stance. The outcome, however, was the erosion of the political unity that made it possible to sustain the low-intensity war for over fifteen years.

Thus, changes in either the inner dynamics of the system or in its surrounding environment illustrate the precarious nature of violent systems at large. The internal sets of tacit rules can be disturbed at any moment leading to their collapse, or as Zartman put it, lead to a "mutually hurting situation."[29] Such a moment is usually the most opportune for third-party mediation, as events in Lebanon demonstrated. By 1990 the warring factions were exhausted by the dramatic escalation in the levels of violence, which made regional and international mediation effective in bringing the conflict to a resolution with the signing of the Taif Accord in Saudi Arabia.

Lebanon exemplified the life cycle of the war system from inception to maturation and to collapse. If a positive political economy is developed under a given military impasse, and this impasse becomes comfortable, the war system can be sustained for a long time.[30] In Lebanon, the war system was not only dependent on actors' behavior, goals, and incentives; it was also shaped by the systemic effects of all of those when they come in contact with other actors' competing goals. Neither Michel Oun nor his opponents could have anticipated the systemic effects of their own actions. Oun was accused of being "mentally unstable" simply because he violated the "standard rules" of the war system by attempting to change the system's boundaries which stirred violence to unprecedented proportions. Whether he was unstable cannot be decided here, but what is more important is that Oun fell victim to systems dynamics that he helped unleash by miscalculating the odds and by not foreseeing the full range of consequences of his aggressive strategies.

Lebanon's case lends support to the thesis that fractionalized societies tend to have wars of longer duration than moderately fractionalized ones, particularly when local actors enjoy the financial support of foreign sources. This finding is contrary to Paul Collier and colleagues' results, which suggest that homogeneous and highly fractionalized societies have shorter civil wars than moderately fractionalized societies.[31] In fact, Lebanon is highly fractionalized and Colombia is a more homogeneous society (80 percent are mestizos and Catholics) in terms of their ethnic and religious social composition. Both countries, however, witnessed protracted wars: Lebanon's war lasted over fifteen years and Colombia's civil war over thirty-five years. Explaining these two cases, as well as the Angolan civil war, as idiosyncratic cases is to avoid the central question: why are some conflicts prone to last longer than others? I have argued elsewhere that these "anomalies" can be explained in terms of the conjunction of the three factors that lead to the formation of the war system discussed above.[32] The previous chapters tackle the Colombian case, demonstrating that these three factors did coincide, which accounts for the long duration of the conflict.

ANGOLA'S WAR SYSTEM

Angola achieved its independence from Portugal in 1975, and before it had a chance to consolidate the state's power, an intra guerrilla conflict ensued among those who fought for independence. The power struggle between the Popular Movement For the Liberation of Angola (MPLA) and the National Union for the Total Liberation of Angola (UNITA) led to a division of power, with the MPLA (as the stronger faction) dominating the state and controlling large parts of the national territory, and UNITA controlling other parts and drawing on the support of then apartheid South Africa and the United States.[33] This is different from the Italian case, but not too dissimilar from Lebanon's case, whose intraelite conflict marred the country's 1943 independence and continued unabated for the remainder of the century, and culminating in a civil war. Intraelite conflicts abounded in Colombia since the country's independence in 1819 and debilitated the state hegemonic capacity.

Angola's civil war has passed through several ebbs and flows since 1975, culminating in the 1992 Agreement facilitated by the international changes brought about by the end of the cold war and the demise of the apartheid regime in South Africa. The agreement would have transformed UNITA into an opposition force with its leader, Jonas Savimbi, serving as a vice president. But soon this agreement collapsed, and UNITA ended up controlling diamond-rich areas in Lunda Sul and

Lunda Norte. The institutional failure of the state to persuade UNITA to agree to a permanent settlement and/or to defeat UNITA decisively has helped to create the first two conditions for a war system, one that thus far has killed five hundred thousand Angolans.

During the course of the civil war, the balance of power has shifted from one side to the other but without either side producing a decisive military victory. After each setback, UNITA was able to regroup and to resume its guerrilla war, drawing on its ethnic base for support and capitalizing on its regional political alliances with the ex-dictator Mobutu Sese Seko of Zaire (now Congo). But most important, what denied the government forces a decisive victory was UNITA's control of the diamond rich areas, which allowed it to build a conventional army with tanks, planes, and other heavy weapons. Such acquisitions have helped to maintain a balance of forces and an impasse that neither side so far has managed to break. In the last eight years (since the breakdown of the 1992 accord), UNITA has raised between $3 and $4 billion from diamond sales.[34] This averages about $300 million per year and constitutes about 3 percent of the GNP's $3 billion in 1998.[35] By controlling the diamond trade, UNITA has been able to develop a positive political economy. The low-intensity war has not yet taxed its forces either politically (in terms of internal dissent or fragmentation) or militarily (in terms of fatalities).[36] Its extraction of diamonds and the protection taxes it levied on companies and on thousands of miners (garimpeiros; amateur diggers) allowed it to strengthen its state-making and war-making capabilities. This was possible from 1994 through 1998, during which time a significant decrease in the intensity of the war took place helping UNITA and the state to regroup and rearm. During that period, UNITA consolidated its power base in the eastern region and improved its administrative capabilities and its war-making machine, that is, it consolidated its counterhegemonic force facing the state. Consequently, and in hindsight, the low intensity war that prevailed during the 1992–1997 period allowed the development of the war system because both parties, given the balance of forces and the costs of war, adjusted to that condition. In Angola, as in Lebanon and Colombia a comfortable impasse settled in for most of the 1990s.

The war system is nonlinear; it is an open system sensitive to changes in its environment. In Angola, the 1998 overthrow of the regime of Mobutu Sese Seko, a supporter of UNITA, changed the dynamics of the war system and transformed the low-intensity war to a high-intensity one where both forces engaged in large battles. The state, capitalizing on the downfall of Mobutu, sought to deliver a decisive blow to UNITA by routing it out from the diamond-rich areas. But the attempt was aborted because Kabila, the successor of Mobutu, was soon under attack, which obliged Angola to come to his rescue. UNITA capitalized on Kabila's crises by allying with Rwanda's Hutu militias and successfully recovered the lost ground, allowing the war system to continue with its ebbs and flows. By early 2000, UNITA's loss of some diamond-rich territory to government forces and the exhaustion of old mining sites led to a 50 percent decrease in its income from $300 million to about $150 million per year.[37] This drop in income diminished the war-making capabilities of UNITA, but it would be premature for the government to rejoice because UNITA's war chest is estimated to be several billions, which would allow it to sustain a menacing military force for a good number of years to come if other conditions remain constant. The war systems of Angola, Lebanon, exhibited a common characteristic of a military impasse that in spite of the ebbs and flows caused by the war system dynamics remained comfortable to the warring factions. This same characteristic is noted in the Colombian case as discussed in the previous chapters.

Angola's state-making process was caught in cold war politics, on which both contending forces drew to consolidate their power struggle. The ruling party (MPLA) was supported by the Soviet Union and Cuba, and UNITA by South Africa and the United States. Such entanglement made the conflict difficult to resolve given that the basic elements of a comprehensive settlement were missing, that is, a power-sharing formula that could allow the exercise of state hegemony. The end of the cold war and the demise of apartheid in South Africa ushered in a new phase in the civil war, with both actors adjusting their goals and strategies to a low-intensity war with occasional flare-ups. My observation is that UNITA's reneging on the 1992 peace accord was predicated on its control of the diamond-rich regions. Accordingly, UNITA rethought its political and military strategy in light of the good prospect of getting a better deal in the future. At that juncture, the state passed a law allowing private individuals to own and sell diamonds, which started a turf war (very similar to the emerald wars in Colombia during the late 1980s) among middlemen: army generals, South African mercenaries, West African traders, exiled Zairian gendarmes, riot police, mining companies, and UNITA fighters.[38] In the subsequent years, however, UNITA managed to become the main force in these two regions (Lundas) regulating the diamond trade.[39]

UNITA, fearing the military, political, and economic ramifications if it were to lose the Lundas, felt that the Lusaka Protocol and the 1998 agreement fell short in defining its privileges in the region and how to legitimize these privileges in a future accord. This became a stumbling block that complicated the application of the accord. To make matters worse, the Angolan civil war became entangled with the political realignments that followed the downfall of Mobutu in Zaire, and the $40 billion diamond trade that includes Angola, Congo, Sierra Leone, and Liberia. UNITA is a major player in this trade, as are the U.S. arms suppliers and the diamond multinationals (such as the South African-based, De-Beers).[40] War systems are open systems with porous borders.

There are important similarities and differences among the Angola, Lebanon, and Colombia civil wars. The warring groups depended on outside financial and military support during the first phase (Lebanon, 1975–80; Angola, 1975–89; and Colombia, 1964–80. The respective states of these countries also relied on foreign aid as well as taxing their own resources in the first phase of the civil war. However, during the second phase, the actors (including the state—especially its armed forces) managed to build their rent-collecting strategies and were able to find enough resources to accumulate a positive political economy. In this second phase, actors capitalized on extracting resources from multiple sources. In Lebanon, for example, the main armed actors relied on levying taxes, investments, contraband of arms and goods, and narco-trafficking. In Colombia, the rebels, the state, and organized crime relied on levying taxes, kidnap-ransom, extortion, oil and gold rents, and narcotrafficking. In Angola, UNITA and the state relied on extracting revenues from natural resources (diamonds and oil).

The ability of actors to accumulate resources to sustain the war system is not a guarantee for its indefinite perpetuation, because systems are susceptible to contingencies and changes in their environment. In the Lebanese case, for example, the emergence of a new actor changed the war system dynamics, leading to the system's destabilization and to its eventual collapse. Here, a new actor adopting aggressive strategies led to counterstrategies from his opponents, which in turn generated unwanted outcomes. This is a typical case illustrating the Prisoners' Dilemma, where actors fail to moderate their conflict strategies, thereby damaging their own long-term interests in maintaining the war system.

In contrast, the Angolan war system is essentially a bipolar system, which has managed to re-equilibrate despite occasional flare-ups. In this respect, it approximates more the condition of a "comfortable impasse" advanced in this book than of Zartman's model of a "fluctuating stalemate."[41] The war system in Angola had long periods (relative to the life span of civil wars) of stability, such as during 1992–97, when the fighting was minimal. Notwithstanding these fluctuations in the intensity of war, the military impasse allowed conflicting forces to adapt, regroup, consolidate their positions, accumulate significant economic resources, and thus prolong the war.

Since 1995, Colombia has been approximating the Lebanese variant with the emergence of a new powerful actor, namely, the paramilitary group led by Carlos Castaño, which disturbed the balance of the war system generating new dynamics and leading to unprecedented escalation in the intensity of war (discussed in chapters 5 and 6). In Lebanon and Colombia, what matters is not the polarity or multipolarity of the war system but rather the actors' behavior and strategies that produced unwanted or unforeseen outcomes.

If states' hegemonic crises constituted the genesis of the war systems, each of the cases discussed acquired its own properties and paths in institutionalizing its respective war system, with the only exception of Italy, which avoided this path altogether. These three paths capture some of the main types of war systems in the world and of which all the other protracted wars are variants. These comparative sketches are intended to bring the Colombian war system into a sharper focus and generate more questions about protracted wars and are worth exploring rigorously in future studies.

APPENDIX

Selection of the Interview Population

The plan of the study for this book called for interviews with the principal actors involved in Colombia's civil war. Interviews and in some cases re-interviews with more than two hundred persons and dozens more informal conversations were carried out between 1994 and1999. These interviews started while I was a Fulbright Scholar at the Department of Political Science at the Universidad de Los Andes in 1994, and then a visiting Professor in 1995, 1996, 1997, and 1998 respectively at the same university and at the Universidad Nacional Institute for Political Studies and International Relations (IEPRI). A number of these interviews were carried out with an understanding that names would be withheld for security reasons.

Interviews were employed to obtain information on four core themes: perceptions on the causes of ongoing civil war, land reform, costs of war and peace, and possibility of a negotiated settlement. Many of the interviews were cited throughout the text. The choice of the sample was based on my consultation with local experts and a thorough review of the literature. Seven main groups were targeted: business groups, labor unions, coca growers, miners, guerrillas, paramilitary officers, military personnel, and state officials involved in the peace negotiations.

After identifying the country's most important business organizations arrangements were made to interview the presidents of these associations. The presidents that accepted to be interviewed were from the Association of Industrial Groups (ANDI), Society of Farmers of Colombia (SAC), Federation of Cattle Ranchers (FEDEGAN), National Association of Exporters (ANALDEX), National Association of Financial Institutions (ANIF), Association of Banks (ASOBANCARIA), and Federation of Coffee Growers (FEDECAFE). Interviews usually took place in the executives' offices and on average lasted two hours each. All were conducted in Spanish with the author taking notes. Recording was generally not used (except in one case) due to the sensitive nature of the questions and to insure comparability with all interviewed. The representatives of the business groups interviewed represent key sectors of the economy such as the industrial sector, financial sector, coffee growers, cattle ranchers, large landlords, and small businesses.

The opinion of the labor movement was also solicited by interviewing presidents of the two most important unions, General Conferation of Democratic Workers (CGTD) and Central Union of Labor (CUT) and representatives of the United Workers Unions (USO), coca growers, and Association of Miners and Farmers of South Bolivar (ASOAGROMISBOL).

The interviews conducted with the guerrillas were the most difficult to arrange and execute due to the guerrillas' clandestine network in urban centers. A total of five informants of FARC were interviewed in Bogota and Bucaramanga, including Yazid Arteta the highest ranking FARC commander currently in captivity. I also obtained two recorded interviews with Mono Jojoy, the chief military commander of the FARC, and Andres Paris, a FARC member of Estado Mayor—the second most important echelon in the organization—both were conducted by students of the Andes University in 1997. I interviewed the ELN's two highest-ranking commanders, Francisco Galan, and Felipe Torres both in the maximum-security prison of Itaqui for over three hours (tape-recorded). Five ELN informants were also interviewed in Bogota, Bucaramanga, and Barancabermeja. Some ex-members of M-19 and EPL (3 commanders) were also interviewed.

I sought to interview the commander of the paramilitary groups in Barancabermeja, alias "Nicolas" but in the eleventh hour, he did not show up. Nicolas is alleged to be involved in various massacres. Instead some paramilitary informants were interviewed with close ties or informed about the paramilitary groups operating in the area. Some other interviews were conducted with large landlords with linkages with right-wing paramilitary groups.

Interviews were also conducted with five active duty military officers in Bogota and Bucaramanga whose names are withheld under their own request. The highest commissioner of peace, Daniel Garcia Penas (1994–98) was interviewed twice. The former attorney general, Alfonso Valdivieso, (1994–98) was also interviewed. Moreover, the president of the Central Bank (Banco de la Republica), Miguel Urrutia, and two other members of the Board of Directors were interviewed for our research purpose.

Finally, a note is in order about the three other civil wars discussed in chapter 7. The section on Lebanon is based primarily on data I collected during my intermittent visits to the country in 1996, 1997, and 1998. These visits allowed me to conduct interviews with a number of political leaders that played a critical role in the 1975–90 civil war. I have supplemented these interviews with other primary source material. The information on Italy and Angola was based on secondary sources.

NOTES

CHAPTER 1

1. This homicide rate per hundred thousand is based on 25,505 homicides registered in 2000 in a country with a population of 40 million.The homicide figure was published in *Medecina Legal* Annual Report, Bogotá, Colombia, January 2001.

2. Such as Gonzalo Sanchez, *Guerra y Politica en la Sociedad Colombiana* (Bogotá: El Ancora Editores, 1991); Charles Bergquist, Ricardo Peñaranda and Gonzalo Sanchez, *Violence in Colombia: The Contemporary Crisis in Historical Perspective* (Wellington, Delaware: SR Books, 1992); Gonzalo Sanchez, *Bandoleros, Gamonales Y Campesinos* (Bogotá: El Ancora Editores,1992); Eduardo Pizarro, *Insurgencia sin Revolucion: La Guerrilla en Colombia en una Perspectiva Comparada* (Bogotá: Tercer Mundo-IEPRI, 1996); Alfredo Molano, Trochas y Fusiles (Bogotá: Ancora, 1994); Alvaro Camacho, Alvaro Guzman Barney, *Colombia Ciudad y Violencia* (Bogotá: Ediciones Foro Nacional, 1990); Francisco Leal Buitrago, *El Oficio de La Guerra* (Bogotá: Tercer Mundo IEPRI, 1994); Daniel Pecaut, Presente, Pasado, Futuro de la Violencia, *Analyisis Politico* no. 30, 1997, pp. 3–36; German Guzman, Orlando Fals Borda, Eduardo Umana Luna, *La Violencia en Colombia* (Bogotá: Puntal de Lanza, 1977); Malcom Deas and Fernado Gaitan, *Dos Ensayos sobre la Violencia en Colombia*, (Bogotá: FONADE-DNP, 1995); David Bushnell makes an important distinction between violence in the last century and the violence of the 1940s. Violence in the 1980s and 1990s is a "third wave" because it can be distinguished from the preceding period of violence (1946–1966) and its ramifications. See David Bushnell, "Politics and Violence in Nineteenth Century in Colombia," in Charles Bergquist, Ricardo Peñaranda, and Gonzalo Sanchez, *Violence in Colombia: The Contemporary Crisis in Historical Perspective* (Wellington, Delaware: SR Books, 1992), p. 12

3. Michael Renner et al., *Vital Signs 1999: The Environmental Trends that are Shaping Our Future* (New York: W.W. Norton and Company, 1999), pp. 112–114.

4. Theda Skocpol, *States and Social Revolutions: A Comparative Analysis of France, Russia and China* (Cambridge: Cambridge University Press, 1979), p. 5. See also Skocpol, *Social Revolution in the Modern World* (Cambridge: Cambridge University Press, 1994); Timothy P. Wickman-Crowley, *Guerrillas and Revolutions in Latin America: A Comparative Study of Insurgents and Regimes since 1956*, (Princeton, NJ: Princeton University Press, 1992); John Foran, ed., *Theorizing Revolution* (London: Routledge, 1996); Cynthia McClintock, *Revo-*

lutionary Movements in Latin America: El Salavador's FMLN and Peru's Shining Path (Washington, DC: USIP, 1998).

5. Nazih Richani, "The Political Economy of Violence: The War System In Colombia" *Journal of Interamerican Studies and World Affairs*, 39, no. 2 (Summer 1997): 37–81, and the "Political Economy of Rent Extraction: The Crisis of the War System in Colombia." *Journal of Conflict Studies* (Fall 2001).

6. See Edward Azar, *The Management of Protracted Social Conflicts: Theory and Cases* (Dartmouth: Dartmouth Publishing, 1990), p. 7.

7. For example see Louis Kriesberg, Terrel A. Mothrup, Stuart J Thorson, *Intractable Conflicts and their Transformation*, (Syracuse, NY: Syracuse University Press, 1989); I William Zartman (ed.), *Elusive Peace: Negotiating and End to Civil Wars* (Washington, DC: The Brookings Institutions, 1995); Roy Licklider (ed.), Stopping the Killing: How Civil Wars End, (New York: New York University Press, 1993); Barabara F. Walter, "The Critical Barrier to Civil War Settlement." *International Organization.* 51, no. 3, (1997): pp. 335–64; David Keen, *The Economic Functions of Violence in Civil Wars* (London: IISS, Adelphi paper, 320, 1998); Mats Berdal and David Keen, Violence and Economic Agendas in Civil Wars: Some Policy Implications." *Millennium: Journal of International Studies,* 26, no. 3, (1997): pp. 795–818; Froncois Jean et Jean Christophe Rufin (eds.), *Econonie des Guerres Civiles* (Paris: Foundacion pour les Etudes de Defense, 1996); Paul Collier and Anke Hoeffler, "On the Economic Causes of Civil War" *Oxford Economic Papers* 50 (1998); and Paul Collier, Anka Hoeffler and Mans Sorbedom, " On the Duration of Civil Wars" Paper. World Bank (1999); Ibrahim Elbadawi, "Civil Wars and Poverty; The role of Extend Interventions, Political rights, and Economic Growth" Paper. World bank (1999); Lincoln P Bloomfield and Allen Moulton, *Managing International Conflict: From Theory to Policy* (New York: St. Martin's Press, 1997); Michel Benson and Jacek Kugler, "Power Parity, Democracy and the Severity of Internal Violence" *Journal of Conflict Resolution* 42. no. 2 (April 1998): 196–209; Nazih Richani, "The Political Economy of Violence: the war System in Colombia." *Journal of Interamerican Studies and World Affairs.*

8. David Berlinski, *On Systems Analysis* (Cambridge: MIT Press, 1976), p. 3; Richard A. Falk and Samuel S. Kim, *The War System: An Interdisciplinary Approach* (Boulder, Colorado: Westview, 1980).

9. See Kenneth Waltz, *Theory of International Politics* (New York: McGraw Hill, Inc., 1979), p. 40.

10. The concept of "comfortable impasse" I developed in this book is the antithesis of I. William Zartman "mutually hurting stalemate theory." The "comfortable impasse" theory I am proposing, given the asymmetry between the conflicting parties, sheds light on a crucial component that can explain protracted conflicts that Zartman's theory did not develop enough. See I. William Zartman, "The Unifinished Agenda: Negotiating Internal Conflicts" in Roy Licklider (ed.), *Stopping the Killing: How Civil Wars End* (New York: New York University Press, 1993), pp. 20–34. \

11. See Waltz, *Theory of International Politics*; Robert Jervis, *System Effects: Complexity in Political and Social Life* (Princeton, NJ.: Princeton Uni-

versity Press, 1999); see also John Weltman, *Systems Theories in International Relations* (Lexington, Mass: D.C. Heath, 1973).

12. See Barrington Moore, *Social Origins of Dictatorship and Democracy: Lord and Peasant in the Making of the Modern World* (Boston: Beacon, 1966); Jeffrey Paige, *Coffee and Power: Revolution and the Rise of Democracy in Central America* (Cambridge, Mass: Harvard University Press, 1998); Paige, *Agrarian Revolution* (New York: Free Press, 1975); Paige "Social Theory and Peasant Revolution in Vietnam and Guatemala," *Theory and Society* 12 (Nov.1983): 699–737; Theda Skocpol, *States and Social Revolutions: A Comparative Analysis of France, Russia and China* (Cambridge: Cambridge University Press, 1979).

13. It is important to note that most internal wars between 1945 and 1990 (about percent) ended with the extermination, expulsion, or capitulation of the losing side. See Barbara Walter, "The Critical Barrier to Civil War Settlement," *International Organization* 51, no. 3, (1997): 335–64; George Modelski, International Settlement of Internal Wars" in James Rosenau (ed.), *International Aspect of Civil Strife* (Princeton: Princeton University Press, 1964). This research, however, intends to explore cases-such that of Colombia and in the last chapter, of Lebanon and Angola—where the balance of power did not allow one side to exterminate another, and the political economy of such conflicts. In these cases the analysis of the political economy is essential to explore how actors adjust to war and the type of political and economic interlacing relations that they construct with one another.

14. The ability of actors to establish a positive political economy could help explain why after a period of the initiation of hostilities the conflict could protract for years. This analysis sheds new light on Collier's, Hoeffler's and Soderbom's contention that after the first year of conflict, the probability of peace is radically lower. See Collier and Hoeffler *On the Duration of Civil War.* Typescript (Washington, DC: World Bank Group, 1999), p. 16.

15. It is reported that in at least 600 municipalities of the 1,071 total, the guerrillas groups exercise various degrees of political influence, ranging from total control to occasional military operations.

CHAPTER 2

1. Antonio Negri, *The Politics of Subversion: A Manifesto for the Twenty-First Century* (Cambridge: Polity Press, 1999), p. 172

2. Ira Gollobin, *Dialectical Materialism: Its Laws, Categories and Practice* (New York: Petra, 1986), p. 164.

3. Ellen M. Immergut, "The Theoretical Core of the New Institutionalism," *Politics and Society* 26, no. 1 (March 1998): 20. (5–34)

4. Leon Zamosc, *The Agrarian Question and the Peasant Movement in Colombia* (London: Cambridge University Press, 1986), p. 9.

5. Gonzalo Sanchez, *Ensayos de Historia Social y Politica del Siglo XX* (Bogotá: Al Ancora Editores, 1984), pp. 130– .

6. Ibid.

7. Zamosc, p. 11.

8. See T. Lynn Smith, *Colombia: Social Structure and the Process of Development* (Gainesville: University of Florida Press, 1967); see also Orlando Fals Borda, *Historia de la Cuestion Agraria en Colombia* (Bogotá: Carlos Valencia Editores, 1985), pp. 83–84.

9. Cathrine LeGrand, *Frontier Expansion and Peasant Protest in Colombia 1850–1936* (Albuquerque: University of New Mexico Press, 1986), p. 68.

10. Ibid., p. 63

11. Ibid.

12. David Forgacs (ed.), *The Antonio Gramsci Reader: Selected Writings, 1916–1935* (New York: New York University Press, 2000), pp. 204–9.

13. Ibid., p. 205. Gramsci articulated three moments in the historical development of a hegemonic force that are relevant to our study. The first and most rudimentary moment is the economic-corporate level: a tradesman feels solidarity with another tradesman, a manufacturer with another manufacturer, and so on, but the tradesman does not feel solidarity with a manufacturer; in other words, the members of the professional group are conscious of its unity and homogeneity and the need to organize it but not in terms of the wider group. A second moment is when consciousness is reached of the solidarity of interests among all members of the social group but only in the economic sphere. During this second moment, the problem of the state is posed but only in allowing equal political-juridical with the ruling groups: the right is claimed to participate in legislation and administration, even to reform these without altering radically the structures. A third moment is that when one becomes aware of one's own corporate interests, in their present and future development, transcending the corporate limits of the merely economic group, and becoming the interests of other subordinate groups. This is the most purely political phase. It is the phase in which previously germinated ideologies become "party," come into confrontation and conflict, until one of them or at least a single combination of them to prevail, to gain the upper hand, to propagate itself over the whole social sphere, bringing about a union in the moral and intellectual areas as well as in the economic and political, posing all the questions around which the struggle rages not on a corporate but on a universal plane, thus creating the hegemony of a fundamental social group over a series of subordinate groups. Colombia's dominant social groups in the twentieth century were mainly in the second moment identified by Gramsci, but it was not until the end of the century that a potential hegemonic force was rising, an issue discussed in chapter 6.

14. *Dominant classes* is a term employed in this research to denote the strategic position occupied by social groups in a number of different institutional hierarchies, including, but not limited to, the organization of production. The land-owning class, for example, controlled not only an important part of the rural economy but political, professional, and social positions, as well as sectors outside of the rural economy. In this book, I employ the term in its plural because no single faction of the dominant class in Colombia exercised hegemony in the Gramscian sense for most of the twentieth century. This definition has been used by Ronald Chilcotte in "Book Review Coffee, Class, and Power in Central America," *Latin American Perspective* 26, no. 2 (March 1999), pp. 169–71.

15. See Jesus Antonio Bejarano, " El Despeque Cafetero 1900–1928," in Jose Antonio Ocampo, *Historia Economica de Colombia* (Bogotá: Tercer Mundo, 1994), pp. 173–207. The increase in coffee production led to the development of an internal market consolidated by new land transportation systems and trains tracks. For example in 1898 there were 593 km of trains tracks of which 71.4 was used for coffee transport; by 1914 it increased to 1.143 km of which 80.4 percent was used for coffee transportation, and by 1922 it increased to 1.571 km and to 89.0 percent.

16. See David Bushnell, *The Making of Modern Colombia: A Nation in Spite of Itself* (Berkeley: University of California Press, 1993), p. 185.

17. Jose Antonio Ocampo, in Ocampo, p. 239.

18. As quoted in Smith, *Colombia*, pp. 248–49.

19. Medofilo Medina, *La Protesta Urbana en Colombia en el Siglo XX* (Bogotá: Ediciones Aurora, 1984), pp. 45–59.

20. Ibid., p. 49

21. As quoted by LeGrand, op. cit. p. 156.

22. Ibid.

23. Ibid., p. 160.

24. Medina, *La Protesta Urabana*, p. 54.

25. For good documentation of the position of the industrial bourgeoisie against Lopez Pumarejo, see Eduardo Saenz Rovener, *La Ofensiva Empresarial: Industriales, Politicos y Violencia en los años 40 en Colombia* (Bogotá: Tercer Mundo, 1992).

26. For a typology of the socioeconmic condition of La Violencia, see Gonzalo Sanchez, *Guerra y Politica en la Sociedad Colombiana* (Bogotá: Ancora, 1991), pp. 121–228.

27. During La Violencia local intermediaries took advantage of the terror to accumulate land and capital at the expense of both small holders and the large landowners. See Carlos Miguel Ortiz Sarmiento, "The Business of the Violence: The Quindio in the 1950s and 1960s in Charles Bergquist, Ricardo Piñaranda, and Gonzalo Sanchez," *Violence in Colombia: The Contemporary Crisis in Historical Perspective* (Wilmington, Delaware: Basic Books, 1992), pp. 125–54; Sanchez, *Guerra Y Politica*, p. 125.

28. Leon Zamosc outlines two paths of capitalist development that maked the agrarian question: one is the landlord path, which features the concentration of land, which creates favorable conditions for a capitalist agriculture based on wage labor and large-scale production; and the other is the peasant path, which is characterized by small land holding, based on family labor. Leon Zamosc, *The Agrarian Question and the Peasant Movement*, p. 7.

29. Gonzalo Sanchez, *Guerra Y Politica en la Sociedad Colombiana*, pp. 125–27.

30. See Nazih Richani, *Dilemmas of Democracy and Political Parties in Sectarian Societies: The Case of the PSP in Lebanon* (New York: St Martin's, 1998); Arendt Lijphart, *The Politics of Accomodation: Pluralism and Democacy in the Netherlands* (Berkeley: University of California Press, 1968); Lijphart, *Democracy in Plural Socieities: A Comparative Exploration* (New Haven, Conn.: Yale University Press, 1977). The main argument presented by these three works is

that societies divided along regional, ethnic, religious, language, and class lines could be either mitigated by elite conciliatory behavior or exacerbated, leading to civil wars. The Lebanese civil war (1975–89) and the Colombian civil wars of the nineteenth century and La Violencia (1948–58) are examples of intra-elite conflicts, which were compounded by the interplay of social divisions based on religion, region, and class divides. Although in Colombia the predominant majority is Catholic, the secular versus sectarian conflict incarnated in the Conservative Party and Liberal Party assumed the functional equivalent of intersectarian conflicts, such the one in Lebanon, due to the ideological impulse that motivates the participants in these types of conflicts. Liberals, for example, were killed because they were perceived as atheist and against God, thus were less human than the Conservative followers.

31. See Daniel Pecaut, Cronicas de dos decadas, and

32. This analysis draws on the insights of Lewis Coser, *The Functions of Social Conflict* (New York: Free Press, 1956) and Georg Simmel, *Conflict* (Glencoe, Ill: Free Press, 1955).

33. This observation supports the view of Rueschemeyer, Stephens, and Stephens, *Capitalist Development and Democracy* (Chicago: University of Chicago Press, 1992).

34. Jorge Cardenas, president of FEDECAFE, interview with author, Bogotá 1996. He reflected on the power passing from the coffee elite to the industrial bourgeoisie and accordingly the FECEDAFE's diminishing influence within the state, while ANDI and the conglomerates gained the space in the 1980s and 1990s.

35. See Miguel Urrutia, "Gremios Y Politica Economica Y Democracia" manuscript, 1981. Urrutia argues that business groups in articulating public policy is overrated, he is inclined to overrate the role of the presidents. For an opposing view and one more consistent with my analysis, see, Bruce Bagley, "Political Power, Public Policy and the State in Colombia, Ph.D. dissertation, University of California, Los Angeles, 1979.

36. Zamosc, p. 36.

37. Ibid.

38. Marco Palacio, *Entre la Legitimidad y la Violencia, Colombia 1875–1994* (Bogotá: Editorial Norma, 1995), p. 194.

39. Ibid., p. 254.

40. Zamosc, p. 46.

41. Ibid.

42. Ibid.

43. Ibid.

44. Zamosc, p. 50.

45. It is noteworthy that Carlos Lleras Restrepo's relationship with the military was also tense. In 1969, when he fired the army commader Guillermo Pinzon Caicedo, brigade commanders of all twenty general officers in the Bogotá area were prepared to overthrow Lleras, but Pinzon told them "bluntly that he did not want a government brought down on his account." This incident reveals that Restrepo's government was under siege, and his reform efforts generated a strong front of opposition ranging from the military to large landlords, to con-

servative political forces. A very similar constellation of forces had faced Lopez Pumarejo couple of decades earlier. The account on the military coup was based on an airgram A-19, January 19, 1973, American Embassy in Bogotá, Department of State Bureau of Interamerican Affairs, National Archives.

46. See Jose Jairo Gonzalez Arias, *El Estigma de la Republicas Independientes 1955–1965* (Bogotá: CINEP, 1992).

47. Departamento Nacional de Planeacion, *La Paz: El Desafio para el Desarrollo* (Bogotá: Tercer Mundo, 1998), p. 122. From 1970 to 1975, ANUC led a vigorous land struggle in which it succeeded in redistributing about twenty-four thousand hectares from forty thousand owned by large landowners, but soon, paramilitary bands such los Pajaros and other family-based armed groups such as los Mendez, los Meza, and los Rodriguez, in alliance with the army, launched an assassination campaign against the peasants and the ANUC organizers. These massacres, the most famous in Ovejas, facilitated the emergence of the guerrillas in these areas. In Ovejas and in the region of Montes de Maria was where the so called Sincelejo radical faction of ANUC emerged in the 1970s. As late as February 2000, sixty-eight peasants were killed in the region: twenty near Ovejas (Sucre) and forty-eight in Salado by paramilitary groups.

48. Ibid.

49. Zamosc, p. 74.

50. American Embassy Bogotá, October 1971, Department of State, Telegram, National Archives.

51. American Consulate in Cali, November 19, 1971. Department of State, Airgram A-26, National Archives.

52. See Dietrich Rueschemeyer, Evelyne Huber Stephens and John Stephens, *Capitalist Development and Democracy* (Chicago: University of Chicago Press, 1992).

53. *Poverty in Colombia*, World Bank Country Study (Washington, D.C.: The World Bank, 1994), pp. 127–28.

54. Ibid. The term *narcobourgeoisie* introduced in this book refers to a fraction of the bourgeoisie that occupies the commanding economic position in the illicit drug industry. Narcobourgeoisie are owners of the means of production and the extractors of the surplus out of the peasantry, wage workers, and those working in their processing plants. The illicit nature of their economic activity affects their behavior and goals. A case in point is their struggle against the extradition of the captured narcotraffickers to the United States, and their staunch support of right-wing paramilitary groups (see chapter 5). The estimated wealth of key narcotraffickers is $76 billion which is about 30 percent of the country's total wealth. These are the estimates of Salmon Kalmanovitz, an economist and member of the Central Bank board of directors. See http://www.unam.mx/cronica/1996/a8096/int006.html.

55. This is based on the UNDCP study as quoted in *El Tiempo*, April 28, 2000. The income of narcotaffickers was estimated to constitute 2 to 3 percent of the country's GDP.

56. Frente a Los Programas Agrarios Conservador Y Liberal, Coordinador Nacional Agrario and Consejo Nacional Campesino, Document, Cartagena, Colombia September 22, 1999. Colombia was self-sufficient in rice production

in the early 1980s, but by 1998, it imported 275,000 tons. Although some improvements in local rice production were recorded in 2000, and imports were reduced, it is premature to conclude that the past trend was reversed. Similar trends in increasing imports are observed in products such as cotton, sugar, and milk. See Oryza Market Report, Colombia, March 13, 2000.

57. Occidental Petroleum, for example, was granted by the government license to drill at a site of about five hundred meters outside the U'was indigenous community (made up of five thousand to seven thousand people) *resquardos*, generating a serious confrontation and threatening the pollution of the community food supply. More important, however, is that their lands also will become targeted for appropriation. The Decree 1122 article of 1999 provides the government a legal mechanism to "redefine" the functions of the land granted to the indigenous communities, which might compromise the legal rights on which the U'was struggle with Occidental Petroleum is based. The peasants whose lands were located close to the Caño Limon pipeline lost their lands because of Law 160 of 1994 and the Public Order Law, which required clearing a five kilometer radius around oil wells and mines. These laws led to the dispossession of thousands of peasants who had their lots close these mines, wells, or pipelines.

58. Ibid.

CHAPTER 3

1. Peter Evans, Dietrich Rueschemeyer and Theda Skocpol, *Bringing the State Back in* (Cambridge: Cambridge University Press, 1985).

2. The regional and international security systems constructed by the United States made the military more dependent on the latter and more autonomous than other state institutions. Such a condition could explain the rapid propagation of the military coup in the region during the cold war era.

3. Alfonso Valdivieso, former attorney general during the Samper Government, interview with author, New York City, May 23, 2000.

4. Ibid.

5. See Francisco Leal Buitrago, *El Officio de La Guerra, La Seguridad Nacional en Colombia* (Bogotá: Tercer Mundo Editores-IEPRI, 1994); see also Framcisco Leal Buitrago and Leon Zamosc (eds.), *Al Filo del Caos, Crisis Politica en La Colombia de los anos 80* (Bogotá: Tercer Mundo Editores-IEPRI, 1991).

6. M-19 is an acronym for the April 19 Movement which emerged in the wake of the alleged rigged presidential election of 1970, in which Rojas Pinilla lost to Misael Pastrana.

7. Betancur succeeding Turbay, under whom the military gained substantial power under the "Estatuto de Seguridad," came to curtail some of these powers by appointing a general from the airforce to the post of minister of defense was offensive to the army. Betancur also antagonized the military by trying to diminish its influence in the police force. Finally, the president wanted to investigate the armed forces' involvement in the formation of paramilitary

groups such as Muertos a los Secustradores (MAS). See Buitrago, *El Oficio de La Guerra*, pp. 109–10.

8. Buitrago, *El Oficio de La Guerra*, p. 112. The analysis is also based on information provided by an informant.

9. Buitrago, "Defensa Y Seguridad Nacional en Colombia" in Francisco Leal Buitrago and Juan Gagriel Tokatlian,(eds) *Orden Mundial y Seguridad, Nuevos Desafíos Para Colombia y America* (Bogotá:Tercer Mundo Editores and IEPRI, 1994), pp. 162–172.

10. Rafael Pardo, *De Primera Mano: Colombia 1986–1994* (Bogotá: CEREC and Grupo Editorial Colombia, 1996) pp 355–56; Alfonso Valdivieso, then minister of education, presented to me another version in which he thought that the attack was authorized by Gaviria because a few days before the attack a rumor was circulated among the ministers that something "big is imminent." Alfonso Valdivieso, Colombia Ambassador to the UN, interview with author, New York City, May 23, 2000. It is believed that prior to the attack the military gave assurance to Gaviria of its ability to capture or kill the leadership of the FARC, then based in Casa Verde.

11. According to Rafael Pardo, then minister of defense, neither he nor the President gave the order to attack, but that attack came as part of delegating to the military issues of Public Order. Thus the military maintained its privilege of conducting counterinsurgency as deemed necessary. See also Pardo, p. 21. Pardo listed other sources of friction between President Batancur and the military, which include: the general amnesty that Betancur declared for the members of the guerrillas under which leaders of the M-19 were released, the truce that treated the guerrillas and the army as equals, the breach of the truce accords. which is on the army yet the government did not define its culpability.

12. Rafael Pardo, p. 133.

13. According to informants and experts consulted by this author the military accepted the peace agreement with the M-19, which paved the way to the Constitutional Assembly in 1991 after it was guaranteed that its privileges, such as managing its budget, justice system, and institution, were left intact.

14. Alfonso Valdivieso, interview.

15. It is important to note that during the Samper mandate, there were rumors of a coup d 'etat that did not materialize. A number of meetings took place between political opponents to Samper and military presonnel who also consulted with the United States Embassy to test the ground for a coup. The coup plotters did not field enough support within the military and without. This account is based on various interviews conducted in Bogotá during that period.

16. Some evidence is surfacing that in fact the military was planning a coup that was aborted because the army failed to gain the endorsement of Police Chief Rosso Jose Serrano, see Alirio Fernando Bustos, *Los Secretos del General Serrano* (Bogotá: Itermedio Editores Libro Virtual, 2000). Again the question is whether this episode was more "Sabre-rattling" to protect the institutional privileges of the military.

17. Interview with informant from the V Brigade, November 1999.

18. In some aspects, this crisis is reminiscent of one that led to the removal of General Pinzon during Carlos Lleras Restrepo's Presidency, which

was caused by the "civilian meddling" with the military budget.

19. This information is based on interviews with a member of the Constitutional Assembly, Bogotá, October 1997.

20. See Eduardo Pizarro, "Reforma Militar Y Democratizacion Politica" in Francisco Leal, *En Busca de La Estabilidad Perdida* (Bogotá: Tercer Mundo Editores and IEPRI, 1995), p. 205.

21. U.S. Embassy in Bogotá, airgram to Department of State, January 19, 1973, A-19. Department of State Bureau of Interamerican Affairs, 1973, National Archives, NND969035.

22. There are a few exceptions under which the military embarked on a sustained offensive over several months in Cauca and Uraba against the M-19 and the EPL respectively. Both campaigns were successful but were not replicated, nor did these campaigns lead to a change in the overall structure or strategy of the armed forces. In 1973, the military also carried a major offensive in which about 30,000 personnel participated against about 150 combatants of the ELN in Anori, Antioquia, which is considered one of the most important achievements of the military ever since its counterinsurgency. The 1973 Anori operation decimated the ELN in northeast Antioquia, and it took the ELN about a decade to recover from that blow. There was a common denominator to these main operations: whenever the guerrillas threatened the interests of dominant local elites and classes, such as the banana and sugar agribusinesses in Uraba and Cauca or the Antioquia's dominant groups, presidents were pressured to act and to put the armed forces into action. But these flare ups remained intermittent episodes and did not change the overall dynamic of the war system, nor did they alter the comfortable impasse.

23. In international terms, there is a ratio of 1:3 between operation and administrative personnel. In Colombia is one of the highest in the world is 1:6. See *El Tiempo,* April 9, 2000.

24. See *Poder Y Dinero,* June 1997. p. 35

25. *El Tiempo,* August 31, 1997, 8A.

26. Ibid.

27. For example, during 1992 and 1997 about $12 million were lost, possibly siphoned to private pockets. In 1997, another case surfaced, involved $6.7 million in the purchase of camping equipment that was never delivered. As a result, twenty five officers, including six generals, were investigated for corruption. Many other cases were recorded, such one of military housing that involved kickbacks and commissions in the amount $33 thousand. See *El Tiempo,* October 28, 1998. 3A.

28. During 1991 and 1994, generals salaries increased by 400.7 percent and lieutenants increased by 200 percent. The personnel serving in areas classified as "red areas" receive a 35% increase in their salaries for the risk. See Richani, "The Political Economy of Violence."

29. *Poder Y Dinero,* June 1997. P. 29.

30. See *Alternativa* 8 (March 15–April 15, 1997): 32–33. Most likely Gaviria's government was trying to appease the military in order to facilitate the changes he was planning to introduce in civil-military relations since most of these moneys were not destined to upgrade armament nor to change the defensive posture of the armed forces.

31. Ibid.

32. Ibid.

33. *Poder Y Dinero,* June 1997. P. 28

34. Department of State, Supplementary Annex to FY 1972 Colombia CASP, National Archives. NND 969035.

35. Ibid., p. 3.

36. In another document also recently declassified by the Department of State, in a telegram from the U.S. embassy in Bogotá, the writer eloquently expressed the degree of the U.S. influence on the military by writing "I think greatest influence on Colombia military in terms of attitudes toward US policy objectives has come through training courses in the U.S. and Panama. At present of nine two-star officers (including army, navy, air and police) six took courses in the US. Of thirty-four one star officers, twenty eight studied in the US, four in Panama, and only two have not." Review of U.S. Military Presence in Latin America, Secret Section, December, 16, 1970, Bogotá 5767.

37. See for example, Francisco Leal Buitrago, *El Oficio de La Guerra,* Eduardo Pizarro Leongomez, La Profesionalizacion Militar en Colombia (1,2,3), no. 1, 2, and 3, 1987 – 88; Andres Davila Ladron de Guevara, El Ejercito Colombiano: Un Actor Mas de La Violencia," in Jaime Arocha, Fernando Cubides, and Myrian Jimeno, *Las Violencias: Inclusion Creciente* (Bogotá: CES, 1998), pp. 92–118.

38. For a review of the literature on National Security Doctrine, see Cesar Torres del Rio, *Fuerzas Armadas y Seguridad Nacional* (Bogotá: Planeta, 2000).

39. For example, see Alfredo Rangel Suarez, *Colombia: Guerra en el Fin de Siglo* (Bogotá; Tercer Mundo and Universidad de Los Andes, 1998), pp. 81–94. Suarez argues that the military strategy is one of elimination.

40. The privatization of security is part of a global trend to subcontract the maintenance of "public order" to private companies. But in Colombia, since the country is in the midst of a civil war this process acquires its own peculiar character since it is tied in with the war system. In the United States, for example, until 1970 there were still more public than private police. The ratio was 1.4:1. By the mid 1990s, there are three times as many private as public police. General Motors has a force of 4,200 private police alone. In Britain, the number of private guards has risen from 80,000 in 1971 to 300,000 by 1997, roughly twice the number of public police. Similar trends are observed in Canada and Austria where the ratio is 1:2. See *The Economist,* April 19, 1997.

41. See Leal, *En Busca de La Estabilidad Perdida,* p. 202.

42. See Richani, "The Political Economy of Violence, p. 56.

43. See Charles Tilly, "War Making and State Making as Organized Crime" in Peter Evans, Dietrich Rueschemeyer and Theda Skocpol, (eds.), *Bringing the State Back in* (Cambridge: Cambridge University Press, 1985), p. 181.

44. Richani, "The Political Economy of Violence"; see also chapter 5.

45. *Alternativa,* (March 15–April 15, 1997): 10 – 16.

46. The hegemonic crisis of the state reached new levels when General Nestor Ramirez alleged that some employees in the office of Attorney General Jaime Bernal Cuellar are guerrillas because of their investigation of the military's human rights abuses and their possible links with paramilitary groups. This is

not an isolated case but rather a pattern reflecting deep inter-institutional disputes representing the fragmentation of the state apparatus. See *El Tiempo,* December 14, 1999. See also Leal, *El Officio de La Guerra.*

47. The negative economic effects of the civil war will be discussed in chapter 7, but for now it is important to note that by 1997, the economy was growing at a lower pace and by 1999 it reached negative growth of 5 percent.

48. As quoted in the *New York Times,* November 6, 1998.

49. See chapter 5.

50. It is estimated that multinational companies' security costs average 4 percent of the companies' operating costs in the developing world. In Colombia the costs are substantially higher, 10 percent. This money is the subject of competition between local and international actors. This figure is taken from *New York Times,* November 6, 1998, p. C3.

51. An informant from BP security revealed to this author yet another facet of a case where a security officer from a multinational company was selling information about the premise of the company to the guerrillas. Interview with author, Bogotá, September 1998.

52. This information is based on the American Consul James Cooper's dispatches, Medellin August 28, 1973. Amb/DCM1 Def.Att, pol.2. National Archives.

53. In comparative terms, the percentages that the respective governments in Colombia allocated to defense were less than Peru, Guatemala, and El Salvador during the high days of their respective insurgencies: Peru dedicated 21 percent of its government budget to defense in 1980 and 11.2 percent in 1990; Guatemala 10.6 percent in 1980 and 15.2 percent in 1995 (a year before the peace treaty; and El Salvador 8.8 percent in 1980 increasing to 24.5 percent in 1990, (a year prior to peace agreement); and in Colombia only 6.7 percent in 1980 increasing to 8.7 percent in 1995.

54. "The Ties That Bind: Colombia and the Military-Paramilitary Links," *Human Rights Watch 2000,* p. 6. What is noteworthy in the case of the Calima paramilitary is the parallels it has with the Muerte alos Secuestradores (MAS) which in turn were instrumental in the formation of the Paras in Puerto Boyaca. The parallel is that Calima group was formed after the ELN seized 140 worshipers from Cali. Among those taken were suspected drug traffickers believed to be part of the business established by the jailed Cali Cartel leaders. The Guerrillas' demand for ransom for some of the hostages is reminiscent of the M-19 kidnapping the sister of the Ochoas' narcotraffickers seeking a ransom for her release, which triggered the creation of the MAS.

55. "The Ties That Bind."

56. It is estimated that more than three thousand Union Patriotica (UP) members were killed since the mid-1980s. The UP was set up in 1985 during the Betancur government as a legal leftist political movement.

57. "The Ties That Bind."

58. Interviews with ELN and FARC commanders by author, Bogotá and Itaqui, November 1997 and November, 1998.

59. Francisco Thoumi, *Poltical Economy and Illegal Drugs in Colombia* (Boulder, Colorado: Lynne Reinner, 1995).

60. Pablo Escobar for example established in 1982 a political movement called "Civismo en Marcha" in Medellin under which he won a seat in the Congress. Rodriguez Gacha on his part established a political base through his paramilitary organization in the Middle Magdalena, Meta, and Llanos Orientales. Pablo Escobar became known in his circles and the popular barrios in Medellin as "el Doctor" while Gacha known as "el Mejicano" "Don," both titles granted because of the admiration of their followers and benefactors.

61. Dario Betancourt and Martha Garcia, *Contrabandistas, Marinmberos y Mafiosos: Historia Social de la Mafia Colombiana 1965–1992* (Bogotá: Tercer Mundo Editores, 1994), p. 191.

62. Francisco Thoumi, "Corruption and Drug-Trafficking: General Considerations and References to Colombia," unpublished paper presented at the United States War College Conference on Colombia, Pennsylvania Carlisle, December 1998, p. 15.

63. For a detailed account of the role of the military in helping to set up a paramilitary group in Mapiripan, see *El Espectador*, "Special Report," March 10, 2000.

64. The air force was involved in a number of uncovered trafficking operations to the U.S. including one that involved the presidential plane.

65. In early 2000 the Bill Clinton's administration was pushing for 1.6 billion in aid ($1.3 billion was later approved that year) to Colombia of which more than 70 percent is designated for military purposes. The United States is actively involved in creating mobile army units, training personnel, which in effect is reinventing a new more modern armed forces to accommodate the regional security interests of the United States. It is also believed that the U.S. military personnel—including special forces, subcontractors, and mercenaries—directly involved in the conflict could reach two thousand.

66. *El Espectador*, November 20, 1998, p. 4A.

CHAPTER 4

1. This is based on my interview with guerrilla leaders from ELN and FARC.

2. Borrowing the expression from Jacques Derrida, *Specters of Marx: The State of the Debt, the Work of Mourning and the New International* (London: Routledge, 1994).

3. This historical account is based on FARC literature. See Jacobo Arenas, *Cese el Fuego: Una Historia Politica de las FARC* (Bogotá: Oveja Negra, 1985); Declaracion Politica de la Octava Conferencia Nacional FARC-EP 1993.

4. Ibid.

5. Yazid Arteta, FARC commander, interview with author, Bogotá, November 1998. See also Alfredo Molano, *Truchas y Fusiles* (Bogotá: IEPRI-El Ancora Editores, 1994).

6. Arteta, Ibid.

7. The only notable development is that in April 2000 FARC appointed a woman commander to the Thematic Committee in charge of negotiation in San Vicente del Caguan.

8. The *secretariado* (secretariat) is the highest position in the FARC's organizational structure, followed by estado mayor central, which is composed of twenty-five commanders of the blocs. The majority of those are of peasant origins. In the lower echelons, almost all leaders are of peasant origins. Yazid Arteta, interview with author.

9. Timothy P Wickman-Crowley, *Guerrillas and Revolutions in Latin America: A Comparative Study of Insurgents and Regimes Since 1956* (Princenton, NJ: Princeton University Press), pp. 327–39; see also Cynthia McClintock, *Revolutionary Movements in Latin America: El Salvador's FMLN and Peru's Shining Path* (Washington, D.C.: USIP, 1998), chapter 6.

10. Felipe Torres and Francisco Galan, interview with author.

11. Based on interviews with ex-guerrillas from M-19 and EPL.

12. Sergio de Zubiria, Member of the Communist Party Central Committee, interview with author, Bogotá December 1998.

13. The hacienda remuneration system was based on paying labor by taking part of their product-use value. Labor was not remunerated by money-exchange value.

14. Karl Marx, *Pre-Capitalist Economic Formations* (New York: International, 1989), p. 67.

15. The role of the FARC with regard to the indigenous population in Marquetalia and U'was in Casanare has yielded mixed results. While FARC's mere military presence in their areas acted as a deterrent or dissuaded foreign intrusion allowing the communities to safeguard their way of life, FARC's recruitments from these communities and attempts to exercise its authority over them generated conflicts that often turned violent. In Marquetalia, for example, where FARC originated, the relationship was conflictive until 1997, when FARC and the Paeces signed a peace agreement. The conflict had begun in 1964 when some Paeces acted as guides for the military during their operation against the peasant armed leagues, referred to as the "Independent Republics." For more details about the 1997 pact, see Maria Cristina Caballero, "El Pacto," *Cambio 16*, no. 218 (August 18–25, 1997): 18–23. A similar case took place in the U'was in Arauca. The U'was, however, have a better relationship with the ELN, since this latter group has been perceived as less intrusive and did not challenge the communal structure of power. In the case of the Afro-Colombian community, however, the relationship was less conflictive, and FARC managed to establish roots in the Chocó, a main concentration area of this community.

16. Alfredo Molano, "Violence and Land Colonization" in Charles Berquist, Ricardo Peñaranda and Gonzalo Sanchez, *Violence in Colombia: The Contemporary Crisis in Historical Perspective* (Wilmigton, Delaware: Scholarly Resources, 1992), p. 198.

17. Ibid.

18. Jesus Bejarano Avila et al., *Colombia: Inseguridad, Violencia y Desempeño Economico en las Areas Rurales* (Bogotá: FONADE and Universidad Externado de Colombia, 1997), p. 134.

19. Front 10 was the only front that operated in Arauca in the 1980s; it was supposed to extract $5 million. FARC, Memo, 1989.

20. Ocampo, *Historia Economica de Colombia* p. 253.

21. The colonos' support of FARC can be explained using Samuel Popkin's argument that peasants are rational utility maximizers who respond to individual incentives offered by the insurgency. The guerrillas offer them protection, security, employment, and services. See Popkin, *The Rational Peasant: The Political Economy of Rural Society in Vietnam* (Berkeley: University of California Press, 1979).

22. Yazid Arteta interview.

23. Arteta explained that before 1996 there were unwritten customary laws that regulated the social and economic spheres and the penal code. In the case of the Rio Caguan, the written laws were introduced under what FARC called "Normas de Convivencia Ciudadana." These norms are applied in all areas where FARC operates.

24. See Jose Gonzalez Roberto Ramirez, Alberto Valencia, and Reinaldo Barbosa, *Conflictos Regionales-Amazonia y Orinoquia* (Bogotá: FESCOL and IEPRI, 1998).

25. As quoted in *El Tiempo*, May 10, 1999.

26. Jose Romero, a peasant/miner from Seranias de San Lucas, south Bolivar, and a spokeperson during their sit-in in Bogotá, interview with author, Bogotá, September 1998. See also chapter 5.

27. This estimate of land acquisition is based on Alejandro Reyes' data.

28. In this context it is important to note that Carlos Castaño presents his paramilitary groups as representatives of the "middle class," and in its defense he articulates the goal of his group. Carlos Castaño, Semana, March 6, 2000. This observation is also based on the Magdalena Medio studies conducted by the Program of Development and Peace.

29. See Nazih Richani, *Dilemmas of Democracy and Political Parties in Sectarian Societies: The Case of the PSP, 1949–1996* (New York: St. Martin's Press, 1998).

30. Ibid.

31. Charles Tilly, "War Making and State Making as Organized Crime" in Peter Evans, Dietrich Rueschemeyer, and Theda Skocpol, *Bringing the State Back In* (Cambridge: Cambridge University Press, 1985), p. 181.

32. See Thomas Biersteker and Cynthia Weber (eds.), *The State Sovereignty as Social Construct* (Cambridge: Cambridge University Press, 1996).

33. For the figures on Shining Path and FMLN see Cynthia McClintock, *Revolutionary Movements in Latin America: El Salavador's FMLN and Peru's Shining Path* (Washington, D.C.: USIP, 1998), p. 73.

34. Informe de Desarrollo Humano Para Colombia, 1998 (Bogotá: Departamento Nacional de Planeacion y PNUD, 1998), p. 143.

35. *El Tiempo*, May 11, 1999.

36. Agrarian bank symbolizes the state bias in favor of large landowners and thus became one of the most favorite target of the guerrillas.

37. See informe special, *Semana*, March 8, 1999, vol. 879. This data is based on information provided by the military.

38. See Thoumi. In 1987 the coca production amounted to 24,000 ha, and in 1989 it increased to 42,000, declining to 40,000 in 1990 an increasing again to 79,500 by 1997. World Wide Statistics.

39. For a detailed account of the history of illicit drug plantations in Colombia, see Francisco Thoumi, *Economia Politica y Narcotrafico* (Bogotá: Tercer Mundo, 1994), chapter 4.

40. This account is based on FARC Seventh Conference and an interview with FARC informants.

41. FARC, Pleno 1989: Conclusiones sobre Plan Militar Estrategico de 8 años, Organizacion, Escuela Nacional Y finanzas. Mimeo.

42. Ibid.

43. Ricardo Vargas (ed.), *Drogas, Poder y Region en Colombia*, volumes 1 and 2 (Bogotá: CINEP, 1994).

44. See Robert Jervis, *System Effects Complexity in Political and Social Life* (Princeton: Princeton University Press, 1999), p. 48.

45. Yazid Arteta, FARC commader interview with author; Felipe Torres and Francisco Galan, ELN commanders, interview with author.

46. This observation is based on my interviews with Jorge Visbal, President of the National Federation of Cattle Raisers (FEDEGAN), Bogotá, Colombia, December 1998, and also President of SAC Jesus Antonio Bejarano. These two organizations and their associates at the regional and municipal levels represent the core interests of the large landowners.

47. High-ranking military informant, Bogotá, September, 1998.

48. FARC informant operating in Bogotá, interview with author, Bogotá, October 1998.

49. This is based on interviews with FARC informants conducted in Barancabermeja and Bogotá in November 1998.

50. FARC for the first time in its history declared in April 2000 that every Colombian with an income of $1 million and more must pay a 10 percent tribute to the guerrillas. This is one additional step to consolidate FARC's status of belligerence competing with state authority complementing its guerrilla army with a command structure similar to the regular army, control part of the national territory, particularly that the government ceded to initiate peace talks in 1998 (a territory of forty-two thousand kilometers, double the size of El Salvador) with a population of one hundred thousand, declaring an independent judicial system in the municipalities under its control (253 municipalities), finally increasing the regional and international recognition of FARC as a defacto belligerent force. It is worth mentioning that the Venezuelan government has been inclined toward granting FARC a belligerent status. See *El Tiempo*, May 2, 2000.

51. Juan Dios Castilla Amel who participated in the negotiation of both cases, interview with author, Baranacabermeja, August 25, 1998.

52. This observation is based on fifteen interviews with five peasants, three university professors and two students, and five workers conducted by author in Bucaramanga, Sangil, Barrichara, and Barancabermeja between August 1997 and September 1998. In terms of gender distribution, five women were interviewed.

53. Among its leaders were three priests, Domingo Laín, Camillo Torres, and Manuel Perez. This latter was its maximum leader until his death in December 1997.

54. See "Che" Guevara, Ernesto, *Guerrilla Warfare* (Lincoln and London: University of Nebraska Press, 1985).

55. In San Vicente de Chucuri, an area of land colonization, the ELN managed to build a social base of support after the 1960s. Jose Ayala and Heliodoro Ochoa both were from San Vicente. San Vicente is well known for the Bolshevic rebellion of 1929 and also for its support to Gaitan. The father of Nicolas Rodriquez Bautista, the current leader of ELN, was a Liberal supporter of Gaitan, who later became a supporter of the ELN was also from San Vicente. See Nicolas Rodrigues Bautista, interview in *ELN: Una Historia Contada a dos voces* (Bogotá: Rodriguez Quito Editores, 1996), pp. 27–59.

56. Carta Militante no. 15, 9/12, Segundo Congreso del ELN Deciembre 1989.

57. Felipe Torres and Francisco Galan, ELN Commanders, taped interview with author November 28, 1997.

58. Ibid. Some other factors that could have played a role in the manner political/ideological differences were resolved were the highly authoritarian character of the then ELN leader Fabio Vasquez and his lack of confidence in his comrades in arms. See Walter J. Broderick, *El Guerrillero Invisible* (Bogotá: Intermedio Editores, 2000).

59. *El Tiempo*, May 19, 1999.

60. Camilo Granada and Leonardo Rojas, "Los Costos del Conflicto Armado 1990–1994" *Planeacion and Desarrollo* 36 (4) (October–December, 1995): 119–51; *El Tiempo*, January 6, 1999. In comparative terms, the ELN annual income is much superior to that of the FMLN, who operated on $50 to $65 million, mainly from kidnapping wealthy businessmen and an annual budget of $5 million; ELN operational costs are estimated at $16 million per year. According to Cynthia McClintock, Shining Path cited estimates ranging from $20 to $500 per year by taxing drug traffickers in the Upper Hualaga valley. Additional amounts were obtained from taxes levied on businesses and citizens; smaller amounts were probably received from various support groups. See Cynthia McClintock, *Revolutionary Movements in Latin America: El Salvador's FMLN and Peru's Shining Path* (Washington, D.C.: USIP, 1998), p. 63.

61. The ELN denies taxing narcotraffickers protection rent, but in areas of its operations such as south Bolivar, and North Santander (Catatumbo), there are coca plantations of 2,800 hectares in La Gabarra (North Santander) and 2,800 in la Serranía de San Lucas (south Bolivar) according to CIA estimates of 1999. The estimates of the number of coca growers is based on a study of Programa Desarrollo y Paz on which it was estimated that about one thousand peasants were involved in coca plantations. From that figure I inferred a similar number of peasants in the Gabarra due to their similar terrains and property structures. In these areas operate fronts of FARC as well.

62. The army claims that from 1997 through 1999 it captured about one thousand of the ELN guerrillas, including some commanders, and about one hundred deserted. These figures, however, most likely are inflated, but there is a

consensus among experts that the ELN has been weakened in the late 1990s. See *El Tiempo*, February 1999, p. 5.

63. *El Tiempo*, April 18, 1997, p. 3A.

64. Carlos Fuente, ex-commander and Member Estado Mayor of EPL, interview with author, Bogotá, November 1994.

65. Maria Victoria A. Uribe, *Ni Canto de Gloria Ni Canto Funebre* (Bogotá: Cinep, 1994), p. 35.

66. FARC imposes a 10 percent tax on local municipalities that should be paid in different forms, such as providing provisions such toothpaste, boots, and food. Municpalities under guerrilla influence also are pressed to subcontract public works to companies owned by guerrilla sympathizers or front companies owned by the guerrillas.

67. This finding is based on interviews conducted with peasants from North Santander, south Bolivar, and Putumayo.

68. Juvencel Duque, officer in Programa Desarrollo y Paz Magdalana Medio, interview with author, Barancabermeja, November 27, 1998.

69. In comparative terms, the FMLN of El Salvador at its highest point in 1989 controlled about 15 percent out of a total 262 municipalities; and the Shining Path at its peak controlled about 28 percent of Peru's municipalities. Figures for El Salvador and Peru are taken from Cynthia McClintock, *Revolutionary Movements in Latin America*, p. 73.

70. As cited in *El Espectador*, November 16, 1998, p. 6–A.

71. See *El Tiempo*, May 20, 1999.

CHAPTER 5

1. Dario Betancourt and Martha Garcia, *Contrabadistas, Marimberos y Mafiosos* (Bogotá: Tercer Mundo, 1994), p. 48.

2. Ibid.

3. See Betancourt and Garcia, p. 54.

4. Representatives of cocaleros from Caqueta and Putumayo, interview with author Bogotá, 1997.

5. *El Tiempo* September 7, 1997, p. 4E. See also *El Espectador* May 29, 1995, p. 10A; News Agency New Colombia, "Farmers are Victims in Colombian Drug War" September 23, 1998. P. 2.

6. Camilo Echandia, "La Amapola en el Marco de las Economias del ciclo Corto," *Analisis Politico* 27 (January-April 1996).

7. Ibid.

8. In Caqueta alone it is estimated that 135,000 (out of 230,000 of total population) almost 60 percent of people live on the coca economy. Jorge Devia, governor of Putumayo, *Semana* December 14, 1999. Sergio Uribe Ramirez in a study based on 1994 coca data production which ranged between 70 and 80 hectares estimated that 38,200 families depended on coca for their livelihood. Sergio Uribe Ramirez " Los Cultivos Ilicitos en Colombia" en Franciso Thoumi et al., (eds.), *Drogas Ilicitas en Colombia: Su Impacto Economico, Politico y Social* (Bogotá: PNUD, 1997), p. 97; Alvaro Camacho using police estimates

puts the figure at 550.000 persons who are involved in coca production this figure includes land owners, colonos, recollectors (raspachines), and wage laborers. See Alvaro Camacho & Francisco Leal Buitrago, *Armar La Paz es Desarmar La Guerra: Herramientas Para Lograr la Paz* (Bogotá: Fescol, IEPRI & CEREC, 1999), p. 272. Hence if we add the coca producers and those who plant poppy seeds and marijuana and traders of the ingredients needed to process the coca into cocaine, the figure will be close to a million colonos, small peasants, and agricultural workers partially or totally depend on illicit plantations.

9. This finding is based on a number of field studies conducted in the Middle Magadalena, south Bolivar, Putumayo, and Guaviare that were made avialable to me. Particularly the studies of the Programa desarrollo y Paz and the Oscar Arcila and Adrina Rodriguez study on Guaviare from the Institute of Amazonic Studies. The price of coca paste has declined from a 1.2 million pesos (about $600) to 900 thousand pesos ($450) in 1999 so it will take the peasant about two years to generate some profits, (this is based on the Putumayo study.

10. Clifford Kraus, "Peru's Drug Success Erode as Traffickers Adapt," *New York Times,* August 19, 1999, p. A3.

11. Clifford Kraus, " Bolivia at Risk of Some Unrests, Is Making Big Gains in Eradicating Coca" *New York Times* May 9, 1999, p. A6.

12. This observation is based on my field observation and interviews with cocaleros from Putumayo, North Santander, and south Bolivar. In fact, in one area I found evidence that the guerrillas are encouraging peasant to substitute illegal crops to legal one. That case was presented in Micoahumado (Middle Magdalena).

13. Francisco Thoumi, *Economia Politica Y Narcotrafico*, p. 133.

14. Interviews with cocaleros; see also Oscar Arcila y Adriana Rodríguez, researchers of Instituto Amazónico de Investigaciones Científicas (Sinchi) on Guaviare. In this study the rearchers found that cocaleros increasing costs of production due to fumigation and other causes have made their subsistence economy similar to the returns they obtained from traditional crops.

15. See Latin America after a Decade of Reforms. Economic And Social Progress in Latin America: 1997 Report (Washington, D.C.: Interamerican Develpoment Bank, 1997), p. 232.

16. Roberto Steiner Sampedro, "Los Ingresos de Colombia Producto de la Exportacion de La Drogas Illicitas" *Coyuntura Economica,* 16 (4) (December 1996): pp. 73–106.

17. Fanny Kertzman as quoted in *El Tiempo,* December 17, 1999

18. Based on interviews with Maria Mercedes De Cuellar, member of the board of directors of the Central Bank, September 1997.

19. Ibid.

20. My choice of defining narcotraffickers as narcobourgeoisie is to denote that this emerging social group not only managed to accumulate vast economic resources which are mostly invested in the "legal economy," but also struggled to legitimate itself through seeking political space. That is to say, its behavior has shifted from a class by itself to a class for itself, conscious of its class and political interest. Hence members' behavior merits treating them as a distinct strata within the bourgeoisie. In the course of this book, the two terms *narcotraffickers*

194   NOTES

and *narcobourgeoisie* are used interchangeably. See also note 54 in chapter 2.

21. Thoumi, *Economia Politica y Narcotrafico*, pp. 165, 215–223.

22. Ibid., pp. 48–9. The government policy toward the narcodollars was supported by the Association of Industrial Groups (ANDI) which argued that narcotraffickers and their fortunes should be amnestied as were the guerrillas during the Betancur government. The ANDI position was supported by the Farmers Association of Colombia (SAC) and the Financial Corporation of the Valle, Association of Small Industrial Enterprises (ACOPI). This demostrates that the state drug policy during the 1980s received the support of key sectors of the dominant class.

23. Evidence has surfaced that at least two influential members of the Congresito Martha Montoya y Álvaro Villarraga, the legislative body that came after the Constituyente in 1991, were involved with the ex-comptroller of the Cali cartel, Guillermo Pallomari, and acted as representatives of the narcotraffickers.

24. Large cattle raisers represented by Acdegam, representatives from the army battalion Barbula, and Texas Petroleum attended the meeting which established paramilitary organization.

25. For security purposes, the name of the high-ranking officer is withheld. In November 1998 I went in a field trip to the Middle Magdalena to interview one of the local paramilitary leaders, and I was surprised that the meeting place was sandwiched between two army positions and that the army patrolling the area does not harass these groups. When, I inquired about the matter I was informed that a good number of paramilitaries live and work in the state's oil company, Ecopetrol, particularly in its drilling plants under the "watchful" eyes of the military forces.

26. Interview with a Colombian army officer, interview with author, Bogotá, August 1998.

27. As quoted by William Ramirez Tobon, *Uraba: Los Inciertos Confines de Una Crisis* (Bogotá: Tercer Mundo, 1997), p. 126.

28. In the 1990s, paramilitaries held at least three summit meetings attended by the representatives from the different regions. A junta of 13 members act as a coordinating council which Carlos Castaño lead. In 1995, the meeting was held in territories controlled by Victor Carranza's paramilitaries and a manifesto was issued in which they declared their support of the military in its fight of the insurgency, and that they constitute a rightist armed political force formed to defend the prevailing socioeconomic order. In the document the United Self-Defense Forces of Colombia (AUC) referred that it receives the logistical and material support of the armed forces, and that the large land owners, cattle ranchers, and some business groups help in financing its project.

29. This largely depended on the type of class differentiation in the municipality which allows the emergence of social groups opposed politically and ideologically to the guerrillas that were affected by the guerrillas protection rent extraction. Mauricio Romero in his study of the Middle Magdalena noted four critical variables that have entered into the formation of a political base for paramilitaries in a number of municipalities: the existence of military and police stations, a well-formed political elite, and differentiated class structure punctu-

ated by the guerrilla protection rent extraction from the more affluent classes. Cases in point are Santa Rosa del Sur, Morales, and Cimitarra.

30. Maria Victoria Uribe Alarcon, *Limpiar La Tierra: Gerra y Poder entre Esmeralderos* (Bogotá: CINEP, 1992), pp. 92–93.

31. See Thoumi, *La Economia Politica del Narcotrafico*, p. 147.

32. This finding is based on testimonies provided to this author by peasant groups from the mentioned areas. It was also cross-validated by human rights groups. See also *Pacificar la Paz Comision de Superacion de la Violencia* (Bogotá: Instituto de Estudios Politicos y Relaciones Internacionales, National University, CINEP and Commision de Juristas, 1992), p. 136–7. In Putumayo "los Masetos" de Gonzalo Rodriguez Gacha established close relations with the local police force that many claimed operated under Gacha orders. This was thanks for the vast economic returns of cocaine trafficking that his men controlled. Moreover, Human Rights Watch 2001 report confirms that some officers are on the payroll of the AUC and salaries are based on rank. Each captain receives between $2,000 and $3,000 per month, majors get $2,500, and a lieutenant receives $1,500 (Human Rights Watch, September 2001).

33. For a account for the formation of the auto defenses of Cordoba and Uraba see William Ramirez Tobon, *Los Inciertos Confines de Una Crisis*, (Bogotá: Planeta, 1997); see also Clara Ines Garcia, *Uraba: Region, Actores y Conflicto 1960–1990* (Bogotá: CEREC, 1996).

34. Alejandro Reyes Posada; and interviews.

35. This figure is widely used by military sources and by experts.

36. In a televised interview Carlos Castaño conceded that 70 percent of his group financing comes from narcotraffickers and also claimed that he has a force of 11,000 men, which most experts believe is an inflated figure. I accepted the commonly used estimate of five thousand to eight thousand men.

37. Police reports as quoted in *El Tiempo*, May 6, 1999.

38. The paramilitary groups of Castaño and his allies operate cocaine processing plants in Aguachica, Rio Negro, Cimitarra, and Puerto Parra, all in the Middle Magdalena according to Juvencel Duque, Middle Magdalena director of the Program Development and Peace, in a talk he presented at George Washington University, May 3, 2000.

39. In late December 1999, the antinarcotics police discovered another major coca processing plant in Tarraza' Antioquia, with an estimated value of $2 million and with a weekly production capacity of a ton of cocaine. This plant was run by paramilitaries linked with the Castaño who operates in the region.

40. Carlos Castaño, televised interview, February 2000; according to police estimates as cited by El Tempo, "Coca Divide Las Autodefen sas," December 2, 2001.

41. Thoumi, *La Economia Politica del Narcotrafico*, p. 134.

42. Ibid., p. 163.

43. Interview with peasants from Guaviare, Putumayo, and Middle Magdalena.

44. This figure is from Direccion Nacional de Estupefacientes, Bogotá, 2000.

45. The coca production in south Bolivar supplanted marijuana because the soil and climate were more suitable for the first. This process started in the mid-1970s and from that date on, coca became one of the main cash crops in

196   NOTES

the area. For example, San Pablo, 75 percent of its income depends on coca production.

46. *Semana,* February 29, 2000. The price calculations of coca paste for 1998 are based on my interviews with coca growers from the region, September 1998.

47. Coca growers from south Bolivar interview with author, Bucaramanga, September 1998.

48. Ibid.

49. See Ricardo Vargas (ed.), *Drogas Y Region en Colombia: Impactos Locales y Conflictos* vol. 2 (Bogotá: CINEP, 1995), p. 196.

50. Ibid; and according to a recent study of the UNDCP they put the figure at 4.4 million hectares that are owned by narcotraffickers with a estimated value of $2.4 billion as quoted in *El Tiempo,* April 28, 2000.

51. *El Tiempo,* May 10, 1999.

52. According Sergio Uribe, a leading expert on coca production in Colombia, commercial coca plantations are those that are those production units of 2 and more hectares with the capacity to produce between 1.6 and 2.8 kilograms of coca paste per hectare per crop with an average of five crops per year. And with the technology employed by these plantations they can extract between eighteen and twenty two grams per arroba of coca. Uribe calculated that in 1994 these commercial plantations constituted about 48 percent of the country's plantations. The commercial plantations employ seasonal wage laborers (raspachines). The remaining 52 percent of the areas were mainly cultivated by small peasants. See Sergio Uribe Ramirez "Los Cultivos ilicitos en Colombia' en Francisco Thoumi, *Drogas Ilicitas en Colombia,* pp. 69–70. In zones of conflict such as Putumayo, Caqueta, Guaviare and Meta, the large commercial plantations increased in the 1990s and often are operated by parmilitary groups.

53. A rentier economy is one where capital formation is mainly based on the extraction of natural resources and land speculation associated with this process and with the overall development of the trade infrastructure as opposed to a diversified economy based on the production of goods. Free trade and the incorporation process into global markets facilitate rentier economies.

54. Ministry of Mining and Energy 1996 and 1998 statistics.

55. Interview by author with two representatives of Asociacion Agrominera del Sur de Bolivar (ASOAGROMISBOL), Bogotá, November, 1998.

56. It is reported that Carlos Castaño has bought lands in Santa Rosa del Sur and that was registered under another name. This is very difficult to corroborate.

57. This is based on this author's calculations of the licenses granted by the Ministry of Mining and Energy in the 1990s.

58. There are a number of multinationals involved in the region, Corona Goldfield (Canada), Oronorte in association with Greenstone (USA), Anchanlgel (Canada).

59. Interviews with miners from south Bolivar, Bogotá, September 1998.

60. Defense Systems is a firm employing British ex-servicemen who have contracts to guard Kuwaiti oil fields and Congo diamond mines.

61. Israeli companies and mercenaries have provided training to paramilitary groups since the 1980s, and their embassy in Bogotá has been active in this respect. See *El Espectador* October 18, 1998, p. 14A.The total length of the pipeline is 480 km from which only about 115 km are not secure. The remaining became in recent years under the control of paramilitary groups and the military with the assistance of security companies.

62. Ibid.

63. Informant from the British Petroleum security service interview with author, Bogotá, October 1998. BP indirectly negotiates with the guerrillas through the local population by furnishing financial assistance to local schools or by providing a certain number of computers or constructing a play ground. The guerrillas in turn pass their demands through local community representatives. It is an implicit modus operandi

64. In addition to the multinational security groups providing their services in Colombia mentioned before, there are the Ackerman Group of Miami, and Kroll-O'Gara based in New York. This latter bought a factory for making armored cars in Colombia. The intertwined relationship between these companies and the military in terms of exchanging intelligence information and cooperation was best described by Enrique Urrea, head of a security committee of the 65 largest multinational companies operating in Colombia, most from the United States. He said, "The Colombian military sends the committee daily intelligence reports and other information while the police provides financial profiles of potential and actual employees." See *New York Times*, November 6, 1998, p C3.

65. Juvencel Duque, Director of the Program Development and Peace in the Middle Magdalena, interview with author November 1998; and also based on his talk at the George Washington University, May 3, 2000.

66. Alejandro Reyes Posada, "Compras de Tierras por Narcotraficantes," in *Drogas Illicitas en Colombia, su Impacto Economico, Politico y Social* (Bogotá: PNUD-DNE, Ariel Ciencia Politica, 1997).

67. Interview by author with an informant active in the region from the armed forces, Bogotá, August 1997; also interview by author with informants Bucaramanga, and Barrancabermeja October 1997 and September 1998 respectively.

68. Dario Betancourt and Martha Garcia, pp. 115–16; the estimates of the amount of narcomoney are largely speculative. Carlos Medina Gallego, using a document of Semana, cited $5.5 billion were invested in lands in Cordoba, Sucre, Antioquia, Meta, and Middle Magdalena areas that also witnessed an increase in paramilitary violence perpetrated against the local peasants. See *Autodefensas, Paramilitares, Y Narcotrafico en Colombia*, p. 260. Incora reported in 1994 that about 3 million hectares were purchased by narcotraffickers whereas Dario Betancourt and Martha Garcia reported 13 million hectares, p. 120.

69. Alejandro Reyes Posada, "Compras de Tierras por Narcotraficantes."

70 Ibid.

71. Fernando Cubides, "Los Paramilitaries y Su Estrategia" *Documento de Trabajo* 8 (Bogotá: Programa de Estudios Sobre Seguridad, Justicia y Violencia, Universidad de los Andes, 1997), p. 37.

72. This fugure is based on an ANUC study conducted in 2001; this study also claims more than 2,500,000 peasants abandoned their lands in the 1990s leaving 1,700,000 hectares mostly under the control of armed actors. As cited in *El Tiempo*, August 5, 2001; see also Comisión Colombiana de Juristas, *Panorama de los derechos humanos y del derecho Internacional humanitario en Colombia 1999*, p. 3. About 1,863 persons lost their lives in the a total of 402 massacres in an average of 34 massacres per month.

73. The 40,000 hectare area of coca plantation (1999) in the Catatumbo provided by the North Santander's governorship exceed by far the more conservative figures provided by the CIA and the Colombian government.

74. Carlos Castaño revealed in a televised interview on April, 2000 that in the Catatumbo there are about 30,000 hectares planted with coca which is financing about thirty-two hundred men (of an estimated five thousand to eight thousand force). This means that this area has become one of the main sources of financing

75. Oil multinationals are compelled to pay protection rent to the guerrilla. These payments are mainly transferred through intermediaries such as subcontractors contracted to perform some work for the company.

76. Reyes, "Compras de Tierras por Narcotraficantes."

77. As quoted in *La Paz: El Desafío para el Desarrollo* (Bogotá: Departamento Nacional de Planeacion, 1998), p. 133–134; the estimates are of the ANUC as cited in "Campesinos, Una Especie en Via de Extincion," *El Tiempo*, August 5, 2001. The cited ANUC study emphasized that the structure of land tenure has changed in the 1990s as much as it did for the entire twentieth century.

78. This account is based on my interviews with displaced peasants from south Bolivar, Bogotá, November 1998.

79. *El Tiempo*, December 30, 1999.

80. *El Espectador*, September 2, 2000.

81. This analysis draws on Robert Jervis, *System Effects: Complexity in Political and Social Life*, p. 39.

82. The figure was cited in "Quien Para los Paras" *Revista Cambio*, January 26, 2001.

83. Since 1995 the paramilitary groups formed the AUC as a unified military structure starting the second phase of the institutional develpoment of paramilitarism; see *La Paz: el Desafío para el Desarrollo*, p. 79. Since then, there has been a notable increase in the paramilitary operations in the south of the country, such as the one on Mapiripan indicating their new national strategy of disputing the guerrillas hegemony in south Colombia and in the north in departments of North Santander, Bolivar (south); and Santander. Castaño considered the Mapiripan attack of 1997 as an inaugurating this new phase, since it was the largest attacks ever carried by the paramilitary against a FARC stronghold. This attack was facilitated by the armed forces which, allowed the transport of troops through the local airport. Carlos Castaño as quoted in *El Tiempo* September 28, 1997, p. 8A.

84. Carlos Castaño, the AUC leader in an interview conceded that his group charges 60% of the market value of the coca produced.

85. This estimate was reached on the following basis: the paramilitary montly pay their men between 160,000 Colombian pesos and 180,000 (1997 pesos, which was equivalent to $106 to $120 at an exchange rate of $1 equaling 1,500 pesos). Depending on rank and seniority, this will average about $113 per man per month. This means that in a year, the paramilitary pay about $6.78 million on salaries alone. The average cost per man between training, food, and equipment, ammunitions and armament is about $250 per month or about $25 million per year. That brings the operational costs of the AUC 5000 fighters to $31.78 million per year or about $50 million for 8,000 men. These calculations took as their base the information provided by Carlos Castaño, in an interview with *El Tiempo*, September 28, 1997, p. 8A. The military hardware and communication equipment could raise the figure to the neighborhood of $100 million per year. This last calculation is my own. See also "Los Paras Ganan La Guerra" *Nota Economica*, 4 (November 17, 1997); and *La Paz: El Desafio Para el Desarrollo*, p. 79. See also E Tiempo, "Coca Divide Los Paras," December 2, 2001.

86. Worker in oilfields of Ecopetrol and ex-member of ELN, interview with author, Barrancabermeja, September 1997.

87. Ibid.

88. Juvencel Duque and Amel Castilla both work in the Programa Desarrollo y Paz para el Magdalena Medio, interview with author, Barancabermeja, November 1998.

89. The total area in the south of Cesar planted with African Palm in 1994 was 10,619 hectares, about 38 percent of the region, south Santander there are about 16,997 hectares (60.8% of the region), the remaining 2 percent are in North Santander, and Bolívar (Morales).

90. Juvencel Duque, interview; and informant, an agricultural engineer working in Puerto Wilches' African palm project, interview with author, Bogotá, November 1998.

91. Carlos Castaño as quoted in *El Tiempo*, March 15, 1999.

92. Ibid.

93. In this respect it is important to mention that commercial districts in cities such as Bogotá, Cali, Medellín, Barrancabermeja, Bucaramanga some large retail businesses do pay protection rent to one group or the other. These groups could be the guerrillas, the paramilitary or another sector of organized crime. The war system has " bandwagon effects" that nourish criminal behavior.

94. Carlos Castaño as quoted in *El Tiempo*, September 28, 1997, p. 8A.

95. Ibid.

96. In one of my field trips in the Middle Magdalena to meet with one of local paramilitary leaders that goes under the name of "Nicolas," I found that his men also work in one of theoil fields of Ecopetrol. Upon investigating this I found that this phenomenon is pervasive. Similar cases were observed in Cesar, Santander, Putumayo, Cordoba, and elsewhere. The significance of this finding is that the actors of the war system are influencing not only the transfer of capital (through taxes) but also and in the allocation of resources and employment in their areas of influence.

97. The guerrillas tax merchants 2 percent of the gold market value and the miners about $8 per month per gram. Manuel Romero, an engineer that works

in south Bolivar, interview with author, Bogotá, October 1998. It is estimated that in 1998(a year after these areas fell under its power) the AUC generated about $9 million from taxing gold miners and the gold trade which is also used as a money laundering operation via Panama.

98. *Informes de Paz*, Junio-Julio 1997. No. 9

99. Ibid.

100. *El Tiempo*, January 30, 2000.

101. The 2000 military deficit is estimated at $130 million which meant a freeze in the Plan 10,000 which is designed to replace 10,000 high school draftees with 10,000 professional soldiers, a reduction in fighting flights from by about fifteen to twenty hours from its current fifty hours, a reduction in the consumption of combustibles, a reduction in the costs of basic services such as water, telephones, electricity, a reduction in 50 percent of intelligence gathering either through contracting informants or buying equipments to intercept communications. These cuts could affect the retirement pension. See *El Tiempo*, January 30, 2000. The United States military aid that came few months later may have saved the military from these cuts.

102. My estimates take as a base line the 1989 FARC's estimation of the costs of maintaining a force of about eighteen thousand fighters divided into sixty fronts necessitated $56 million. Now this is in addition to the major military operations, which involve 300 and more fighters which per year have been averaging ten operations since 1996 with an average cost of a million each, then we will have a total of $66 million per year. *FARC Pleno de 1989: Conclusiones Sobre Plan Militar Estrategico de 8 anos, Organizacion, Escuela Nacional y Finanzas*, Mimeo.

103. The military estimates the FARC income of $450 million per year with $50 million costs, which I think overestimates the income and underestimates the costs. See *Semana* March 8, 1999, no. 879.

104. *Semana* September 6, 1999, no. 905.

105. *El Tiempo*, August 22, 2000.

106. *El Tiempo*, December 29, 2000.

CHAPTER 6

1. Data obtained from Deparamento Nacional de Planeacion, *La Paz: El Desafío para el Desarrollo* (Bogotá: Departamemto de Planeacion, 1998), p. 62.

2. As quoted in Jesus Antonio Bejarano, *Colombia: Inseguridad, Violencia y Desempeño Económico en las Areas Rurales* (Bogotá: FONADE, 1997), p. 30.

3. Myra Buvinic and Andrew Morrison, "Living in a More Violent World," *Foreign Policy*, 118 (Spring 2000): 58–72.

4. Robert Putnam, *Making Democracy Work: Civic Traditions in Modern Italy* (Princeton, N.J.: Princeton University Press, 1993).

5. Mancur Olson, *Power and Prosperity: Outgrowing Communist and Capitalist Dictatorships* (New York: Basic Books, 2000)

6. Property rights are not only contested in the rural areas, but also in urban centers and middle sized cities where families looking for better oppor-

tunities or escaping persecution migrate to these centers and a number of them occupy public lands or private lands. In the latest incident was in Montería, Cordoba where 3,000 families occupied 22 hectares owned by Mario Geraldo, a contractor. The squatters were dislodged after police and army forces intervened with the help of paramilitary groups, who assassinated various persons and threatened the remaining. In other cities such as in Medellín 250,000 occupy public and private lands illegally, as in Cali where 6,000 persons annually illegally occupy lands. In Bucaramaga there are 79 squatters' barrios with a population of 49,000, and in Neiva there are 15,000 squatters. Bogotá is where squatters of "invasion," or pirate, expand about 180 hectares per year or about 3.5 hectares per week. The population of these barrios is no less than 2,000,000. By the early 1970s 46 percent of Bogotá residents lived in homes illegally constructed. A legal dislodging procedure with the backlog and judicial inefficiency might take up to twelve years for a process that does not need more than six months. Again, for our purpose, the use of violence in Monteria to dislodge the squatters reveals two things, violence of the state and private groups (paramilitary) supplements the lack of a more democratic mechanism and procedures to solve disputes over private or public property. More important, rural land conflicts are transported to urban areas, which makes it even more urgent to put in place conflict-solving-mechanisms other than violence. In this context, the guerrillas in squatters' barrios assume the task of protecting the squatters such as in Medellín, Bogotá, Barrancabermeja, and Bucaramanga, and this again feeds into the war system as a modality of conflict resolution similar to its function in areas of colonization in rural areas. See *El Tiempo*, March 8, 2000. See also Francisco Thoumi, *Derechos de Propiedad en Colombia: Debilidad, Ilegitimidad y Algunas Implicaciones Economicas* (Bogotá: CEI, Universidad de los Andes, 1995).

7. Mauricio Rubio "Crimen y Crecimiento en Colombia," *Conyuntura Economica.* (March, 1995): 101–125.

8. *Racionalizacion del Gasto Y de Las Finanzas Publicas*, Bogotá, 1999.

9. These figures were obtained from two sources, *The Economist* Conferences Round table with the Government of Colombia, Conclusion Paper, Bogotá, Colombia, April 14 –15, 1997; Minister of Commerce Marta Lucia Ramirez as quoted in *El Tiempo*, October 5, 2000.

10. *Economist Intelligence Report*, February 2000.

11. As reported in *El Tiempo*, April 30, 1999, p. 1.

12. Ibid.

13. These are the tangible costs. The intangible costs are harder to evaluate and to quantify, costs such as how much people pay to avoid the insecurity associated with the civil war and the costs of leaving the country or changing residences.

14. A 1993 survey was found that in 4 percent of those interviewed belonging to the upper class there was incident of ransom-kidnapping in the family, whereas, only 2 percent of the lower class; in the case of extortion, the percentage increased to 11 percent of those in the upper class and to 4 percent in the lower class. See Juan Luis Londono de la Cuesta, "Violencia, Psiquis, Y Capital Social," *Revista Consigna*, 450 fourth semester, 1996, pp. 7–8.

15. Mauricio Rubio, "Crimen y Crecimiento en Colombia,' *Coyuntura Economica* (March 1995).

16. This finding supports Paul Collier's finding based on all civil wars which took place during 1960–92 GDP per capita declines at an annual rate of 2.6 percent relative to its counterfactual. See Paul Collier, "On the Economic Consequences of Civil War" *Oxford Economic Papers* 51 (1999): 168–183.

17. Montenegro and C. Posada, "Criminalidad en Colombia," *Coyuntura Economica*. (March 1995): 82–95.

18. For GDP indicators see note 10, Economic Intelligence Rport 1998, 1999, and 2000. It is important to note that prior 1998, the effects of the civil war went unnoticed because the country was witnessing a steady economic growth. But when the economic growth declined the civil war and its escalation started having a multiplier effect on the economy. A sharper decline in GDP, from $102.9 billion in 1998 to $86.6 billion in 1999, is reported in the Human Development Report, 2001, UNDP (New York: Oxford University Press, 2001), p. 179.

19. As quoted in *El Espectador*, March 22, 1999.

20. Representative of the Santo Domingo group met with the FARC in Costa Rica in 1998, and in 1999, Nicanor Restrepo of the Sindicato Antioqueno, a member of the cacaos formed part of the government negotiating team. And again in March 2000, the conglomerates met with Manuel Marulanda, the FARC leader.

21. The cacaos and the industrial bourgeoisie have come to this conclusion as is evident in their political discourses.

22. This is based on Antonio Gramsci's conception of hegemony. See *Prison Notebook*, vol.2 (New York: Columbia University Press, 1996).

23. See *Semana*, March 20, 2000.

24. See Entering the 21st century World Development Report, 1999/2000, *World Bank 2000* (New York: Oxford University Press, 1999), pp. 260–1.

25. Ibid., p. 268.

26. Ibid., pp. 268–69.

27. Luis Carlos Sarmiento, from Grupo Aval, Edmundo Esquenazi, from the Group Sanford, and Andrés Obregón, from Grupo Bavaria were among the founders of the Foundation of Ideas for Peace.

28. This idea was influenced by Michelle Garfinkel and Stergio Skaperdas, "Contract or War? On The Consequences of a Broader View of Self-Interest in Economics" paper presented in the Conference of Economics of Violence, Princeton, N.J. January 2000.

29. *El Elespectador*, March 17, 2000. This newspaper is owned by Santo Domingo, one of the cacaos, and one of the participants in the meeting.

30. *See Hacia Una Politica de Desarrollo Colombiano*, (Bogotá: Consejo Gremial Nacional, 1994).

31. For example I interviewed the president of the ANDI in 1995 he favored a more aggressive military strategy against the guerrillas. A few years later (1998) ANDI was favoring a negotiated settlement as mentioned before. See Richani, "The Political Economy of Violence: The War System in Colombia."

32. The findings were published in *El Tiempo*, February 7, 1999, p. 1.

33. Ibid.

34. Jorge Visbal, President of Federation of Cattle Ranchers (FEDEGAN), interview with author, Bogotá, December 3, 1998

35. *El Tiempo*, February 7, 1999. P. 1.

36. The president of ANALDEX, the group that incorporates the leading export-businesses, expressed in his group convention that now more than ever before they are convinced that finding a peaceful negotiated settlement occupies even higher priority than negotiating regional or international economic plans, after all, who is going to invest on Colombia if the conflict continues. As quoted in *El Tiempo*, October 5, 2000.

37. *World Bank 2000*, p. 252.

38. I interviewed Jorge Visbal president of FEDEGAN in December 1998, and SAC's president Jesus Bejarano in November of the same year (assassinated in 1999). I also interviewed Representatives of SAC in August of 1996. Jorge Cardernas, the president of FEDECAFE was interviewed a year earlier, in August 1995. These interviews sought to define the FEDAGAN, SAC and FEDECAFE positions on a possible negotiated settlement and the concessions they were willing to make in the area of land reform.

39. FEDEGAN data.

40. Visbal, interview with author.

41. Based on FEDEGAN's estimates for 1998.

42. See Gallego Medina, *Autodefensas, Paramilatares y Narcotrafico en Colombia Origin, Desarrollo y Consolidacion el Caso Puerto Boyaca* (Bogotá: Editorial Documentos Periodisticos, 1990).

43. This is based on the UNDCP study as quoted in *El Tiempo*, April 28, 2000. The income of narcotaffickers was estimated to constitute 2 to 3 percent of the country's GDP.

44. It is important to note that the guerrilla groups increased their military presence in municipalities where latifundios and large cattle ranchers property structures dominate such as in the Caribbean littoral from nine municipalities (8 percent)in 1985 to sixty three municipalities (59 percent) in 1995.

45. These figures might be inflated for political purposes.

46. Visbal interview. Banco de Bogotá is owned by Grupo Aval.

47. For example, cattle Ranchers exported less than 0.60 percent of meat mostly to Venezuela and Ecuador. The highest point of exported meat was reached in 1975 when it amounted 10.11 percent. But since then the trend has been a steady decline. Paradoxically, and because of the lifting on trade restrictions, Colombia started importing milk and other dairy products, affecting negatively its local production. *La Ganaderia Bovina en Colombia 1997–1998*, (Bogotá: FEDEGAN, 1998), pp. 52–64; 201–204.

48. Visbal interview; Jesus Bejarano, interview with author, Bogotá, November 24, 1998.

49. Marx defined objectified labor as "the constantly self-renewing condition and means for the worker to obtain a part of the value he has produced and hence a portion of the social product measured by his portion of value, his necessary means of subsistence. (profit for capital, rent for land, and wage for labor)

are also sources of revenue in the sense that capitalist fixes one portion of the value of a year's labor and hence of its product in the form of profit, landed property fixes another part in the form of rent and wage labour a third portion in the form of wages. The three are nothing more than objectified social labour. Marx, *Capital* vol.3. (London: Penguin Classics, 1991), p. 961.

50. This forms part of an Andean trend, in the region of Chapare in Bolivia, for example, peasants and coca growers are also being expelled from "prime" lands that are rich with hydrocarbons and in which multinationals are investing. In Ecuador, particularly in the oil-rich region bordering Colombia, the authorities in collaboration with multinationals and the U.S. military are increasingly creating a security system complementing to that in place in Putumayo and Caqueta in Colombia which in turn is putting pressure on the peasants' economy and disrupting their communities. In Putumayo, for example, abundant in oil, coca, and important reserves of gold and copper, has also become a major theater of war with an active military participation of the U.S. from its bases in Ecuador and Colombia. The discovery of important gold and copper reserves in Putumayo was made by the Ministry of Mining. See *El Tiempo*, March 6, 2001.

51. The banana plantations in Uraba were strong supporters of the Castaño paramilitary groups since the early 1980s, when the guerrillas and their union supporters once enjoyed significant political power. The paramilitary defeated the EPL and the FARC and weakened considerably the plantations workers' unions. A similar case is exhibited by the palm plantations that also depend on their ties with right-wing paramilitary groups for "defending" them against the guerrillas and their leftist sympathizers in unions. The flower businesses that are mainly concentrated on the plains of Bogotá are largely owned by traditional wealthy families from the capital and form an integral part of the traditional ruling elite. This sector is very conservative ideologically in spite of its export-oriented interests and linkages with global capital.

52. Fernando Devis comes from Augura (the group that represents about three hundred banana plantations from the Uraba). Augura is well known for its right wing tendencies and for its links with the Castaño paramilitaries. SAC includes representatives from fifty business groups, including Association of Flower Exporters, Association of Cultivators of Sugar Cane, Producers of Rice, Producers of Cotton, Chicken Farms (FENAVI), and Federation of Palm Oil.

53. Fernando Devis was quoted saying on October 2, 2000 that "I never believed in the guerrillas peaceful intentions . . . and that I was a strong opponent to the creation of the demilitarized zone." See *El Tiempo*, October 2, 2000.

54. Figures are obtained from FEDECAFE, *Estudios Especiales*, March 10, 1997.

55. Jorge Cardenas, president of FEDECAFE, interview with author, Bogotá, August 1995.

56. Ibid.

57. Ibid.

58. The U.S. military assistance known as the "Colombia Plan" consist of a $860.3 million to Colombia, $170 million to Colombia's neighbors; $270.8 million to enhance the US bases in Uraba, Curazao and Ecuador. More than 70 percent of this assistance is for military purposes.

59. Between 1997 and 1999, about 550 massacres were committed by paramilitary groups against the peasant base of the guerrillas taking the lives of 600 persons. See *Semana* March 27, 2000. See also chapter six particularly section on massacres.

60. In April 2000, FARC issued its Law 002, which requires that all individuals with an income of $1 million and more to pay the organization a 10 percent tax.

61. In 1998 the kidnap-ransom acts reached a record level of 2,609 cases, registering an increase of 31% from 1997. The guerrillas (FARC and ELN) were the main perpetrators. Organized crime committed 857 of those kidnappings. Antioquia and Cesar are the departments where the highest number of kidnap-ransoms were committed. The increase in the number of kidnap-ransom acts is motivated by the increasing costs of the conflict precipitated by the destabilization of the war system in the late 1990s. It is important to mention that in 1996 ELN, FARC and EPL committed 651 kidnap-ransoms only, while this practice increased significantly in 1998 to 1,752 which demonstrates an increase of 24 percent. Data is based on figures of National Police, Foundacion Pais Libre. The previous highest record was scored in 1991 when the guerrillas kidnapped 854 persons for ransom. Pais Libre calculates that 50 percent of the guerrillas' income for 1999 was through kidnap-ransom activity.

62. See Richani, "The Political Economy of Violence," p. 46.

63. *El Espectador* September 2, 1999.

64. The information provided in this paragraph is based on interviews with guerrilla informants, military sources, and also on *El Espectador*, September 13, 1999, and *El Tiempo, January* 6, 1999.

65. *Semana,* September 6, 1999, no. 905.

66. If my analysis is correct, then this confirms Roy Licklider's summary of seven cases of negotiated settlements in his edited volume *Stopping the Killing* in which he argues that a "mutually hurting stalemate" is not enough for a negotiated settlement. But what matters is the perception of the belligerent parties that the current situation as untenable and unlikely to improve in the future. Roy Licklider (ed.), *Stopping the Killing: How Civil Wars End,* p. 309. For a similar argument, see Cynthia Arnson (ed.), *Comparative Peace Processes in Latin America* (Washington, D.C.: The Woodrow Wilson Center Press, 1999), pp. 1–28.

67. This condition is similar to the one reached by EL Salvador's and Guatemala's elite prior to signing the peace agreement in 1991 and 1996 respectively. See Cynthia Arnson, *Comparative Peace Processes.* Arnson's analysis, however, did not call attention to the important effects of kidnap-ransom and homicide rates on the dominant classes and their decision to engage in a peace process. In Guatemala, for example, on average three to four wealthy individuals were kidnapped for ransom per month, that is between thirty six and forty eight persons were kidnapped per year. In 1994, the result was about $35 million of money transfers to the guerrillas and organized crime. The political/economic and psychological effects of this on dominant social classes are not difficult to imagine. Data on Guetemala were obtained from Steve Macko, "Security Problems in Latin America," ENN Daily Report 08/24/96 vol. 2, no. 237.

68. In reference to Zomosc thesis, see chapter 2.

69. Zamosc, p. 7.

70. Jeffrey Paige, *Coffee and Power*, pp. 1 – 10, 315–361.

71. Moore, *Social Origins of Dictatorship and Democracy*, p. 460.

72. My contention that the increasing importance of the investments in rural lands for speculative purposes constitutes a new aspect of land conflicts does not negate that extracting surplus from peasants and agricultural workers employed by large plantations (coca and other illicit plantations) and agro industries (such as palm-oil enterprises, flower plantations, diary production) constitutes also part of the capital formation and another source of land conflicts. Narcotraffickers, for example, extract the surplus out of the peasant coca planters and at the same time invest their surpluses in lands for speculative purposes. In this connection, it is important to keep in mind that buying land is one modality of money laundering employed by the narcotraffickers.

73. Organizations such as ANUC, coca growers' organizations, and the guerrillas provided the peasantry with vehicles to organized their response to the rentier-capital encroachments.

74. The constitutional reform of 1991 resulting from the peace process with the M-19 and the Quintin Lame could be interpreted in the vein of the armed left opening political spaces in an exclusive political system.

75. In cases such as El Salvador, Nicaragua, and Guatemala, criminal violence and homicides increased after signing peace agreements. In the case of El Salvador, its homicides rates exceeded that of Colombia in the late 1990s.

76. Gramsci, p. 219.

77. Luis Carlos Villegas, president of the ANDI, *Agenda Empresarial por Colombia, El Primer Paso es la Paz*, 151, (March-April 1998): pp. 4–6.

78. Ibid

79. Edgar Ruveiz, economist, interview with author, Bogotá, August 1995.

80. See Patrick Baert, Unintended Consequences: A Typology and Examples," *International Sociology* 6 (June 1991): pp. 201–10; Also Philippe Van Parijes, "Perverse Effects and Social Contradictions: Analytical Vindication of Dialectics?" *British Review of Sociology* 33 (December 1982): pp 589–603.

81. The environment of a system "is the set of all things not components of the system that act or acted on by the components of the system." see Alicia Juarrero, *Dynamics in Action, Intentional Behavior as a Complex System* (Cambridge, Mass.: MIT Press, 1999), p. 110.

82. See Francis Clines, " Maryland Farmers Turn from Tobacco to Flowers," *The New York Times*, February 25, 2001, p. A12.

83. Clifford Kraus, "Desperate Farmers Imperil Peru's Fight on Coca," *The New York Times*, February 23, 2001, p. A4. The coca prices sharply increased from eight dollars for twenty five pounds of coca leaves in 1997 to eighteen dollars in early 1999 to forty dollars by late 2000. The price increase is attributed to a number of factors, including better routes for trafficking employing river, road and sea and also better aerial communications.

84. The $23 billion figure was cited in Francisco Thoumi "Las Drogas Ilegales Y Relaciones Exteriores de Colombia: Una Vision Desde el Exterior" in Alvaro Camacho, Andres Lopez, and Francisco Thoumi, *Las Drogas: Una Guerra Fallida: Visiones Criticas* (Bogotá: Tercer Mundo, 1999), p. 120.

CHAPTER 7

1. Malcom Deas, " Reflections on Political Violence: Colombia" in David Apter, (ed.), *The Legitimatization of Violence* (New York: New York University Press, 1997), p. 352.
2. John A. Davis, *Conflict and Control: Law and Order in Nineteenth Century Italy* (London: Macmillan Education LTD, 1988).
3. Ibid., p. 314.
4. Deas, p. 386.
5. Ibid.
6. Ibid., p. 51.
7. Ibid., p. 55.
8. Judith Chubb, *The Mafia and Politics: The Italian State under Siege,* Western Societies Program, occasional paper no. 23, Center for International Studies, Cornell University, 1989, p. 14.
9. Ibid.
10. Ibid., p. 16
11. Ibid.
12. Ibid., p. 25.
13. Ibid., p. 26.
14. Pino Arlacchi, "The Mafioso: From Man of Honour to Entrepreneur," *The New Left Review*118 (November-December 1979): pp. 53–72
15. Peter Gran, *Beyond Eurocentrism: A New View of Modern World History* (Syracuse: Syracuse University Press, 1996), pp. 94–95; for organized crime's relationship during and after the Second World War with the anti-Fascist coalition see Vittofranco Pisano, *The Dynamics of Subversion and Violence in Contemporary Italy* (Stanford, CA: Hoover Institution Press, 1987), pp. 92–96. The Allied landing in Naples was facilitated by the Mafia and the Mafia gained from resisting fascist key municipal positions.
16. See Pino Arlacchi, *Mafia Business: The Mafia Ethic and the Spirit of Capitalism* (London: Verso, 1986); *Commissione Parlamatare sul fenomeno della Mafia, Relazione di Maggioranza* (Rome: Camera dei Deputati, Senado della Republica).
17. Ernesto Savona (ed.), *Mafia Issues: Analysis and Proposals for Combating the Mafia Today* (Milan, Italy: International Scientific and Professional Advisory Council of the United Nations Crime Prevention and Criminal Justice Programme, 1993); and E. Savona and Phil Williams, *The United Nations and Transnational Organized Crime* (London: Frank Cass, 1996).
18. See Emanuele Macaluso, *Giulio Andreotti Tra Stato e Mafia* (Messina, Italy: Rubettino Editore).
19. This is the most recent figure on homocides rates. See *Human Development Report 1999* (New York: Oxford University Press, 1999), p. 221, Canada had for the same year a 1.9 per 100,000; and France a similar 4.7 per 100,000; whereas Colombia had a 75.9 per 100,000.
20. Williams and Savona, p. 14.
21. Richani, *Dilemmas of Democracy*, particularly chapter 2.
22. Samir Tanir, "Al-Iktisad al-Lubnani bain Harbain," *Assafir*, May 31, 1993.

23. Nazih Richani, "Comparative Protracted Wars, Lebanon and Colombia" paper presented at the International Institute of International Studies Conference on Civil-Military Relations, Beirut, September 1998; Richani, "The Political Economies of the War System in Lebanon and Colombia,"paper presented at the World Bank and Peace Research Institute Oslo (PRIO) Conference on the Economics of Civil Wars, Oslo, Norway June 11–12, 2001.

24. The 1980s the local production of hashish and opium amounted $1 billion by 1987 which was about one-third of the GDP. In this sense, Lebanon became second to Colombia in the international drug trade. Crack cocaine was also produced in Lebanon with material imported from Colombia particularly during the intensification confrontation with drug traffickers. Foreign Broadcast International Service (FBIS), Near East Service, February 9, 1990, p. 48.

25. It was estimated that close to $2 billlion related to the war economy circulated through the banking system prividing liquidity and enough reserves with hard currency preventing the devaluation of the Lebanese Liras (LL). This latter was sharply devalued from an exchange rate of 5 LL to one dollar to 2000 LL to one dollar by the second half of the 1980s. This devaluation was precipitated by the withdrawal of PLO funds and the dwindling foreign aid to the warring faction by the mid-1980s. The PLO withdrew from Lebanon in the aftermath of the 1982 Israeli invasion.

26. Al Hayat, February 4, 1990.

27. "Hukum al Milishiat," Alhayat, January 31, 1990.

28. Harb al Sharkiya fi Takdirat al-Uman al Mutahida, AnNahar, November 11, 1990.

29. I. William Zartman, "The Unfinished Agenda: Negotiating Internal Conflicts" in Licklider, pp. 20–34.

30. Richani, Dilemmas of Democracy, chapter 6. Leaders of Lebanese Forces, for example, thought that the low-intensity war could serve best their political and ideological interests rather than accepting a compromise, which could entail political and economic concessions to the other side. Kareem Pakradouni, member of the central council of the Lebanese Forces, interview with author, Beirut, 1996.

31. Paul Collier, Anke Hoeffler, and Mans Soderbom, "On the Duration of Civil War" typescript (Washington, D.C.: World Bank, Development Economic Research Group, 1999).

32. See Richani, The political Economy of Violence, Richani, "How Can a War System Break Down?" Paper presented at the United States War College, Carlisle Penn., December 1998.

33. It is important to note that UNITA recruits most of its followers from its leader's Jonas Savimbi Ovimbundu homeland and from the Chokwe, Lunda, Nganguala, and other southern Angolan groups who are seeking to preserve elements of their own cultures. Some of the southerners maintained centuries-old legacies of distrust toward northern ethnic groups. This allows a better appreciation to some ethnic aspects of the conflict. See Thomas Collelo (ed.), Angola: A Country Study (Washington, D.C.: Library of Congress, 1991), pp. 187–88.

34. A United Nations committee on Angolan sanctions estimate. See The New York Times, Sunday, August 8, 1999, p. 3.

35. *Human Development Report 1999.* (New York: Oxford University Press, 1999), p. 183.

36. At the end of 1998 two break-away factions emerged, one headed by Abel Chikumuvu, the leader of the Unita's parliamentary delegation formed after the 1994 Lusaka Protocol, and the Unita-Renovada (Renewed Unita). Neither faction commands any considerable support within Unita's hard core forces, and Jonas Savimbi's leadership seemed unwavering. See Donald Rothchild and Caroline Hartzell, "Interstate and Intrastate Negotiations in Angola" in Zartman, pp. 175–203.

37. *Financial Times*, March 30, 2000, p. 4.

38. *Financial Times*, May 3, 1996. P. 4.

39. A Lebanese diamond trader with business in Unita's controlled areas explained to me that Unita exercised total control on diamond trade until the date of the interview in the late 1998. Interview with author, Beirut, September 1999.

40. See *African Business* 249 (December 1999): pp. 8–11.

41. Zartman argues that the condition of a mutually hurting stalemate is hard to find because of the conflict dynamics. He explains that the moment government sees a small improvement in its favor to reestablish its authority over the country, the insurgency may see it as the beginning of justified self-determination. If the insurgency weakens, it draws back to the hills, bush, or marqueis, and if the government weakens, it withdraws to the capital and where it can exercise its sovereignty over a slighter smaller part of the country, yet neither party has the power to dislodge the other completely, a fluctuating stalemate becomes a way of life. Zartman in Licklider, *Stopping the Killing*, p. 26. But in the cases of Lebanon, Angola and Colombia there are military forces with significant fire power, large base of support, and access to vast economic resources, consequently increasing the price of peace aided by a comfortable low-intensity war. The disincentives for a peaceful settlement are downplayed in Zartman's model.

BIBLIOGRAPHY

Al Hayat February 4, 1990.

Alarcon, Maria Victoria Uribe. *Limpiar La Tierra: Gerra y Poder entre Esmeralderos*. Bogota: CINEP, 1992.

Alonso, Manuel Alberto. *Conflicto Armado y Configuracion Regional: El Caso Del Magdalena Medio*. Antioquia: Universidad de Antioquia, 1995.

Alternativa, no. 8 (March 15–April 15, 1997), pp. 10–16, 32–3.

Amel, Juan Dios Castilla. Program Officer, Programa Desarrollo y Paz Middle Magdalena. Interview with author, Barranacabermeja, August 25, 1998.

American Consul James Cooper dispatches, Medellín August 28, 1973. Amb/DCM1 Def.Att, pol.2. National Archives. Washington, D.C.

American Consulate in Cali, November 19, 1971. Department of State, Airgram A-26 National Archives, Washington, D.C.

American Embassy in Bogotá, October 1971, Department of State, Telegram. National Archives. Washington, D.C.

American Embassy in Bogota,January 19,1973 Department of State Bureau of Interamerican Affairs, Airgram A-19. National Archives, Washington, D.C.

Andi: *Agenda Empresarial por Colombia, El Primer Paso es la Paz*, no. 151 (March-April 1998): 4–6.

Angel, Carlos Arturo, president of the ANDI, interview with author, August 1995, Bogota.

Arcila, Oscar, and Adriana Rodríguez, Researchers of Instituto Amazónico de Investigaciones Científicas (Sinchi) on Guaviare. Unpublished Study.

Arenas, Jacobo. *Cese el Fuego: Una Historia Politica de las FARC*. Bogota: Oveja Negra, 1985.

Arias, Jose Jairo Gonzalez. *El Estigma de la Republicas Independientes 1955–1965*. Bogota: CINEP, 1992.

Arlacchi, Pino. *Mafia Business: The Mafia Ethic and the Spirit of Capitalism*. London: Verso, 1986.

———. *Mafia, Peasants and Great Estates: Society In Traditional Calabria*. London: Cambridge University Press, 1983.

———. "The Mafioso: From Man of Honour to Entrepreneur." *New Left Review*, no. 118 (November-December 1979): pp. 53–72.

Arnson, Cynthia (ed.). *Comparative Peace Processes in Latin America*. Washington, D.C.: The Woodrow Wilson Center Press, 1999.

Avila, Jesus Bejarano, Camilo Enchandia Castilla, Rodolfo Escobedo, and Enrique Querez. *Colombia: Inseguridad, Violencia y Desempeño Economico en las Areas Rurales*. Bogota: FONADE and Universidad Externado de Colombia, 1997.

Azar, Edward. *The Management of Protracted Social Conflicts: Theory and Cases*. Dartmouth: Dartmouth Publishing, 1990.

Baert, Patrick. "Unintended Consequences: A Typology and Examples" *International Sociology*, no. 6 (June 1991): pp. 201–10

Bagley, Bruce. "Political Power, Public Policy and the State in Colombia(Ph.D. Dissertation, University of California, Los Angeles, 1979.

Bautista, Nicolas Rodrigues. *Interview in ELN: Una Historia Contada a dos voces*. Bogota: Rodriguez Quito, 1996.

Batatu, Hanna. *Syria's Peasantry, the Descendants of Its Lesser Rural Notables, and Their Politics*. Princeton, N.J.: Princenton University, 1999.

Beck, Nathaniel, King, Gary and Zeng Lancgche. " Improving Quantitative Studies of International Conflict: A Conjecture," *American Political Science Review* 94, no. 1 (March 2000): 21–35.

Bejarano, Jesus Antonio. *Colombia: Inseguridad, Violencia y Desempeño Económico en las Areas Rurales*. Bogota: FONADE, 1997.

———. President of the SAC, interview with author, Bogota, Colombia, December 1998.

———. " El Despeque Cafetero 1900–1928" en Jose Antonio Ocampo, *Historia Económica de Colombia*. Bogota: Tercer Mundo, 1994.

Benson, Michael, and Jacek Kugler. "Power Parity, Democracy and the Severity of Internal Violence" *Journal of Conflict Resolution* 42, no. 2 (April 1998): 196–209.

Berdal, Mats and David Keen. Violence and Economic Agendas in Civil Wars: Some Policy Implicatoins." *Millennium: Journal of International Studies* 26, no. 3, (1997): 795 – 818.

Berlinski, David. *On Systems Analysis*. Cambridge, Mass.: MIT Press, 1976.

Betancourt, Dario and Martha Garcia. *Contrabadistas, Marimberos y Mafiosos*. Bogota: Tercer Mundo, 1994.

Biersteker, Thomas and Cynthia Weber.(eds.). *The State Sovereignty as Social Construct*. Cambridge: Cambridge University Press, 1996.

Bloomfield, Lincoln and Allen Moulton. *Managing International Conflict: From Theory to Policy*. New York: St. Martin's, 1997.

Broderick, Walter J. *El Guerrillero Invisible*. Bogotá, Intermedio, 2000.

Brough, Wayne and V. Lelliot. "The Economics of Insurgency." in Mwangi Kimenyi and John Mbaku (eds.) *Institutions and Collective Choice in Developing Countries: Applications of the Theory of Public Choice*. Aldershot, England: Ashgate, 1999.

Buitrago, Framcisco Leal and Leon Zamosc (eds.) *Al Filo del Caos, Crisis Politica en La Colombia de Los años 80*. Bogota: Tercer Mundo and IEPRI, 1990.

Buitrago, Francisco Leal. "Defensa Y Seguridad Nacional en Colombia" in Francisco Leal Buitrago and Juan Gagriel Tokatlian,(eds) *Orden Mundial y Seguridad, Nuevos Desafios Para Colombia y America*. Bogota:Tercer Mundo Editores and IEPRI, 1994.

———. *El Officio de La Guerra, La Seguridad Nacional en Colombia*. Bogota: Tercer Mundo and IEPRI, 1994.

Bushnell, David. *The Making of Modern Colombia: A Nation in spite of Itself*. Berkeley: University of California Press, 1993.

————. "Politics and Violence in Nineteenth Century in Colombia" in Charles Bergquist, Ricardo Peñaranda and Gonzalo Sanchez, *Violence in Colombia: The Contemporary Crisis in Historical Perspective*.Wellmington, Del.:SR Books,1992.

Bustos, Alirio Fernando, *Los Secretos del General Serrano*. Bogotá: Itermedio, Libro Virtual, 2000.

Buvinic, Myra, and Andrew Morrison. "Living in a More Violent World." *Foreign Policy* 118 (Spring 2000): 58–72.

Camacho, Alvaro Guizado and Barney Alvaro. Colombia: Ciudad y Violencia. Bogota: Ediciones Foro Nacional, 1990.

Camacho, Alvaro Guizado and Andres Lopez Restrepo. "Perspectivas Criticas Sobre los Cultivos Ilicitos en Colombia. Paper presented at the IEPRI, Bogota, Colombia, 1998.

Camacho, Alvaro Guizado, Andrez Lopez, and Francisco Thoumi. *Las Drogas: Una Guerra Fallida*. Bogota: Tercer Mundo Editores & IEPRI, 1999.

Carta Militante no. 15. (December 9,1989). Segundo Congreso del ELN.

Castaño, Carlos. "Esta Guerra no da mas." *Cambio 16* no. 235 (December 15, 1997): 22–27,

Child, Jorge. *Fin del Estado*. Bogota: Editorial Grijalbo, 1993.

Chubb, Judith. *The Mafia and Politics: The Italian State under Siege*. Western Societies Program. Occasional Paper no. 23, Center for International Studies, Cornell University, 1989.

Collelo, Thomas (ed.). *Angola: A Country Study*. Washington DC: Library of Congress, 1991. Pp. 187–88.

Collier, Paul and Anke Hoeffler."*On the Economic Causes of Civil War*." *Oxford Economic Papers* 50 (1998).

Collier, Paul, Anke Hoeffler, and Mans Soderbom, "On the Duration of Civil War" Typescript. Washington, D.C.: World Bank, Development Economic Research Group, 1999.

Collier, Paul. "On the Economic Consequences of Civil War" *Oxford Economic Papers*, 51 (1999): 168–183.

Comisión Colombiana de Juristas. *Panorama de los Derechos Humanos y del Derecho Internacional Humanitario en Colombia 1999*. Bogota: Commision de Juristas, 2000

Consejo Gremial Nacional. *Hacia Una Politica de Desarrollo Colombiano*. Bogota: Consejo Gremial Nacional, 1994.

Coser, Lewis. *Continuities in the Study of Social Conflict*. New York: Free Press, 1962.

————. *The Functions of Social Conflict*. New York: The Free Press, 1956.

Cubides, Fernando."Los Paramilitares y Su Estrategia" *Documento de Trabajo* no. 8 Bogota: Programa de Estudios Sobre Seguridad, Justicia y Violencia, Universidad de los Andes, 1997.

Davis, John A. *Conflict and Control: Law and Order in Nineteenth Century Italy*. London: Macmillan Education, 1988.

De Guevara, Andres Davila Ladron. "El Ejercito Colombiano: Un Actor Mas de La Violencia" in Jaime Arocha, Fernando Cubides and Myrian Jimeno." *Las Violencias: Inclusion Creciente*. Bogota: CES, 1998.

Deas, Malcom. "Reflections on Political Violence: Colombia." In David Apter (ed.), *The Legitimatization of Violence*. New York: New York University Press, 1997.

Deas, Malcom and Fernando Gaitan. *Dos Ensayos Sobre la Violencia en Colombia*. Bogota: FONADE and DNP, 1995.

Declaracion Politica de la Octava Conferencia Nacional FARC-EP 1993.

Del Rio, Cesar Torres. *Fuerzas Armadas y Seguridad Nacional*. Bogota: Planeta, 2000.

Department of State, *Supplementary Annex to FY 1972 Colombia CASP*. NND 969035. National Archives, Washington, D.C.

Derrida, Jacques. *Specters of Marx: The State of the Debt, the Work of Mourning and the New International*. London: Routledge, 1994.

De Zubiria, Sergio. Member of Communist Party Central Committee, interview with author, Bogota, December 1998.

Duque, Juvencel. Director of the Program Development and Peace in the Middle Magdalena, interview with author, Barrancabermeja, November 1998; and also based on his talk at George Washington University, May 3, 2000.

Echandia, Camilo. "La Amapola en el Marco de las Economias del Ciclo Corto." *Analisis Politico*, no. 27 (January-April 1996).

Economist Intelligence Report, February 2000.

The Economist, April 19, 1997.

Elbadawi, Ibrahim "Civil Wars and Poverty; The role of Extend Interventions, Political rights, and Economic Growth." typescript. World Bank (1999).

Entering the 21ˢᵗ century: World Development Report, 1999/2000, World Bank 2000. New York: Oxford University Press, 1999.

El Espectador, 29 Mayo, 1995, p. 10A; 18 October 1998, p. 14A; November 20, 1998. P 4A; March 10, 2000, Special Report;

Evans, Peter, Dietrich Rueschemeyer and Theda Skocpol. *Bringing the State Back in*. (Cambridge: Cambridge University Press, 1985).

Falk, Richard and Samuel S. Kim. *The War System: An Interdisciplinary Approach*. Boulder, Colorado: Westview, 1980.

FARC informant operating in Bogota, interview with author, Bogota, October 1998.

FARC. *Pleno de 1989: Conclusiones Sobre Plan Militar Estrategico de 8 anios*, Organizacion, Escuela Nacional y Finanzas. Mimeo.

———. Seventh and Eighth Conferences Documents.

FEDEGAN, *La Ganaderia Bovina en Colombia 1997–1998*. Bogota: FEDE-GAN, 1998.

Financial Times, May 3, 1996. P. 4; March 30, 2000, p. 4.

Foran, John (ed.). *Theorizing Revolution*.London: Routledge, 1996.

Froncois, Jean and Jean Christophe Rufin (eds.). *Econonie des Guerres Civiles*. Paris: Foundacion pour les Etudes de Defense, 1996.

Fuente, Carlos. Ex-comander and Member Estado Mayor del EPL. Interview with author, Bogotá, November 1994.

Garfinke, Michelle and Stergio Skaperdas. "Contract or War? On The Consequences of a Broader View of Self-Interest in Economics." Paper presented at the Conference of the Economics of Violence. Princeton, January 2000.

Gallego, Carlos Medina. *Autodefensas, Paramilatares y Narcotrafico en Colombia Origin, Desarrollo y Consolidacion el Caso Puerto Boyaca.* Bogota: Editorial Documentos Periodisticos, 1990.

Galan, Francisco. ELN Commander, interview with author, Itaqui, November 1997.

Gollobin, Ira. *Dialectical Materialism, Its Laws, Categories and Practice.* New York: Petra Press, 1986.

Gramsci, Antonio. *Prison Notebook*, vol. 2. New York: Columbia University Press, 1996.

Gran, Peter. *Beyond Eurocentrism: A New View of Modern World History.* Syracuse, NY: Syracuse University Press, 1996.

Granada, Camilo and Leonardo Rojas. " Los Costos del Conflicto Armado 1990–1994." *Planeacion & Desarrollo* 36, no. 4 (October-December1995).

Guevara, Ernesto, "Che." *Guerrilla Warfare.* Lincoln and London: University of Nebraska, 1985.

"Harb al Sharkiya fi Takdirat al-Uman al Mutahida," *AnNahar,* November 11, 1990.

Hartlyn, Jonathan. "Civil Violence and Conflict Resolution: the Case of Colombia." In Roy Licklider (ed.), *Stopping the Killing: How Civil Wars End.* New York: New York University Press, 1993.

———. *The Politics of Coalition Rule in Colombia.* New York: Cambridge University Press, 1988.

"Hukum al Milishiat," *Alhayat,* January 31, 1990.

Human Development Report 1999. New York: Oxford University Press, 1999.

Immegurt, Ellen M. "The Theoretical Core of the New Institutionalism." *Politics and Society,* 26, no. 1 (March 1998).

Informe de Desarrollo Humano Para Colombia, 1998. (Bogotá: Departamento Nacional de Planeacion and PNUD, 1998), p. 143.

Informes de Paz, Publication of the office of the high commissioner of peace, November, 1996 no. 3; December 1996, no. 4; February 1997, no. 5; April 1997, no. 7; March 1997, no. 6; May, 1997, no. 6; June-July 1997, no. 9; June-July, 1997, no. 9.

Interview by author with informant from the V Brigade operating in Santander and North Santander, November 1999.

Interview with two representatives of Asociacion Agrominera del Sur de Bolivar (ASOAGROMISBOL) with author, Bogotá, November, 1998.

Interviews with miners from South Bolivar, Barrancabermeja, September 10, 1998.

Jervis, Robert. *System Effects Complexity in Political and Social Life.* Princeton, N.J.: Princeton University University Press, 1999.

Juarrero, Alicia. *Dynamics in Action, Intentional Behavior as a Complex System.* Cambridge, Mass.: MIT Press, 1999.

Kalmanovitz, Salmon. *La Encrucijada de la Sinrazon y otros Ensayos.* Bogota: Tercer Mundo Editores, 1989.

Keen, David. *The Economic Functions of Violence in Civil Wars.* London: IISS, Adelphi paper, 320, 1998.

Kraus, Clifford. "Peru's Drug Success Erode as Traffickers Adapt." *New York Times,* August 19, 1999, p. A3.

————. " Bolivia at Risk of Some Unrests, Is Making Big Gains in Eradicating Coca." *New York Times*, May 9, 1999, p. A6.

Kriesberg, Louis. Terrel A. Mothrup, and Stuart J. Thorson. *Intractable Conflicts and their Transformation*. Syracuse, N.Y.: Syracuse University Press, 1989.

Latin America After a Decade of Reforms. Economic And Social Progress in Latin America: 1997 Report. Washington DC: Interamerican Develpoment Bank, 1997.

LeGrand, Catherine. *Frontier Expansion and Peasant Protest in Colombia, 1850–1936*. Albuquerque: University of New Mexico, 1986.

Licklider, Roy (ed.). *Stopping the Killing, How Civil Wars End*.New York: New York University Press, 1993.

Lijphart, Arendt. *Democracy in Plural Societies: A Comparative Exploration*. New Haven, CT: Yale University Press, 1974

————. *The Politics of Accommodation: Pluralism and Democacy in the Netherlands*. Berkeley: University of California Press, 1968.

Lomperis, Timothy. *From People's War to People's Rule: Insurgency, Intervention and the Lessons of Vietnam*. Chapel Hill, N.C.: The University of North Carolina Press, 1996.

Londoño, Juan Luis. "Violencia, Psiquis, Y Capital Social: *Revista Consigna*, no. 450 (1996): 7–8.

Macaluso, Emanuel. *Giulio Andreotti tra Stato e Mafia*. Messina, Italy. Rubettino, Editore. Year na.

Maria Mecedes, De Cuellar, member of the board of directors of the Central Bank, interview with author, September 1997.

Marx, Karl. *Capital*. Vol. 3. London: Penguin Classics, 1991.

————. *Pre-Capitalist Economic Formations*. New York: International Publishers, 1989.

McClintock, Cynthia. *Revolutionary Movements in Latin America: El Salvador's FMLN and Peru's Shining Path*. Washington, D.C.: USIP Press, 1998.

Medina, Medofilo. *La Protesta Urbana en Colombia en el Siglo XX*. Bogotá: Ediciones Aurora, 1984.

Ministry of Mining and Energy Statistics, 1995–1998.

Modelski, George. "International Settlement of Internal Wars" in James Rosenau (ed.). *International Aspect of Civil Strife*. Princeton: Princeton University Press, 1964.

Molano,Alfredo, *Truchas y Fusiles*. Bogota: IEPRI and El Ancora Editores, 1994

————. "Violence and Land Colonization" in Charles Berquist, Ricardo Penaranda and Gonzalo Sanchez. *Violence in Colombia: The Contemporary Crisis in Historical Perspective*. Wilmington, DE: Scholarly Resources Inc, 1992.

————. *Aguas Arriba: Entre La Coca y el Oro*. El Ancora Editores, 1992.

Montenegro, A and C. Posada. "Criminalidad en Colombia." *Coyuntura Economica*. (March 1995): 82–95

Moore, Barrington. *Social Origins of Dictatorship and Democracy: Lord and Peasant in the Making of the Modern World*. Boston: Beacon, 1966.

Nasr, Salim. No. 162 "Lebanon's War: Is the End in Sight?" *Middle East Report* (January-February 1990).

Negri, Antonio. *The Politics of Subversion: A Manifesto for the Twenty-First Century.* Cambridge: Polity, 1999.

————. *Insurgencies: Constituent Power and The Modern State.* Translated by Maurizia Boscagli. Minneapolis: University of Minnesota, 1999.

Negri, Antonio and Michael Hardt. *Empire.* Cambridge, Mass.: Harvard University, 2000.

News Agency New Colombia, "Farmers Are Victims in Colombian Drug War," September 23, 1998, p. 2.

New York Times, November 1998, p C3; August 8, 1999, p 3.

Nota Economica, 4 (November 17, 1997)

Ocampo, Jose (ed.). *Historia Economica de Colombia.* Bogota: Tercer Mundo, 1994.

Olson, Mancur. *Power and Prosperity: Outgrowing Communist and Capitalist Dictatorships.* New York: Basic Books, 2000.

Pacificar la Paz Comision de Superacion de la Violencia. Bogota: Instituto de Estudios Politicos y Relaciones Internacioaneles, National University, CINEP and Commision de Juristas, 1992.

Paige, Jeffrey. *Agrarian Revolution.* New York: Free Press, 1975.

————. *Coffee and Power Revolution and the Rise of Democracy in Central America.* Cambridge, Mass: Harvard University Press, 1998.

————. Social Theory and Peasant Revolution in Vietnam and Guatemala. *Theory and Society* 12 (Nov.1983): 699–737.

Palacio, Marco. *Entre la Legitimidad y la Violencia, Colombia 1875–1994.* Bogota: Editorial Norma, 1995.

Pardo, Rafael. *De Primera Mano: Colombia 1986–1994.* Bogota: CEREC and Grupo Editorial Colombia, 1996.

Pisano, Vittofranco. *The Dynamics of Subversion and Violence in Contemporary Italy.* Stanford, CA: Hoover Institution Press, 1987.

Pecaut, Daniel. "Guerrillas and Violence."In Charles Berguist, Ricardo Peñaranda, Gonzalo Sanchez (eds.). *Violence in Colombia.* Wilmington: SR Books, 1992.

————. *Orden y Violencia: Colombia 1930–45* (Vol.1). Bogotá, Colombia: Siglo XXI Editores, 1987.

Pizarro, Eduardo. "Reforma Militar Y Democratizacion Politica." in Francisco Leal *En Busca de La Estabilidad Perdida.* Bogota: Tercer Mundo Editores and IEPRI, 1995.

————. "Revolutionary Guerrilla Groups in Colombia." In *Violence in Colombia,* ed. Charles Bergquist, Ricardo Peñaranda, and Gonzalo Sanchez. Wilmington: SR Books, 1992.

————. "Los orígenes del movimiento armado comunista en Colombia." in *Análisis Político,* no. 7, (May-August 1989).

————. La Profesionalizacion Militar en Colombia. *Analisis Politico.* Nos. 1, 2, 3 (1987–88).

Poder Y Dinero, June 1997.

Popkin, Samuel. *The Rational Peasant: The Political Economy of Rural Society in Vietnam.* Berkeley: University of California Press, 1979.

Posada, Alejandro Reyes. "Compras de Tierras por Narcotraficantes." In Francisco Thoumi et al. *Drogas Illicitas en Colombia, su Impacto Economico, Politico y Social.*" Bogota: PNUD-DNE, Ariel Ciencia Politica, 1997.

Poverty in Colombia, World Bank Country Study. Washington, D.C.: The World Bank, 1994.

Putnam, Robert. *Making Democracy Work: Civic Traditions in Modern Italy.* Princeton, N.J.: Princeton University Press, 1993.

Racionalizacion del Gasto Y de Las Finanzas Publicas, Bogota, 1999.

Ramirez, Jose Gonzalez Roberto, Alberto Valencia, Reinaldo Barbosa, *Conflictos Regionales-Amazonia y Orinoquia.* Bogota: FESCOL and IEPRI, 1998.

Renner, Michael et al. *Vital Signs 1999: The Environmental Trends that are Shaping Our Future.* New York: W.W. Norton and Company, 1999.

Resistencia no. 109 (April 1995), pp 12–13; no. 112 (May 1997), p. 20; no. 18 (August 1998), p. 19.

Review of U.S. Military Presence in Latin America, Secret Section, December 16, 1970. Bogotá 5767. National Archives, Washington, D.C.

Revista Cambio, January 26, 2001

Richani, Nazih. "Political Economy of Rent Extraction: the Crisis of the War System in Colombia." *Journal of Conflict Studies.* (Fall 2001).

———. "The Political Economies of the War System in Lebanon and Colombia." Paper presented at the World Bank and Peace Research Institute Oslo (PRIO) Conference on the Economics of Civil Wars, Oslo, Norway June 11–12, 2001.

———. *Dilemmas of Democracies and Political Parties in Sectarian Societies: The case of the PSP in Lebanon.* New York: St. Martin's, 1998.

———. "*How can a war system Breakdown*" paper presented at the United States War College, Carlisle Penn., December 1998.

———. "The Political Economy of Violence: The War System In Colombia." *Journal of Interamerican Studies and World Affairs.* 39, no. 2 (Summer 1997).

———. "The Druze of Mount Lebanon: Class Formation in a Civil War." *Middle East Report.* No. 162 (January-February 1990).

Romero, Manuel. Geologist who works in south Bolivar, interview with author, Bogotá, October, 1998.

Romero, Mauricio. *Unpublished Paper on South Bolivar.* Bogotá, 1997.

Rovener, Eduardo Saenz. *La Ofensiva Empresarial: Industriales, Politicos y Violencia en los años 40 en Colombia.* Bogota: Tercer Mundo, 1992.

Rubio, Mauricio "Crimen y Crecimiento en Colombia' *Coyuntura Economica* 1995.

Rueschemeyer, Dietrich, Evelyne Stephens, Huber and Stephens, John. *Capitalist Development and Democracy.* Chicago: University of Chicago Press, 1992.

Ruveiz, Edgar. Economist, interview with author, Bogotá, August 1995.

Sampedro Roberto Steiner. "Los Ingresos de Colombia Producto de la Exportacion de La Drogas Illicitas" *Coyuntura Economica.* 16 no. 4 (December 1996).

Sanchez, Gonzalo. *Guerra y Politica en la Sociedad Colombiana.* Bogotá: El Ancora, 1991.

——. Ensayos de Historia Social y Politica del Siglo XX. Bogota: El Ancora, 1984.

Sarmiento, Carlos Miguel Ortiz. "The Business of the Violence:" The Quindio in the 1950s and 1960s in CharlesBergquist, Ricardo Pinaranda and Gonzalo Sanchez" *Violence in Colombia: The Contemporary Crisis in Historical Perspective* (Wilmington, Delaware: Basic Books,1992.

Savona E. and Phil Williams, *The United Nations and Transnational Organized Crime.* London: Frank Cass, 1996.

Savona, Ernesto. *Mafia Issues: Analysis and Proposals for Combating the Mafia Today.* Milan, Italy: International Scientific and Professional Advisory Council of the United Nations Crime Prevention and Criminal Justice Programe, 1993.

Schirmer, Jennifer. *The Guatemalan Military Project: A Violence Called Democracy.* Philadelphia: University of Pennsylvania Press, 1998.

Semana March 27, 2000; March 8, 1999, no. 879; September 6, 1999 no. 905; August 17, 1998, no. 850; August 24, 1998, no. 851; November 30 no. 865.

Simmel, Georg. *Conflict.* Glencoe, Ill.: Free Press, 1955.

Skocpol, Theda. *Social Revolution in the Modern World.* Cambridge: Cambridge University Press, 1994.

——. *States and Social Revolutions: A Comparative Analysis of France, Russia and China.* Cambridge: Cambridge University Press, 1979.

Smith, T. Lynn. *Colombia: Social Structure and the Process of Development.* Gainesville: University of Florida Press, 1967.

Suarez, Alfredo Rangel. *Colombia: Guerra en el Fin de Siglo.* Bogota: Tercer Mundo and Universidad de Los Andes, 1998.

Tanir, Samir. "Al-Iktisad al-Lubnani bain Harbain" *Assafir* May 31, 1993.

The Economist April 19, 1997.

The Economist Intelligence Report 1998, 1999, and 2000.

The 'Sixth Division': Military-Paramilitary Ties and U.S. Policy in Colombia. Human Rights Watch September 2001.

The Ties That Bind: Colombia and the Military-Paramilitary Links, Human Rights Watch 2000. Human Rights Watch February 2000.

Thoumi, Francisco. Paper Presented at the United States War College Conference on Colombia, Carlisle, Pennsylvania, December 1998.

Thoumi, Francisco, Sergio Uribe, and Alejandro Reyes. *Drogas Ilicitas en Colombia: Su Impacto Economico, Politico, y Social.* Bogota: PNUD, 1997.

——. *Economia Politica y Narcotrafico.* Bogota: Tercer Mundo, 1994.

——. *Derechos de Propiedad en Colombia: Debilidad, ilegitimidad y Algunas Implicaciones Economicas.* (Bogota: CEI, Universidad de los Andes, 1995).

El Tiempo, April 18, 1997, p. 3A; August 31, 1997; September 7, 1997, p. 4E; September 28, 1997, p. 8A; October 28, 1998; February 10, 1999, p. 5A; February 7, 1999, p. 1; April 30, 1999, p. 1; May 6,10, 11, 19, 1999; December 17, 30, 1999; January 30, 2000; March 8, 2000; April 9, 28, 2000; May 2, 2000.

Tilly, Charles. "War Making and State Making as Organized Crime" in Peter Evans, Dietrich Rueschemeyer and Theda Skocpol (eds.). *Bringing the State Back in.* Cambridge: Cambridge University Press, 1985.

Tobon, William Ramirez. *Uraba: Los Inciertos Confines de Una Crisis*. Bogota: Tercer Mundo, 1997.

Torres, Felipe. ELN commander, interview with author, Itaqui, November 1997.

Uribe, Maria Victoria A. *Ni Canto de Gloria Ni Canto Funebre*. Bogota: Cinep, 1994.

Urrutia, Miguel. *Gremios Y Politica Economica Y Democracia*. Manuscript, 1981.

Valdivieso, Alfonso. Colombia's Ambassador to the UN and former attorney general (1994–1998), interview with author, New York City, May 23, 2000.

Van Parijes, Philippe. "Perverse Effects and Social Contradictions: Analytical Vindication of Dialectics?" *British Review of Sociology*. no. 33 (December 1982): 589–603.

Vargas, Ricardo Vargas (ed.). *Drogas Y Region en Colombia: Impactos Locales y Conflictos*. vol. 2 Bogotá: CINEP, 1995.

Visbal, Jorge. President of Federation of Cattle Ranchers (FEDEGAN), interview with author, Bogotá, December 3, 1998.

Velazquez, Alejo Vargas. *Colonizacion y Conflicto Armado: Magdalena Medio Santadereano*. Bogota: CINEP, 1992.

Walter, Barbara. "The Critical Barrier to Civil War Settlement." *International Organization*. 51, no. 3. (1997): 335–64.

Waltz, Kenneth. *Theory of International Politics*. New York: McGraw Hill, Inc., 1979.

Weltman, John. *Systems Theories in International Relations*. Lexington, Mass: DC Heath, 1973.

Wickman-Crowley, T. *Guerrillas and Revolutions in Latin America: A Comparative of Insurgents and Regimes Since 1956*. Princeton, N.J.: Princeton University Press, 1992.

Yazid Arteta, FARC Commander, interview with author, Bogota, November 1998.

Zamosc, Leon. *The agrarian Question and the Peasant Movement in Colombia*. London: Cambridge University Press, 1986.

Zartman, William (ed.). *Elusive Peace: Negotiating and End to Civil Wars*. Washington, D.C.: Brookings, 1995.

INDEX

African-Palm, 31; sector of, 125
Afro-Colombians, 13
Agrarian leagues, 67; Cundinamarca
  agrarian leagues, 67; economy, 94;
  Sincelejo Radical Faction, 31;
  Tolima agrarian leagues, 67
Agribusiness, 75, 123–124, 145;
  agrarian economy, 150; agrarian
  elite, 141, 146, 150
Algeria, 73
Alternative crop: State of Maryland
  prototype(United States), 154–155
Alvaran, Luis Alberto, 57
ANAPO (Alianza Nacional Popular),
  29
Andi, 27, 103
Angola, 7, 9, 167; war system in,
  167–169; balance of power in, 168;
  positive political economy in, 168;
  low-intensity war in, 168; high
  intensity war in, 168; diamond in,
  168; war-making capabilities of
  belligerent forces in, 169; Lusaka
  Protocol, 169; National Union for
  the Total Independence of Angola
  (UNITA), 167; Popular Movement
  for the Liberation of Angola, 167
Anori, department of Antioquia, 85
Antioquia, 128
Antioquian Syndicate, 47
ANUC (National Association of
  Peasant Users), 28–31; Sincelejo
  Radical faction of, 31, 149
Apertura, 143
Ardila Lulle, Carlos, 137; see also
  economic conglomerates
Argentina, 54; military, 38
Arteta, Yazid, 71

Aurodefensas Campesinas de
  Cordoba y Uraba-ACCU, 108, 123
Autodensas Unidas de Colombia-
  AUC, 108; composition of,
  108–109, 115–116; Paramilitaries
  of, 111, 124, 147–148; first
  summit of, 122–123; operational
  costs of, 124; narcotrafficking
  income of, 124
Ayala, Turbay, 43

Barrancabermeja, 80
Bautista, Nicolas, 82; see also ELN
Bedoya, Harold, 40
Bejarano, Jesus, 115, 145; see also
  SAC
Blue cartel: air force, 56
Bolivar-Serrania de San Lucas, 87,
  south Bolivar, 89; coca production
  in, 95–96, 110–111; coca growers,
  112; San Pablo in, 111–113;
  subsistence peasant economy in,
  110–113; global economy impact
  on, 113; mining in, 114;
  multinational corporations in,
  114–116; Mineros de Antioquia,
  115; paramilitaries in, 115; miners
  mobilization in, 115, 148; gold
  production in, 114–115, 148
Bolivia, 76; coca production, 76; coca
  producers, 96, 98, 155; peasant
  resistance, 98
Bourbon reform, 12
Bourgeoisie class, 29
Boyaca (department), 78, 85; emerald
  in, 105–106; Green War in, 106;
  Puerto Boyaca in, 107
Brazil (military dictatorship), 38

221

SUNY series in Global Politics
James N. Rosenau, editor

List of Titles

American Patriotism in a Global Society—Betty Jean Craige

The Political Discourse of Anarchy: A Disciplinary History of International Relations—Brian C. Schmidt

From Pirates to Drug Lords: The Post–Cold War Caribbean Security Environment—Michael C. Desch, Jorge I. Dominguez, and Andres Serbin (eds.)

Collective Conflict Management and Changing World Politics—Joseph Lepgold and Thomas G. Weiss (eds.)

Zones of Peace in the Third World: South America and West Africa in Comparative Perspective—Arie M. Kacowicz

Private Authority and International Affairs—A. Claire Cutler, Virginia Haufler, and Tony Porter (eds.)

Harmonizing Europe: Nation-States within the Common Market—Francesco G. Duina

Economic Interdependence in Ukrainian-Russian Relations—Paul J. D'Anieri

Leapfrogging Development? The Political Economy of Telecommunications Restructuring—J. P. Singh

States, Firms, and Power: Successful Sanctions in United States Foreign Policy—George E. Shambaugh

Approaches to Global Governance Theory—Martin Hewson and Timothy J. Sinclair (eds.)

After Authority: War, Peace, and Global Politics in the Twenty-First Century—Ronnie D. Lipschutz

Pondering Postinternationalism: A Paradigm for the Twenty-First Century?—Heidi H. Hobbs (ed.)

Beyond Boundaries? Disciplines, Paradigms, and Theoretical Integration in International Studies—Rudra Sil and Eileen M. Doherty (eds.)

Why Movements Matter: The West German Peace Movement and U. S. Arms Control Policy—Steve Breyman

International Relations—Still an American Social Science? Toward Diversity in International Thought—Robert M. A. Crawford and Darryl S. L. Jarvis (eds.)

Which Lessons Matter? American Foreign Policy Decision Making in the Middle East, 1979–1987—Christopher Hemmer (ed.)

Hierarchy Amidst Anarchy: Transaction Costs and Institutional Choice—Katja Weber

Counter-Hegemony and Foreign Policy: The Dialectics of Marginalized and Global Forces in Jamaica—Randolph B. Persaud

Global Limits: Immanuel Kant, International Relations, and Critique of World Politics—Mark F. N. Franke

Power and Ideas: North-South Politics of Intellectual Property and Antitrust—Susan K. Sell

Money and Power in Europe: The Political Economy of European Monetary Cooperation—Matthias Kaelberer

Agency and Ethics: The Politics of Military Intervention—Anthony F. Lang, Jr.

Life After the Soviet Union: The Newly Independent Republics of the Transcaucasus and Central Asia—Nozar Alaolmolki

Theories of International Cooperation and the Primacy of Anarchy: Explaining U. S. International Monetary Policy-Making After Bretton Woods—Jennifer Sterling-Folker

Information Technologies and Global Politics: The Changing Scope of Power and Governance—James N. Rosenau and J. P. Singh (eds.)

Technology, Democracy, and Development: International Conflict and Cooperation in the Information Age—Juliann Emmons Allison (ed.)

The Arab-Israeli Conflict Transformed: Fifty Years of Interstate and Ethnic Crises—Hemda Ben-Yehuda

Systems of Violence: The Political Economy of War and Peace in Colombia—Nazih Richani

Debating the Global Financial Architecture—Leslie Elliot Armijo

Political Space: Frontiers of Change and Governance in a Globalizing World—Yale Ferguson and R. J. Barry Jones (eds.)

Crisis Theory and World Order: Heideggerian Reflections—Norman K. Swazo